This World Is Not Your Home

By Chad Sychtysz

© 2021 Spiritbuilding Publishers

All rights reserved. No part of this book may be reproduced in any form or by any means, including photocopying and electronic reproduction, without the written permission of the publisher.

Published by
Spiritbuilding Publishers
9700 Ferry Road, Waynesville, OH 45068

(800) 282-4901

THIS WORLD IS NOT YOUR HOME
By Chad Sychtysz

ISBN: 978-1-955285-33-9

Printed in the USA by D & E Printing, Brownsburg, IN
dandeprinting.com

Spiritbuilding
PUBLISHERS

spiritbuilding.com
Spiritual equipment for the contest of life

Dedication

To Debra ("Debbie") Isbelle (1950—2020), my dear mother-in-law and a fine Christian lady, who has gone home to be with the Lord forever.

Acknowledgements

While no one assisted me in actually *writing* this book (although I would have welcomed the help!), several people helped me in *producing* it. I will admit, this book began as an intensely personal project, one that has been on my mind for a number of years in one form or another.

Matthew Allen, my publisher (and fellow minister in Ohio), is always so full of encouragement and support. He often asks what I'm working on, and then is excited to get it published when it is done. I deeply appreciate his friendly candor, while always remaining professional, in dealing with me and my "projects." Jamey Hinds in Florida is Matthew's "layout guy," and does all of the manuscript layout and formatting for most (if not all) of Spiritbuilding Publishers' books. I've known Jamey personally for nearly 20 years, and I know I am in good hands with his work.

I had several "readers" go through the original manuscript, which is a difficult thing to do, especially for those who are not accustomed to such work. Yet, they all happily agreed to do it, and for this reason, deserve to be thanked: Darrell Beane, another fellow minister of the gospel; Heather Hafer, a personal friend; and David Bryan Smith, another personal friend. In particular, David offered substantial responses to my manuscript. Sometimes these were praises; other times, they were calls for clarification or more explanation. In either case, he proved himself to be quite the gentleman, and I have enjoyed our coffeeshop discussions over this manuscript as well as my other writings. I also want to thank Brenna Price (in Montana) for editing the manuscript and catching many of my writing mishaps and grammatical gaffes.

My family—my wife (Honey), daughter (Larissa) and her husband (Tim), and son (Logan), are always supportive of my writing. Their love for me is unconditional, as is mine for them. Larissa has been especially helpful, as she designed the covers for the last several of my books. She is more talented and "artsy" than I am in that work.

Table of Contents

Part One: The Afterlife and Its Implications
   Chapter One: Is There an Afterlife? 1
   Chapter Two: Thoughts on the Afterlife 14
   Chapter Three: You Will Be in the Afterlife 29
   Chapter Four: As Heaven Is Real, So Is Hell 40
   Chapter Five: What the "Rich Man" Wants You to Know 52

Part Two: Satan's World and How It Affects You
   Chapter Six: The World of the Darkness 64
   Chapter Seven: The Influence of the Darkness 74
   Chapter Eight: Satan May Not Be Who You Think He Is 89
   Chapter Nine: Satan Wants to Destroy You 104

Part Three: Christ Has Overcome the World
   Chapter Ten: Christ, the Light of the World 118
   Chapter Eleven: The Finest Man to Have Ever Lived 128
   Chapter Twelve: What Happened at the Cross 140
   Chapter Thirteen: "And There Was War in Heaven" 150

Part Four: Preparing for the Afterlife
   Chapter Fourteen: The Problem of Your Evil 162
   Chapter Fifteen: Christ Can Overcome Your World 172
   Chapter Sixteen: A Message to Christians 183

Appendix I: The Problem of Evil 192
Appendix II: Near-death Experiences 207

Sources Used for This Study 224
Endnotes 227

Scripture taken from the NEW AMERICAN STANDARD BIBLE ®, Copyright © 1960, 1962, 1963, 1968, 1971, 1972, 1973, 1975, 1977, 1995 by The Lockman Foundation. Used by permission.

Author's Preface

This book, probably like a lot of books, was not created in a vacuum, unaffected by the world in which it was written. I actually began researching it prior to 2018, taking copious notes from numerous books and other sources. Incidentally, I have fully read nearly every book listed in the bibliography—a task which, in itself, takes a great deal of time and effort. And many "writing sessions" at coffee shops.

I began writing the original manuscript in 2018, and got about a third of the way through, but other things seemed to be more pressing at the time. Concurrently, I was working on other writing projects—namely, finishing my workbook series on the New Testament epistles, and a massive re-write of my previously-published book, *The Gospel of Grace*. Both of these projects were completed in early 2020. And then there was 2020 itself—a year that will live in infamy, to be sure—in which the world seemed to lose its mind, fear seemed to overcome the faith of many Christians, and propaganda, polarizing politics, and violent protests besieged our country. It was a distressing and very difficult time to endure, especially for church leadership (of which I was a member). While I purposely avoided mentioning specific events of 2020 (and thereafter) in my manuscript, you can be sure that a lot of these were on my mind.

In some ways, however, it was an ideal time for me to write about what the New Testament refers to as "the darkness," its seductive power, and its chief puppet, Satan himself. I was not just writing theoretically about the darkness and what it does, I was witnessing it up close and personally. This insidious darkness was not just affecting people indirectly, it was *indoctrinating* them, *reprogramming* them, and thus *changing* them. This was happening to Christians and non-Christians alike. It seemed like a dark and ominous cloud had settled over the entire country, blinding many to what was really happening. Those who could "see" were those enlightened by God's truth; many others "saw" only what they wanted to see, or believed what others told them to believe.

On the other hand, I felt a strong and passionate need to magnify the work of Christ in the midst of all this fear, madness, and capitulating of human faith. The spiritual world of darkness is powerful and influential, to be sure, but it feeds on the fears and submission of those who give their allegiance to it rather than to Christ. Even so, Christ is infinitely greater, stronger, and more successful than the darkness can ever claim to be. Christ has already been victorious over Satan and the darkness—despite the fact that so many Christians *and* non-Christians have seriously questioned this. My purpose, then, was to lay out this great cosmic drama between good and evil, Satan and Christ, and darkness and Light. I did my best to avoid giving Satan any meaningful credit, but went out of my way to exalt Christ and His victory over Satan, the world, and the darkness—a victory that will be celebrated for the eternity to come.

But I could not talk about Satan *or* Jesus (or even God Himself) without spending at least some time validating the existence of the spiritual realm—specifically, the afterlife. If there is no afterlife, then discussions concerning spiritual beings (however evil or virtuous) are just a waste of time. If there is an afterlife, then such discussions are completely relevant and bear directly upon the spiritual future of every person who has ever lived. This book's thesis—*this world is not your home*—intentionally and regularly bubbles up to the surface of the text.

As I said, things got in the way, so to speak, of writing the full manuscript for this book. Some of these things were personally tragic: in June, 2020, my reclusive father died under deplorable conditions; in December, 2020, my dear mother-in-law died suddenly of a heart attack; and in January, 2021, my youngest brother died in hospice as a result of untreatable liver cancer. Things like this, especially so compacted as they were, do not leave us untouched. Instead, they jar us to the core, causing massive introspection as well as profound re-examination of the world we live in—in essence, of life itself. This happened to me, as it might well have happened to anyone else in similar circumstances, and some of this introspection and external clarity poured into the manuscript. It could not help but do so. Instead of pulling inward and hiding (though the urge seemed at times irresistible), I chose to confront my pain, my questions, and faith—my faith as well as "the" faith—directly and openly. As you read through some of the chapters, you will likely pick up on some of the raw, unfiltered, and very straightforward results of those confrontations.

The "what doesn't kill you, makes you stronger" meme is generally true, but only if you have a strong faith to begin with. Living with a weak faith in God—or worse, with no faith at all—is not a sign of strength. Instead, it is a false sense of security in deceptions promoted by godless people, Satan, and the darkness. God has given us every reason to believe in Him, not only when things are going well, but especially when everything around us is falling apart. I have chosen to remain steadfast in my commitment to Christ. Even so, I have tried very hard in this book not to promote my own faith, but to promote *the* faith—the truth that God has revealed to all people. You cannot be saved from this perverse world by adopting my faith. You can, however, and *will* be saved by living by faith in Christ, the Savior of all who are redeemed by His blood.

For those who need their faith in Christ reinforced, this book is written with you in mind. For those who are not yet Christians but are honestly seeking the truth, this book is written with you in mind also. It bothers me greatly that most of the human population is not comprised of either one of these people—Christians or truth-seekers. So many people—*so many people*—have been deceived by the darkness and have unwittingly resigned themselves to an awful future existence. I don't want to be one of those people. Regarding my own spiritual afterlife, I cannot *afford* to be one of those people.

But then, neither can you.

Your feedback on this book is welcome—but *be nice*. If you disagree with whatever has been written, do so respectfully, not viciously. You can contact me directly: *chad@booksbychad.com*.

Chad Sychtysz
September 3, 2021

Part One: The Afterlife and Its Implications
Chapter One: Is There an Afterlife?

The afterlife is a subject that is as emotionally-charged as it is radically interpreted. Some believe that it exists; others aren't sure. Some see it as a glorified extension of this earthly life; others want to customize it to their own liking. It is amazing to hear people speak so casually or carelessly about the afterlife, as though it is something that will just happen on its own, like puberty or old age. It is equally amazing that so many people are *indifferent* about what lies ahead. Perhaps they think it will be someone else's problem; perhaps they think it will take care of itself—out of sight, out of mind.

Is there any proof that the afterlife does exist? If not, then there is no need to worry about it. On the other hand, if sufficient proof *does* exist, it would be foolish to dismiss it with unconcern. This proof cannot be in the form of "I think" or "I feel" or "I believe," because our thoughts, feelings, and private beliefs prove nothing. If we have no authoritative standard by which to know for certain what awaits us after death, then everyone's opinions on this subject would be equally valid (or equally pointless, depending on how you look at it). If we do have such a standard, then all human opinions are to be rejected simply because they *are* opinions—unauthorized, unprovable, and flippant guesses on the subject, nothing more.

Any authorized standard must be something more than one's personal conviction, especially with regard to a subject so important as the afterlife. Personal convictions certainly seem rewarding to the one who has them, but they often fall apart under objective criticism. Contemporary claims of private revelations from God, visions of heaven, angelic encounters, revised gospels of Jesus Christ, miraculous performances, and messages from the dead all fall into this category. Passionately-held opinions and strong convictions about the afterlife are not equal to well-constructed, evidence-based, and logical arguments. Religious fervor is no replacement for relevant proofs and sound reasoning.

The subject of the afterlife is so critically important because, if it does exist, *every human soul* will experience it, and this experience will be either very good or very bad. There is no neutral existence in the afterlife, unless everyone is exactly the same, everyone's situation is exactly the same, and nothing ever happens—like being sound asleep for all eternity. Even if someone thinks this is the case, it remains to be proven, and no such proofs exist. On the contrary, everything we do know about the afterlife leads us in a very different direction than this.

The Disposition of the Human Soul

Like any other realm of life, the afterlife—in order *to* exist—requires authority (someone in charge), structure (for design and functionality), and a reason *for* its existence (purpose). It could not have just "happened" any more than *you* just happened. You did not just pop into existence one day for no reason, but you were brought to life through a process that no person created but which exists and functions nonetheless. The fact that you have a conscience, a spiritual awareness, and an innate desire to worship something greater than yourself—in fact, greater than all of us—implies that there is something otherworldly about you. Your parents did not impart this to you; they do not even fully understand it themselves. You did not create this spiritual part of you, either—you do not have that kind of power, authority, or ability. Someone greater and higher than you— someone *transcendent* of human life—imparted this otherworldliness to you.

Human life itself—its conception, programmed design (in DNA), and spirituality—forces us to look beyond this physical world for its origin and explanation. Someone had to conceive of life itself—not only of each individual person, but of the very *concept* of "life." Someone had to do all the programming: all attempts to justify the theory of Evolution here fall apart. Information, codes, blueprints, engineering, intelligence, and decision-making cannot "just happen," and anyone who approaches the subject honestly and with an open mind will admit this. We cannot *explain* human life in mere biological, physiological, or even material terms. Love, hate, righteousness, wickedness, guilt, forgiveness, justice, and a yearning for God (or even "a" god) cannot be explained with a purely materialistic or mechanical model of the world. Human thoughts are not just random firings of neurons in the human brain, but manifestations of our spiritual nature.[1]

If this is true about the living, then the question becomes: what happens when you die? Perhaps we should clarify: when "you" die, is it really *you* that is dying, or is it merely the physical *part* of you that dies? Is your physical death really the end of *you*? Or, does the spiritual part of you go on living beyond the grave, having entered into a world very different than this one? Therein is the essence of the discussion about the afterlife. Even if the afterlife does exist, it does not automatically mean you will personally participate in it. Maybe you will not be allowed? Maybe you will not be invited? Maybe you will not be worthy? Each of these factors (allowed, invited, and worthy) require a decision by someone with authority. You or I cannot be this "someone," since we could know nothing about the afterlife except what someone in charge of it *told* us.

So then, first of all, we need to determine whether or not the afterlife exists. Second, we need to know whether we will have any conscious experience in it. Third, we need to know *how* we will experience it. Such questions are not limited to the afterlife itself, but necessarily involve the existence (or non-existence) of the human soul. We know that no one participates *physically* in the afterlife, since their bodies remain here, and we bury or cremate them. Thus, the only way anyone can participate in the afterlife is spiritually—as a soul-being, not a flesh-and-blood being. Otherwise, we just simply disappear from *all* existence, as though we had *never* existed.

This question about the human soul—the spiritual part of you— necessarily involves God. If you did not give yourself your own soul, then who did? If your parents did not give you a soul, then who did? If the theory of Evolution provides zero explanation for or ability to produce a soul, then where did it come from? If the human soul is merely a figment of our own imagination, then how do we explain a universally-experienced imagination that came up with the concept of God, a soul, and the afterlife in the first place—where did all *that* come from? If the human soul *and* our imagination are simply manifestations of some neurological experience of the human brain, then what about all the other evidence that says otherwise—including the universal concept of a Higher Being, the biblical record, and all the teachings of Jesus Christ?

The existence of God—an all-powerful and all-knowing Creator—sufficiently answers all these questions.[2] If God exists, then it is God who gave each of us a human soul, just as He also designed the blueprint for the human body in our DNA. If God exists and gave us a human soul, then He did so for some distinct purpose. It also stands to reason that He expects something *from* us, since no purpose would make sense that did not require some measure of responsibility on our part. And, if He exists and we are responsible to Him, then it also stands to reason that He will evaluate our performance concerning this responsibility at some time in our existence. To give someone a responsibility without holding them accountable is illogical and pointless. Not surprisingly, the Bible confirms all that has just been said—something we will pursue later.

If God exists, then the human soul exists; if the human soul exists, then the afterlife exists. It is logically, intellectually, and even biblically impossible to hold to any one of these beliefs without necessarily accepting the others. One simply cannot claim that the soul exists but not God, since the ultimate proof for the soul's existence equally affirms God's existence. Likewise, one cannot claim that God exists but not the afterlife, since the ultimate proof for the existence of one (God) equally affirms the existence of the other (afterlife). These three things rise or fall together; they cannot be separated. To attempt otherwise would be like saying gravity exists, but not laws of physics; or, that visible light exists, but not the electromagnetic spectrum. Just as illogical would be to deny the existence of gravity and visible light when clear and irrefutable evidence exists to confirm them both.

"Reasons" Why God Does Not Exist

Atheists claim that there is no God—no divine, supernatural, and sovereign Being that is responsible for and presides over the physical universe. For example, Richard Feynman (1918–1988), Nobel Prize-winning physicist, wrote:

> God was invented to explain mystery. God is always invented to explain those things that you do not understand. Now, when you finally discover how something works, you get some laws which you're taking away from God; you don't need him anymore.[3]

This attempts to reduce God to a primitive, superstitious mindset that is blinded by fairytale-like mysticism. However, we have yet to hear a convincing and irrefutable argument that *confirms* that God does not exist. There are no such proofs, only subjective reasoning.[4] Such reasoning is always selective and inconsistent. For example, when a person finds an arrowhead or pottery shard in the ground, or observes the statues of Easter Island or the Sphinx in Egypt, he does not for a moment assume that these things "just happened." But when an Evolutionist—and all modern atheists are Evolutionists—considers the complexity and interdependence of the human body, he claims that it "just happened" over myriads of accidents, chance mutations, and eons of time. This kind of duplicity is not only unscientific; it is insincere. It is not *supportive* of science as much as it is *against* any supernatural intervention in the natural world. The atheist "[trusts] his mind when reasoning about evolution, but not about God!"[5]

Atheistic positions (posing as truth-based arguments) ultimately rest upon whether or not a person buys *into* the atheist's premise. Buying into a premise does not prove it to be true, but only assumes it to be true. This is like Evolutionists laying out a series of skulls, bones, and fossils and telling you that one "evolved" into the other. This proves nothing except what they choose to believe and what they tell you. You must accept the premise of Evolution in order to "see" it from where they stand. From where I stand, these people simply laid out a bunch of bones and fossils, then created a fanciful story to connect them all. This is not science, as it is claimed to be, but mythology.[6] It is no different than ancient pagans claiming that there is one god responsible for successful crops, another god in charge of fire, yet another god that oversees war, etc. Without actual proof, it is just one person's opinion (imagination) over another's.[7]

Instead of conclusive proofs about the non-existence of God, the soul, and the afterlife, modern atheists commonly unleash hateful diatribes against God (even though, allegedly, He is not even supposed to exist).[8] Atheists are fond of writing long manifestos pouring forth scathing critiques of God's decisions, what He did or did not do, and how *dare* He not conform to their personal expectations.[9] But this is all simply opinionated rhetoric, nothing more.[10] May the atheist have his opinion about God, etc.? Of course. But this is no replacement for factual evidence to the contrary.

There are at least three well-worn "reasons" given as to why there is no God (and thus, no soul and no afterlife). First, there is evil in the world, and the God of the Bible is supposed to be "good" (Mat. 19:17). Since it is allegedly impossible to rectify an evil world with a good Creator or a good Creation (Gen. 1:31), God cannot exist.[11] Admittedly, the problem of evil has confounded philosophers and moralists for centuries, but it is illogical to assume that human wickedness automatically negates divine goodness. (Please see "Appendix I: The Problem of Evil.") Instead of rejecting the reality of evil, atheists have instead rejected the reality of God—even though are both, ironically, *spiritual* in nature. This is like the Sadducees asking Jesus about what happens with resurrected souls, even though they did not believe in spirits or resurrection (Mat. 22:23–32, Acts 23:8). For what it's worth, Jesus said that they were "mistaken" about everything concerning these subjects.

Personal expectations of a Divine Being have nothing to do with critical, objective, and irrefutable evidence against His existence. Choosing not to believe something is no argument against its existence. For example, there are many good, honest, and decent people in the world, but there are also rapists and child molesters. I do not claim that good people cease to exist just because evil people also exist. I also do not eliminate whatever *influenced* all these people to be good simply because all the *evil* people were influenced by something else.

The second reason atheists present is that they are very unhappy about how God (who, remember, is not even supposed to exist) has performed in the Bible—particularly in the Old Testament. He is characterized as a capricious, egomaniacal, bloodthirsty, genocidal, murderous, petty tyrant, among other things. He brings famine and drought; He brings fire down upon entire cities; He floods the world, exterminating most of humankind. Since no good God could possibly behave the way the God of the Bible has behaved (so they reason), He must be a figment of people's imagination. Since this biblical God offends the unbeliever's personal beliefs about how the world ought to be governed if God *did* exist, therefore He must *not* exist.

This again is a subjective assessment of God's character, not a proven fact of His non-existence. Just because God disappoints one's personal expectations of Him does not mean He does not exist. For example, the President of the United States may sorely disappoint my expectations *of* a president, but this does not mean that he simply ceases to exist (or *never* existed). Adolf Hitler has disappointed my personal expectations of a human being, but I don't pretend that he did not really exist because of this. Opinions—even the shared opinions of very intelligent and educated people—do not constitute an irrefutable argument.

The third common reason for which atheists deny God's existence is because He holds people accountable to a moral standard and punishes those who refuse to live up to it. The subject of divine mercy and grace is often ignored in this picture, because those who hate God and Christians—as many atheists pointedly do—are seldom interested in a balanced view. If you step out of line, God will condemn you; if you do not worship Him the way He wants, He will destroy you; if you do not love Him the way He wants, He will cast you into fiery hell. Since no good God should be so demanding, exacting, and judgmental (so they reason), the good God of the Bible cannot possibly be real. He is, they will say, a crutch for the weak-minded, a savior for the weak-willed, and a default answer for people too ignorant to think for themselves.[12]

The Biblical Record Demands an Intelligent Response
Having allegedly etched God out of existence, atheism has also etched the reality of the human soul *and* the afterlife out of existence. Betty Brogaard, an atheist, says that "insofar as I can logically ascertain, no one exists in any cognizant form after death."[13] But how did she "logically ascertain" that conclusion? What is this based upon? Certainly, it is not her own personal experience or the testimony of those who have died. What does that leave? Her opinion, nothing more. Yet, people's opinions about the afterlife cannot create, disprove, or customize it. All they can do is give us some small but unfounded comfort that we think we know what we're talking about. This terribly irrational approach will have catastrophic results.

If we are all the product of Evolution, then there can be nothing *actually* spiritual about us.[14] To believe in Evolution is to deny your own soul's existence. If you have no soul, then this life is literally all there is for you. Yet, there is no evidence that this is true, except for the atheist's "logical" ascertainment. Nearly everyone believes—intuitively, if nothing else—that they do have a soul. The Bible not only confirms this, but tells us how this soul came to be (or, what gives life to it). It is impossible to argue for the existence of the soul and/or afterlife without the existence of a Higher Power having given you that soul in the first place, since the material world is incapable of giving us something that it does not already possess.[15] But if there is a Creator of human life—a self-existent, timeless, all-knowing, and all-powerful Being that is not the imaginary product of human life—then this same Being can impart a living and eternal soul to every human that He brings to life.

This latter scenario is the Bible's depiction of God. He is an omnipotent, omniscient Creator; He is a sovereign deity that answers to no one outside of Himself; He is not bound to the physical or human limitations of our earthly realm. If the Bible is true and factual, then everything it says about God—and everything God says about Himself—is also true and factual. The Bible declares itself to be "inspired" [lit., God-breathed] literature, thus a sacred record (2 Tim. 3:16–17).[16] This means that the authority behind it is God Himself, and its essential message has been revealed by God to man, rather than men having dreamed up their version of Him (Gal. 1:10–12). The Bible reveals the "eternal purpose" of God (Eph. 3:11–12), which is summed up in the recurring statement throughout the Old and New Testaments, "I will be their God and they [those who live by faith in Him—MY WORDS] will be My people" (see Lev. 26:12, Jer. 7:23, 2 Cor. 6:16, Rev. 21:3, etc.).

Everything we know *factually*—not assumedly, possibly, or deductively, but *factually*—about God, the spiritual realm, the soul, sin, salvation, angels, demons, and the afterlife is found only in the Bible. No other record has proven to be so reliable and convincing; no other record offers evidence on par with what the Bible offers. Everything that *anyone*—atheists, agnostics, pseudo-Christians, and true believers alike—can know factually about God and His attributes is found in the Bible. Unless Jesus had explained God to us, and unless we had a record of that explanation in the New Testament [NT], no one would be able to know God as well as we do now (John 1:18). We could make general deductions about God (e.g., He is all-powerful, all-wise, the Creator, a proficient engineer, etc.) by examining the physical world and human nature. But the only way we could know of His personality, love, wrath, patience, forgiveness, and message for humankind is if He revealed these things to us, recorded that revelation, and preserved it for us through the ages. This is what the Bible claims to be: a timeless documentation of the Creator's benevolent communication to all those made "in His image" (Gen. 1:27).

The Bible is not only a book of religion, but of literature, poetry, wisdom, history, law, and genealogical records. It is supported by internal evidence, including:

- A consistent and united theme (despite being written over a 1,500-year span by over 40 different unrelated authors).
- A central figure (Jesus Christ), who is depicted as Lord and Savior of the world.
- Prophecies both stated and fulfilled, most of which are hundreds (some even thousands) of years apart.
- A consistent and universal moral code, irrespective of individual covenants God made with different people or nations.
- Numerous accounts of miraculous events which are supported by many eyewitnesses and are not denied by many detractors.

The Bible is also supported by external evidence, including:

- Historical evidence that corroborates many of the events described in it.
- Archaeological evidence corroborating many of the people, cities, and cultures described in it. The Bible has been shown to be more accurate than secular sources once led us to believe.
- Physical evidence of a world-wide flood, as described in the Bible (Gen. 6—8).
- Critical analysis—the Bible has been subjected to withering

criticism and meticulous examination by both believers and critics alike, yet has never been discredited. In fact, many who set out to disprove the Bible ended up becoming believers because its integrity is so convincing. No other alleged account of God and His works (e.g., Apocrypha, Quran, Book of Mormon, etc.) can withstand the same blistering critical scrutiny that men have unleashed against the Bible.
- The Bible stands head and shoulders above any other ancient text regarding style, eloquence, consistency, credibility, codification of law, specific details (genealogical records, names of places and cities, census accounts, etc.), and structure.

Other writers have examined each of these points in great detail.[17] Yet, the question remains: if the Bible is not what it says it is—what the evidence declares it to be—then what is it? Many people have chosen not to *believe* the Bible, but none have been able to *disprove* it. Again, not wanting to believe in something and proving that thing to be untrue are not on the same page. One is an opinion, a choice; the other is a sound conclusion based upon relevant evidence and objective reasoning. For example, people have had 2,000 years to prove that Jesus is not who He said He was, did not do what the Bible claims that He did, and does not possess the authority that He demonstrated in His miracles. To date, no one has offered a cogent argument that the biblical claims of Jesus—or even His actual existence—are untrue. People have scoffed, belittled, criticized, tried to discredit, and outright blasphemed Jesus, but none have provided conclusive evidence that compels all of us to throw away our Bibles.

This brings us back to an earlier point: if the Bible confirms the existence of and gives personality to the same God whose handiwork we see everywhere in the physical world, then these are not two unrelated or coincidental conclusions. God does exist—He may not satisfy every person's expectation of Him, but He *does exist*. The burden of proof is not upon me to prove that He exists, given all the evidence that the physical world and biblical texts provide, but is upon the one who says otherwise. First, that person must prove that:

- A complex, interdependent, and (in the case of human beings) intelligent world accidentally came to be without any outside (supernatural) intervention;
- Our moral intuition (or, innate sense of right and wrong), sense of guilt, longing for forgiveness, and all other spiritual aspects of the human condition, are also accidental, imaginary, and irrelevant;
- The Bible, despite all previous efforts to disprove it and destroy its credibility, is false, imaginary, and irrelevant.

Second, that person must fill this void—the giant hole created by expelling a Creator, morality, and the biblical record—with a *superior explanation* to all of this, *and* with evidence and proofs that are also superior to what the biblical record offers. This burden of proof—first, *prove the status quo wrong*; and second, *prove something better instead*—rests upon the shoulders of the unbeliever. To date, no one has done any of this. Atheists are quick to deny God's existence, but they have no good reason for this. They are quick to dig holes, but have nothing with which to fill them. In the end, they have a philosophy filled with speculation, emptiness, and hopelessness—but they want you to believe in their "logical" ascertainments! "Truth cannot be denied unless some truth is being affirmed."[18]

If someone says, "The Bible is *not* the word of God," how does he know that for certain? How *can* he know this? Is he willing to bank his future—particularly, his future existence in the afterlife—on this? What can he know—or not know—about God, his soul, and the afterlife apart from the Bible? How can he claim (as the agnostic does) that God is "unknowable" when the knowledge of God is sitting there right in front of him in the Bible? How can he know for certain that God and the afterlife are "unknowable" in the face of evidence to the contrary?[19]

If a person is not convinced by the Bible that there is a God, he has a soul, and he will participate in the afterlife, then what *is* he convinced of? If he does not believe the Bible's message, then what message *does* he believe? Everyone believes something about himself and his future, even if it is that he just "happened" through evolutionary chance and that all consciousness ceases to exist upon death. This is an uninformed and groundless belief, but it is a belief all the same.

But even if this is one's belief, what so *convinced* him of it? Has he taken the time to examine the Bible in detail to know for certain that it is not true? This is unlikely. It is far more likely that he has simply listened to others tell him what to believe, and—since what they said allows him to live as he pleases—he adopted their opinion as his own. This is both illogical and irresponsible, given what is at stake. He hopes that he is right, of course, but he has no good reason to have such hope.[20]

People's opinions about God—even my own—are just that: *opinions*. The Bible reveals that God is not interested in personal opinions. He concerns Himself only with truth, justice, and righteousness, and He proves Himself to be the authoritative standard for these things. Do we need faith in order to believe in God? Absolutely. Faith provides the link between where we stand now and what will happen to our souls in the future. But faith ought to be based upon facts and evidence, not feelings and opinions. Blind faith in religion is no better than the Evolutionist's often-cited blind forces of nature being credited with guiding a single-cell organism to produce a complex and intelligent human being. Both are fictitious, mythological, and imaginary beliefs that are founded on nothing more than wishful thinking and false conclusions. Both belief systems are hopeless, and lead their followers to ruin (Mat. 15:14).

Summary Thoughts

If God exists, then the human soul *and* a conscious afterlife exists. It is logically and biblically impossible to maintain any one of these without the other two. The same source material (the Bible) from which we learned about God also speaks of the reality of the human soul. The same logic and reason by which we can sufficiently know that God exists can be applied to that of the human soul and the afterlife. These three—God, the soul, and the soul's afterlife—all rise or fall together.

Of course, not everyone chooses to believe that God exists. This decision is based upon personal preference rather than sound reasoning. Some people simply do not like a "God" whom they cannot control, does not meet their expectations, or will not let them live like they please. An amoral, mundane, and purely theoretical "god"—like a blind force of nature—caters to their personal expectations. Choosing *not* to believe in a blind force of nature brings no consequence. On the other hand, choosing not to believe in one's own Creator brings the severest of consequences, especially in the life to come.

The Bible is not our only source of information about the existence of God, but it is a unique and irrefutable one. It carries within it numerous proofs, evidences, and testimonies. The Bible gives a name, personality, and depiction of this God that we already know exists by observing the marvel of the physical world and all living creatures—human beings in particular. As clearly, directly, and unapologetically as it defends God's existence, so the Bible also defends the existence of the human soul *and* the realm where all souls go when separated from the human body.

Atheism and apathy are on the rise, so it has become fashionable to etch God out of the picture and dismiss any concern for an afterlife. Yet, while truth can be suppressed, maligned, or ignored, it cannot be killed and will not remain silent. The evidence for God, one's soul, and the afterlife is not going away and demands our attention. This has nothing to do, up front, with religion or even Christianity, but with the basic moral responsibility that all of us have as human beings. What you read from this point forward is factual information concerning what will be the most important part of your existence.

Chapter Two: Thoughts on the Afterlife

The question—"Is there an afterlife?"—is relatively straightforward. The answer is either "yes" or "no." If "yes," then we can move on to aspects *of* this afterlife, and how we can possibly know them. A "no" answer, on the other hand, requires a sufficient amount of objective proof. If we do have a soul that is heading for a future existence, then we cannot just ignore all of this at someone's word.

If we can know that there is an afterlife, the next logical question is: what *constitutes* this afterlife? And, on the heels of this question are a number of other questions, including: what kind of consciousness will I have in that life? What will I do there? Will this afterlife be radically different than the life I am experiencing right now or simply an extension of this one? How can I be a human being in a context outside of my physical body, this three-dimensional physical world, and the natural laws that govern my earthly existence? Is the human soul truly immortal, unable to be annihilated? Does everyone who has ever lived go on to live *forever*?

These are all fair questions. And, at the risk of sounding very disappointing, no one (on earth) has the full answer to any of them. On the other hand, there *are answers*. While some of these answers may be deductive or even intuitive, it is the Bible that provides the only revealing, factual, and authoritative source of such information. Unless God had revealed these answers to us in His word, we could only blindly speculate on what lies ahead of us. As it is, we can know enough to be fully prepared for it instead.

Since there is another life for you in a world beyond this one, then what is happening here and now is not the entirety of your existence. This can be very unsettling or very exciting, depending upon what you think this future life is going to be—particularly, what you think it is going to be for you.

Many people are deeply concerned with the questions "what will happen to me?" or "what has happened to my loved ones who have already died?" There is good reason for such concern, for the subject of the afterlife is a sobering view of the future. Your beliefs about the afterlife—or whether there even is an afterlife—should have a profound effect on how you live this life. The two subjects are inextricably related.

The "Afterlife" Defined

To condense a long and complex discussion into a relatively short one and simple one, "afterlife" is synonymous with whatever your soul will consciously experience *after* this life. Your existence beyond your physical death constitutes your "afterlife," regardless of what happens in that realm and existence. If you did not have a soul, but only possessed an illusion of consciousness (as Evolutionism necessarily demands), then you would have no afterlife. To clarify: there still may be a spiritual realm in which *non*-humans dwell, but *human souls* will not be among them if our existence is entirely limited to an earthly one. There is no "after" for us if what we are experiencing now is the fullness of our being.

The afterlife goes by various names. Some call it the "hereafter," to distinguish it from the "here and now." Others call it the "underworld," an allusion to a common ancient belief that departed souls literally went to a world under the earth. It is "the great beyond," "the world to come," "eternal bliss" or "eternal destruction" (depending on how things go for a person), "the realm of the dead," "the grave," or simply "death." Regardless, "The notion that life continues on in some form after death is one of the oldest concepts held by human beings."[21]

Nearly every distinct culture or civilization has its own depiction of the afterlife. It is often a realm from which no one can ever leave, and is overseen by some higher authority—a god(s) and/or goddess(es). Often in these realms are sacred symbols, extension of archetypes from this life: a colossal world tree, its branches reaching to the heavens (where gods live) and roots descending to the underworld (the grave); a river dividing the realm of the living and dead; a majestic mountain; a vast and ethereal field or meadow; a great sea; legendary animals; beautiful, angelic maidens; etc. Most views of the afterlife incorporate some form of judgment, justice, reward, or punishment. There is a prevalent belief among many cultures that what is lacking here will be taken care of in the hereafter; what is crooked here will be straightened in the world to come (see

Eccles. 1:15, 12:14). The "higher authority" in that realm—whether God or gods—will make certain that this is done.

The ancients regarded themselves within the context of a great family, clan, or tribe. This idea, they believed, carried over into the afterlife. The newly dead went to join the already dead, being "gathered to their fathers" (2 Kings 22:20, etc.), recreating and expanding over multiple generations the family that was once begun on earth. Thus, there was often less concern with the individual soul than with a grand continuation of the soul's relatives. Each person sees himself (or herself) as part of a never-ending relationship with his ancestors. "Having shared in the life of the group, the individual participates in its ultimate destiny, a destiny that can transcend even death."[22]

Even so, there was no universally shared view of the afterlife among the ancients. The Hebrews (and others) simply referred to it as *Sheol*, meaning "the grave" or the unseen realm of the dead (Psalm 18:5 and 89:48, for example). This was not a state of unconsciousness, but was regarded as a shadowy, gloomy, and inactive state of being—in contrast to the sunlit and active realm of human activity on earth. "Such conceptions, it need hardly be said, did not rest on revelation, but were rather the natural ideas formed of the future state, in contrast with life in the body, in the absence of revelation."[23]

The ancient Greeks had very similar ideas in their realm of the dead which they called Hades. Properly, "Hades" was the name of the god of the underworld. The realm of the dead was thus known as "the house of Hades."[24] The NT uses the word *tartaroo* (commonly referred to as "Tartarus") which seems to correspond to this realm (2 Peter 2:4). "[This] word appears in classical Greek to refer to a subterranean region, doleful and dark, regarded by the ancient Greeks as the abode of the wicked dead. It was thought of as a place of punishment. In the sole use of the word in the NT it refers to the place of punishment for rebellious angels."[25] The Greeks believed that souls of the deceased were sent to one of three realms: Elysium, for blameless warriors; Tartarus, for the wicked; and the Fields (or Meadows) of Asphodel for everyone else.

Ancient Egyptians had one of the more elaborate and fanciful depictions of the afterlife, but largely (it appears) for their pharaohs and other renown men. The pyramids and similar funerary temples were meant to become the eternal dwelling places of these men; tomb pictures could magically supply the wants of the deceased. Osiris was the god of the netherworld and oversaw, along with his wife, Isis, all of the departed spirits. Generally speaking, the masses of human souls continued to "sow and reap bountiful harvests, and enjoy the pleasures formerly had on earth. He [Osiris] held the promise of a continued existence in this afterworld," giving Egyptians an anticipation for a relatively comfortable promise of the future.[26]

Eastern religions, particularly Hinduism and Buddhism, believe in reincarnation: a dead person's soul is reborn into another earthly existence. Hinduism assumes that people return to earthly life as *different* people, often in a different social standing (or caste), or even as animals. Ultimately (or hopefully), a person will reach a state of Nirvana in which all desire is extinct and one becomes liberated (whatever that means, or whatever that looks like). Buddhism follows Hinduism, but says that we do not have individual souls. Rather, we have a bundle of memories and desires that need to be purged from consciousness, and then a person enters a blissful state of being. The one who oversees all this decision-making remains conspicuously absent or unidentified.

Norse mythology speaks of Valhalla [lit., hall of the slain] for valiant warriors. Muslim men look forward to a heavenly bliss, being surrounded by their wives and a company of "beautiful, dark-eyed, female companions."[27] Muslims also believe in a "soul sleep" until the Judgment Day when Allah (their version of the biblical God) judges all souls. Until then, righteous souls will have visions of Allah, and wicked souls will have visions of torment. Sufiism, a branch of original Mohammedism, adds a personal element: a departed soul can "find" itself and move from lower levels of the afterlife to higher levels.

Modern Judaism's depiction of the afterlife, depending on who you ask, ranges from reincarnation to a heavenly existence to the annihilation of the soul. Spiritualism teaches that, depending on the quality of your spiritual "vibrations" in this life, you will experience either a dark and unpleasant existence in the life to come, or an extremely beautiful and joyous one. A so-called Law of Progress allows souls from lower realms to gradually ascend to upper realms, no matter how many eons of time it takes.

Traditional Christian Views of the Afterlife

Christian theology provides a clear and distinct disposition of the dead: all souls are judged by God, then sent either to heaven or hell, depending on how they lived while on earth (all to be discussed later). This thought has permeated much of the world's understanding of the afterlife, even though not everyone or every culture accepts its conclusions. What is different between Christianity and ancient ideas is that now we have veritable information from those who have *seen* the afterlife: Paul, in his vision of Paradise (2 Cor. 12:1–4); John, in his detailed but symbolic vision of the spiritual realm (Rev. 4—21); and, most notably, Jesus Christ, who came *out of* the spiritual realm, was resurrected *from* the spiritual realm, and returned *to* the spiritual realm after His resurrection (John 1:1–3, 14, Acts 17:30–31, and Acts 1:9–11). These claims are all supported by the miracles produced by those who made them. In the case of Jesus' resurrection, He is the subject of His *own* miraculous event.

Americans have been heavily influenced by centuries of Catholicism, which claims to be the authentic representation of biblical Christianity despite its glaring lack of biblical support. Catholicism has introduced modifications to the afterlife that many adherents have come to accept as fact. These include: different levels of both hell and Paradise, notably detailed in Dante's *Divine Comedy;* Purgatory, in which souls can be purged (or cleansed) of sin through a finite period of suffering; and Limbo [lit., edge or boundary], a realm of the dead who are guilty of Original Sin (of Adam) and yet are neither assigned to hell nor allowed into heaven. Such traditions, born in the Middle Ages, have persisted to this day, and have given the impression that there may be a second chance after death for sinners to make things right with God.

Other more modern teachings have influenced our understanding of the afterlife. Universalism, which is increasingly popular among evangelicals, has deleted hell from existence and claims that everyone will ultimately be in heaven. Calvinism claims that God has already decided who will be saved or condemned in the hereafter, so ultimately there is nothing anyone can do about it: the lost cannot be saved, and the saved cannot be lost.[28] Mormons believe that those who are sealed in an earthly temple ceremony will reign with God. Good people will live apart from God; some sinners will suffer a temporary hellish existence, but can repent of their sins and escape this; and really wicked people will join Satan in an eternal torment. Mormons also allow living people to be baptized on behalf of departed souls (so-called "baptism for the dead"), allegedly saving those condemned souls from ruin.

Jehovah Witnesses (and other Sabbatarian denominations) believe that all human souls experience a kind of "soul sleep" until after the alleged thousand-year reign of Christ on earth. Upon completion of that millennium, all souls will be judged. Of these, 144,000 select souls who were faithful to God on earth will live with Him in heaven; the remaining faithful will be sent back to a rejuvenated earth to live forever; the unfaithful will be consumed by fire and annihilated. Annihilation means that the soul will altogether cease to exist—a teaching that is completely foreign to the NT.

Modern Responses to the Afterlife

If you asked people today what they believe about the afterlife, their answers would likely fall into one of the following responses:

- **I'm not interested in the subject.** The irreligious person does not seem to care whether there is an afterlife—or so it appears. Perhaps he merely suppresses the idea, or masks it over with what he thinks are more pressing things, or thinks that there will be time enough later in life to dwell on such matters. He carelessly dismisses any proofs of an afterlife, or thinks such proofs somehow do not affect him personally. He is simply a man of the world—*this* world—and he will deal with an afterlife if or when it happens.
- **There is no afterlife.** The atheist claims—conclusively, he believes—that there simply is no God, eternal soul, or afterlife. "Atheist" is derived from *a-* [against] and *theos* [God]. Atheists do not merely disagree with what God has said or done, but they

allegedly do not believe that there *is* a God or *any* gods. The world is purely material and mechanical, having evolved to its present state over eons of time. There are no souls, there is no higher moral authority than that of human beings, and we simply cease to exist after death. The atheist does not *prove* that there is no afterlife; he simply argues God and the afterlife out of existence by his own intellectual rationalism.

- **We cannot know if there is an afterlife.** The agnostic claims that he cannot know for certain that there is a God, an eternal soul, or an afterlife. "Agnostic" is derived from *a-* [against] and *gnosis* [knowledge]. He assumes that, since these things cannot be proven—invariably, to his personal *expectations*, not to the degree that is necessary for drawing an intelligent conclusion—he can safely dismiss them altogether. As a result, he lives with indifference toward any spiritual future, even though he has failed to prove how or why this is unknowable in the first place. Ironically, he claims to know *with certainty* what is knowable or unknowable based upon his own arbitrary logic.
- **There *is* an afterlife, but it will be on one's own terms.** People may not use these exact words, but they certainly hold to this opinion. Many have a customized view of the "great beyond," usually based on a blend of emotional and religious beliefs (see below). Some of these versions include: a happy reunion with loved ones; a glorified earthly existence; a happy existence, but without God and angels—simply a glorified conscious awareness; or life in which everyone becomes his own god and gets to create his own universe.
- **There *is* an afterlife, but no hell—only God's heaven.** There is no punishment in the afterlife, only (apparently) reward. If you don't go to heaven, then you simply cease to exist. Or, heaven is simply where *everyone* goes, no matter what. The premise is: since a loving God cannot possibly send anyone to eternal torment, therefore everyone is already "saved"—they just may not yet know it.
- **There *is* an afterlife, and every soul will be either in heaven or hell.** This is what the Bible actually teaches, however unpopular it may be and whether one chooses to believe it. But it is easy for people

to use common terms that carry very different meanings. Compare a Christian's conception of heaven with that of a Muslim's conception of *his* heaven, for example—or a Mormon, or the member of a charismatic cult. Just because two people agree on the same terminology does not mean they believe the same thing.

In order for an afterlife to exist, it requires a universal standard of authority to determine the truth about it. If such a standard did not exist, then no truth about the afterlife could be known at all. Most personal or religious views of the afterlife lack consistent, credible, authentic, and evidential authority. Many religious authorities claim to "know" one thing or another, but have little or nothing to back it up. In many cases, people are just *making stuff up*, then peddling it as though it is "the truth" or wanting so badly to believe in it that it becomes *a* "truth" to *them*. Sadly, the subject of an afterlife is often complicated by various theories, philosophies, worldviews, personal opinions, and religious beliefs. It is even further complicated by pride, conflicts of interest, erroneous teachings, indifference, and fear.

Of course, if there is *no* afterlife, then it is a waste of time to pursue the matter—but we need to know for certain that this is true. If there is no afterlife—and thus, no soul—then we have nothing to worry about with regard to moral responsibility, moral accountability, answering to a Higher Authority for what we did in this life, reward, punishment, or any other details. We simply accept that there is no afterlife—period. When we die, we are completely, irretrievably, and permanently *non-existent*. We have no more consciousness, no memories, no ability to think or make decisions, no emotions, no personality, and no *life*.

If there is no afterlife, then whatever we now perceive to be "spiritual" is actually a projection of neural impulses of the physical brain, nothing more. When the brain dies, so do its projections—its thoughts, consciousness, memories, and "soul." When we close our eyes in death, our soul—or, what we call the "soul"—simply vanishes into nothing. It is as if we had never lived. When you die, it will be as though *you* had never lived. Our present lives, then, have no meaning or importance beyond what is going on in the here and now. Ultimately, since everyone dies—and even the physical world is destined to die—all of humanity will have been for nothing. In the future, humankind will be less than a faded memory; it will be as though it had never happened. No one needs to be saved or forgiven, since everything and everyone will be lost and forgotten.

On the other hand, if there *is* an afterlife, then we ought to do everything in our power to prepare for it, if indeed our decisions here have any impact on the life to come. This is not something we want to guess at, given what is at stake.

The Customized Approach

The Bible claims absolutely that there is an afterlife—a spiritual, human consciousness that endures beyond this earthly life. Even so, the Bible only partially answers our questions concerning it, and never to our full satisfaction. Other questions remain unknown and, unless we have someone from the afterlife to answer them, are unknowable. To clarify: these things are unknowable to *us*, but not to those (human souls, heavenly beings, angels, demons, and God Himself) who already dwell there.

For the earth-bound human being, however, it is very difficult—if not impossible—to fully grasp what it must be like in a realm he cannot comprehend and with a consciousness he has never experienced. Instead of accepting the biblical view of the afterlife as a glimpse into something we were never meant to fully understand in this life, people tend to impose earthly expectations upon it—in essence, *customizing* the afterlife to meet their own desirable expectations. While it is likely that we all do this to some extent (in an attempt to understand it), some of these customized views have been elevated to a virtual doctrinal status.

In a typically-held view of the afterlife, deceased loved ones, relatives, and friends will be there to welcome you, already having (somehow) found each other and recreated the friendship circle that you all enjoyed here on earth. Virtually everyone whom you loved dearly on earth will be there, ready to resume your earthly relationship with them. You will laugh together, eat and drink together, and carry on in whatever way you used to when you were alive. Families will all get together and, as the saying goes, "the circle will be unbroken." Never mind that many of these family members were a bunch of irreligious, irresponsible, foul-mouthed adulterers when they were here. In the hereafter, God will (allegedly) see the good in everyone and automatically forgive them of their crimes.

This customized view often assumes that we will resume in heaven whatever identity we chose for ourselves on earth. For example, if you were a biker on earth, you will ride a glorified Harley in the hereafter. You will still wear blue jeans, a studded leather vest or jacket, and a skullcap or bandana on your head. You will still wear very cool shades, gold chains, studs, and/or big, gaudy rings. You will still sport big biceps, colorful tattoos, and a handlebar mustache. People will still be slightly afraid of and at the same time very respectful toward you. Or, if you were a celebrity singer or an actor here on earth, then you anticipate reuniting with all your singing and acting buddies that preceded you in death. Souls in your customized heaven will throng together to hear your beautiful singing voice, just as they did on earth. Or, you will perform great theatrical roles on a heavenly stage as you simply extend your celebrity status into the great beyond.

If you listen to people talk at funerals and memorial services, you will see that people really believe these things. They say things like, "I bet Joe is up there right now fishing along a beautiful stream with an awesome flyrod." Or, "I can just see Aunt Sue up there right now carrying on with all of the old relatives, telling jokes and tall tales while sipping red wine and smoking cigarettes." Or, "Ol' Bill is probably up there right now playing pool, drinking beer, and flirting with all the ladies—just like he always used to do here!" In some inexplicable way, the deceased are always "looking down" on the living, either with anticipation for the rest of their friends and family to join them, or at least with curiosity as they see how things turned out after they had died. All of this sounds so promising, so idealized, and so romantic—in essence, so *humanized*. Yet, there is not a shred of evidence (biblical or otherwise) to back up any of it.

Even those who are more spiritual-minded tend to embellish and customize. They may think that their own church or denomination is the only group that will be there, and that they will simply resume their churchly lifestyle in the hereafter. Or, they think that their form of contemporary church worship—heads bowed, hands in the air, a rhythmic swaying of the crowd, the euphoric rush of "the Spirit" overtaking everyone, the band playing cutting-edge Christian rock on the stage, the sound system and lighting all creating a powerfully emotional experience—will be recreated for them in heaven. Everything will be "awesome," and Jesus will likely stand on the stage dressed in blue jeans, a casual shirt, and Birkenstocks—just like many preachers do today.

All such constructions and customizations fail to consider one enormous factor: *we have no authority in the afterlife.* We cannot assume that, upon death, our souls are suddenly in charge of themselves, and can continue to make decisions and dictate circumstances like we did on earth. This is pure fiction; there is no reason to believe it; no one can justify it. No existence is possible without authority, and we are clearly *not* an authority in a realm we did not create, have never seen, cannot even fathom, and cannot enter into by our own volition. The fact that we could not will ourselves into existence *or* stop ourselves from ever dying proves this. If we cannot have absolute authority in this life, what makes us think that we will have it in the life to come?

The Reason for Our Existence

One of the profound ideas in considering the afterlife is that "life" never really ends. It is simply continued in a completely different context. Death certainly is the end of this present life, but it is not *the* end. Not only do we die to this present world, but this world will be as dead to us, since we will never return to it. We now live in a physical, tangible, three-dimensional world; the afterlife does not conform to this. We now live in a time-based world; the afterlife, if it is the final phase of our existence, is either eternal in nature (so time is unknown) or simply ends for reasons that we do not know. I'm speaking here without reference to what the Bible teaches, but simply as a preface to the subject.

No matter what will or will not happen in the afterlife, someone must be in charge of it. The God of the Bible is also presented as the Creator of the physical universe, all life on earth, and human life in particular. He is also the One in charge of the invisible spiritual realm to which the afterlife belongs. If there is no God, then another being must be responsible for the afterlife in order for it to even exist, because it is impossible for it to exist without someone (or something) being in charge of it. While Evolutionism seems to work for those who wish to believe in it, it is absurd to think of the spiritual realm having "evolved" over time into what it is now or what it will be once we see it. Besides, Evolution does not even recognize a spiritual realm.

The Bible does offer an explanation not only of this present life but also (to a limited degree) the life to come. Just as the God of the Bible oversees this world, so He oversees the world to come. Just as God is responsible for having created *our* world (the physical universe; see Gen. 1), so He is responsible for having created *His* world (the spiritual realm). To accept some ancestral belief, cultural legend, words of some religious authority figure, or even one's own personal "think so" over the impressive and irrefutable testimony of the Bible is to reject the very best testimony on this subject for a significantly inferior one. Such a rejection is irrational and inexplicable. This is especially true given what is at stake—one's eternal future existence.

In the Creation account of the origin of Man (Gen. 2), God is responsible for designing the human body *and* imparting life to Man, the only creature who bears the "image of God" on earth (Gen. 1:27). "Then the LORD God formed man of dust from the ground, and breathed into his nostrils the breath of life; and man became a living being" (Gen. 2:7). This is an English translation of the original Hebrew text. The Hebrew word here for "being" [*nephesh*] means "alive" in the same sense that you are alive right now. The emphasis in this passage, however, is that man's physical body is lifeless until God gives it life. Once the life is removed from the body, then what is left is no longer a person (or, a living thing), but is dead (James 2:26).[29] *Nephesh* is often translated "soul" in the Old Testament, but almost invariably refers to one's physical life, not his spirit or soul that continues after death. Even so, the idea that living souls on earth do continue after death is a staple biblical teaching. Jesus Himself said that God "is not the God of the dead but of the living; for all live to Him" (Luke 20:38). In other words, God does not preside over a cosmic cemetery of dead bodies, but surrounds Himself with living souls.

Imbedded in these few passages is the idea that a person's life on earth is only a phase of his existence, not the entirety of it. This does not mean that the afterlife is merely "phase two" of one's existence, but something far more profound: it is the main reason why we were given life in the first place. God does not intend for us to live here on the earth forever; He intends for us to be with *Him* forever. What we call "heaven" is not merely a nice place to be; it is where God dwells, and therefore is where those who are made "in His image" are supposed to be once they leave this earth. In that future existence, we will be freed from the limitations of the body, earthly knowledge, and the material world that presently restrain us. "For now," the apostle Paul says, "we see in a mirror dimly, but then [in the next phase of our existence—MY WORDS] face to face; now I know in part, but then I will know fully just as I also have been fully known" (1 Cor. 13:12).

We are meant to be with God, and God is meant to be with us; "They shall be My people," He says over and over throughout the Bible, "and I will be their God" (Jer. 32:38, 2 Cor. 6:16, etc.). This gives our earthly existence not only closure, but a destination; we are not just aimlessly plodding through a mundane existence on this planet, we are bodily-yet-spiritual beings preparing to be with the One who created us. This also gives our earthly life meaning, purpose, and *hope*—if indeed we regard it in the way God expects us to. Since He will "require" our spirits from us (Luke 12:20) and bring us to judgment (John 5:28–29, 2 Cor. 5:10), we are meant to live responsibly to Him while we are here. His intention is not to bring us to ruin, but to bring us *home*. Nevertheless, He allows us to make that decision rather than making it for us.

The (assumed) annihilation of one's existence is not merely a dark outlook on humanity, but it sucks all meaning and purpose out of it. If this present existence is all that we will ever know, then earthly life descends into a hopeless, irrational, and senseless every-man-for-himself experience (a.k.a. "survival of the fittest"). Likewise, there will be no ultimate justice for wicked people and no vindication of the righteous. In fact, wickedness and righteousness would have no objective meaning, no point of reference outside of our own imagination. It is the afterlife—a future existence—that *completes* this life. It is the afterlife that brings closure, finality, and *completion* to what we experience in the here and now. And it is the afterlife that gives weight, substance, and purpose our present lives. Take away the afterlife, and everything else implodes.

Summary Thoughts

Many different opinions exist concerning the afterlife. Without a fixed, timeless, and universally-applied standard of authority to reference, we are free to imagine whatever we want about what will happen to us after we die. This means that we are also free to imagine that *nothing* happens to us, since no one can know that something *does* happen unless he has good reason to do so. Every culture has its own take on the subject. The irreligious, atheist, agnostic, universalist, and many other "-ists" all wade in with their particular views. In the absence of a definable standard, nothing can be known for certain *about* the spiritual realm or whether there even *is* one. We may as well choose whatever "-ism" or fairytale that makes us happy in this life, since we can do nothing to prepare for or avoid what happens to us after we leave it.

The Bible, however, does not offer yet another opinion about the existence of the human soul and its survival after physical death, but confirmation of it. Not only this, but the Bible declares what will happen to each soul after death, based upon the decisions that each soul made in this present life. There are only two paths in this life, and only two destinations of those paths in the life to come. What begins here will be ended there; whatever "God" we serve here will determine whether or not we will be with the God of the Bible there.

One might think that people would take the subject of the afterlife far more seriously than they do. As it is, many people go about their lives with little concern for it, even when facing their own mortality. In the absence of biblical information, this would be acceptable; yet, since we have such information, a cavalier approach is irresponsible. Even if one does believe in an afterlife, it is intellectually careless to assume that the future spiritual realm caters to his own fanciful depiction of it. We have no authority to make such assumptions; we have no authority to customize the afterlife to our own liking; we have no authority in the world to come, period. If there is an afterlife, then there must be a God (and vice versa); if there is a God, then He is in charge of what will happen to our souls, not us.

To some, death reveals the meaning of one's life; to others, this life is all there is, and so death is the end of all there is. "Our philosophy of life influences our philosophy of death. Conversely, how we perceive death and what meaning we give it affect the way we live."[30] In any case, *death* marks the end of this life. Whatever waits for us on the other side—if anything—will not be known personally to us until we die to this life.

Chapter Three: You Will Be in the Afterlife

The idea of a life beyond our earthly existence is a difficult thing to wrap one's mind around. After all, this earthly life is all we have ever known; we have never seen or experienced anything different. The idea of being in (or even going to) another "life" seems incomprehensible, no matter how strongly one believes it to be true. The incomprehensibleness of the idea does not make it any less true; still, we have nothing to compare it to in our earth-bound, human existence.

The idea of immortality in this future life—an eternal consciousness, in whatever state we find ourselves—is equally difficult to comprehend. No one here has ever experienced eternal life; everything in our world has a beginning and an end. The concept of living *forever* can be as frightening as it is fascinating. Yet, the Bible speaks directly to this fact: "For this perishable must put on the imperishable, and this mortal must put on immortality" (1 Cor. 15:53). The apostle Paul was speaking to Christians and their hope to be with God, but the statement has universal application: the physical human experience will be replaced by a fully spiritual one. In this spiritual future, we will have a body, but it will not be like the one you now occupy.

So then, there are three major things to consider: a new kind of existence in the future; an immortal existence, which will never change or end; and a new body in which to experience this new and immortal existence. This is a lot to take in all at once. But if it is all true, then it is something that deserves our careful attention. It makes no sense to ignore it altogether, for any reason. People make all kinds of plans—reservations, itineraries, schedules, events, etc.—for a future vacation. No one just blindly embarks on a trip to nowhere without having a good idea of what to expect. If this is true about an earthly vacation, it should be considerably more so concerning one's future existence.

The information you are being confronted with now (in this life) is meant to prepare you for what is coming. And, regardless of whether you choose to believe it, you cannot stop, avoid, or excuse yourself from what is coming. All you can do is be ready for it or enter into it blindly and completely unprepared. In any case, the future—*your* future—will be here before you know it.

Major Events in Your Future

There are two endings that every person will face: the ending of his physical life on earth, which is deeply personal; and the ending of the world, which is cosmic or universally-shared.[31] Our death will bring about this first ending; according to the Bible, the Second Coming of Christ will bring about the second (2 Thess. 1:6–9, 2 Peter 3:7, 10–12, etc.). Both of these endings—even the idea of them—have never been personally experienced by us. We are alive; the earth has always existed in our lifetime. We cannot fathom—even though we have every reason to believe it is true—the cessation of our earthly life or of the earth itself.

Neither one of these events—the death of you, or the death of the physical universe—is something a person can opt out of. Choosing to deny your mortality does not suddenly make you immortal any more than choosing to deny your humanity makes you a tree or a bird. And just because one chooses to deny the Second Coming of Christ does not mean that God's plans for this will evaporate, or that they will not affect him personally. Many people today are doing exactly what was predicted in Scripture (2 Peter 3:3–7):

> Know this first of all, that in the last days mockers will come with their mocking, following after their own lusts, and saying, "Where is the promise of His coming? For ever since the fathers fell asleep, all continues just as it was from the beginning of creation." For when they maintain this, it escapes their notice that by the word of God the heavens existed long ago and the earth was formed out of water and by water, through which the world at that time was destroyed, being flooded with water. But by His word the present heavens and earth are being reserved for fire, kept for the day of judgment and destruction of ungodly men.

Such people "set nature and its law above the God of nature and His revelation and argue from the past continuity of nature's phenomena to the conclusion that there can be no further interruption to them."[32] They argue, in effect, "I don't see how the world can end. It's never ended before!" But this is like saying, "I don't believe that I will die. After all, I've never died before!" It is a position based solely on personal experience, not facts, evidence, and an authority greater than themselves. This is not merely a weak argument; it is not an argument at all. It is simply an unfounded opinion. It sounds authoritative, yet speaks with an authority that the one saying it does not have. It also ignores the universal human experience: *your* death will be unique to *you*, but death itself is hardly unique to anyone.

Likewise, someone says, "I don't believe Jesus Christ is coming again—He's never appeared in the clouds to judge the world before!" This person simply ignores what has happened in human history, what has been recorded and preserved in the Bible, and what has been promised by a God who has never broken any of His promises. This also masquerades as an authoritative statement, but the one who speaks it has no authority to talk this way. A person cannot just start saying things that affect all of human history, the future of the world, and the future of every human soul without being qualified to say them. And no one on earth is qualified on his own credentials to predict these things.

So then, your life here will indeed end. Look around you—it is happening all the time to people who anticipated it, doubted it, resisted it with all their might, or simply disbelieved it would ever happen to them. All those people—young and old, Christians and atheists, sophists and the irreligious, princes and paupers, black and white and everything else—all these once were here, but now they are not. Walk through a cemetery sometime and you get a sense of this. Perhaps everyone buried there thought at one time that they would live on earth forever. But it does not matter what they once thought about their mortality, for they had no control over it. Indeed, they all finally succumbed to something that was bigger than all of them—something that none of them could evade, avoid, opt out of, or stop altogether.

However, these same people still exist—no longer in the flesh, but certainly in the spirit. Popular books about death "leave the general impression that dying is a beautiful experience regardless of one's life style or relationship to Christ. That certainly is not in harmony with either traditional Christian belief or Biblical pronouncements."[33] Those who chose not to believe in God now regret such a decision; those who chose not to believe in God's existence now have been proven wrong; both groups will stand trial before the God whom they rejected. Those who *did* believe in God will also be judged on the substance of their belief (or, faith), and whether their souls have been redeemed by the blood of Christ. Not everyone who claims to "believe" stands righteous before God, since "the demons also believe, and shudder" at what lies ahead of them (James 2:19).

Two Very Different Futures

As sure as you will die, so your soul will continue to exist consciously in the afterlife. The same Bible that clearly, unapologetically, and unequivocally maintains that there is an afterlife also declares this realm to be comprised only of heaven and hell. Thus, there will be only two groups of people in the hereafter: those who will dwell forever with God in heaven, and those who will forever be separated from Him in hell. Both endings are equally incomprehensible to us, yet one is incomprehensibly *wonderful* and the other incomprehensibly *awful*.

According to the Bible, those who are ushered into eternal life with God ("heaven") will be engulfed in the warmth, beauty, and fellowship of His presence. The earthly life will not be recreated for them, for they will enjoy an entirely new and completely spiritual existence rather than a physical one.[34] All the burdens and sorrows of this life will be removed; they will never be known again. The "great multitude" of human souls that will dwell with God (Rev. 7:9) will not be concerned with earthly family and friends, or with trying to recreate or replicate their earthly identity or experiences. "Behold," God says, "I am making all things new" (Rev. 21:3–5). These souls will have a new identity, a new body, and a new level of spiritual fellowship that they could not fathom when they were still on earth. Much of this is described for us with earthly imagery, of course, because we could not understand a literal explanation.

In the biblical depiction of heaven, God is the center of all life, the center of all attention, and the center of *everything* (Rev. 4:1–11).

His angels and other "living creatures" encircle His throne; His Son sits at His right hand. The saints—the souls of those redeemed by the blood of Christ—all come before their Creator, praising, worshiping, and adoring Him. There is no need for looking up old friends and old relatives; *all* will be friends and relatives who are united in the spiritual brotherhood of Christ. Christ's church—and *only* His church—will be as a Bride for Him, to be forever joined with Him in an eternal marriage, the wedding feast of which will never end (Rev. 19:7–9, 21:2–3).

These people—the ones "purchased for God with [Christ's] blood" (Rev. 5:9)—will be a "city of God," also known figuratively as the "New Jerusalem" (Heb. 12:22). There will be no need for tabernacles, temples, or church buildings; God will dwell before them, among them, and in them. They will be His people, and He will be their God, just as He had intended all along (2 Cor. 6:16). His heaven will be filled with light, joy, peace, and fellowship. There will be music and singing; there will be abundance and prosperity. No one will be forgotten, overlooked, or excluded; all will be showered with divine love and attention. There will no longer be any need of faith or grace, since we will see God with our own eyes and grace will have served its purpose (i.e., to deal with sin).

This is a beautiful picture, and speaks to the deepest longings of the human soul. We all want to be taken care of, protected, and comforted. We all want to be accepted, appreciated, and completed. We all want to live forever in an existence that cannot deteriorate or be taken away from us. If we are fully honest with ourselves, we all want to be *with God*—and God, thankfully, wants all of us to be with Him.[35] The entire reason for creating humankind, giving us the Bible, sending us His Son, and providing us with a means of salvation is so that we *can* be with Him.

Those who are not with God in His heaven will be forever separated *from* Him in a miserable, painful, and horribly sad existence. This is known to us as "hell," and there have been many attempts to eradicate such an awful scenario. People love the idea of heaven, of course, but hell appears unthinkable. Modern preachers, liberal theologians, and even those who make no claim on Christianity denounce the very idea of (in their words) "a loving God sending people to burn in hell for all eternity." This misrepresents the concept of "a loving God," but also completely ignores what people *do* to this loving God in the first place. Even so, no person in the Bible spoke more directly on the reality of hell than Jesus Himself—the only One who has the credentials to do so.

Such are the two destinations in the afterlife, according to the Bible. There is no third or alternate destination for one who does not like these two. The Bible says that Jesus came *from* the afterlife (the spiritual realm) to inform us that our souls do exist, the afterlife is real, we really are going there, and no one is exempt from this (John 5:28-30). If we dismiss the biblical record, then we have no credible account of what happens to us after we die, since no one has ever come back from the dead to tell us about it.[36] (See Appendix II: "Near-death Experiences.")

Questions Concerning the Afterlife

As stated earlier, the subject at hand is emotionally-charged, riddled with traditional thinking, and difficult to grasp. Even the biblical portrayal of a heavenly afterlife is sparse in comparison to what we know of earthly life *and* what our curiosity longs to have revealed to us. It is fair, then, to acknowledge some of the common questions people raise in thinking about the afterlife. On the other hand, the sheer volume of such questions reveals what has already been stated—namely, that we cannot expect to wander into this realm on our own authority and think that we have full control of the situation. In fact, quite the opposite is true.[37]

- How does the human soul—something we have never even seen—get to the afterlife? How do we know the way? Who or what takes us there? What does it look like there—not just symbolically (as in Revelation) but *literally*? How will we live? Will we breathe air—or will we breathe at all? Will we eat and drink—or will we need any nourishment? What will keep us *alive* in the afterlife?
- Many believe that the afterlife is merely an extension of earthly life, but in a different context. But is this true? Will there be land and sky, mountains and valleys, continents and oceans, a sun and other celestial bodies, and gravity? How will we move about—will

we walk, run, swim, or fly? Will we merely "think" or teleport ourselves to different locations? Will there even *be* "locations" to go to? Will we have our own homes in which to dwell, or will we simply be a massive throng of souls with nowhere to go?

- What will be our identity in the afterlife? Will we have glorified human bodies—and if so, what will they look like? Will we have limbs and hands and feet—or even eyes and ears and a mouth? Or, will we be (as some think) a kind of floating ghost-like apparition that is bodiless, formless, and indistinct? How will we be known in the afterlife—will we have distinct features that link us to our earthly existence? Will we retain our earthly gender, ethnicity, and skin color? Will our names remain the same—and who decides one way or the other? How will we be identified? How will we communicate? What language will we speak? *Whose* language will we speak—and how will we know it? Will we use words, or will we simply read each other's thoughts?
- Many people believe in some form of reward or punishment in the afterlife that is based upon how we live in this life. But is this reward eternal? Will the wicked suffer forever? Will God make everyone suffer equally even though not everyone sinned equally? Likewise, will the righteous forever *be* righteous? If angels can fall from their proper domain (2 Peter 2:4), can righteous saints fall from theirs? Will salvation ever be possible for the condemned, and will sin ever be possible for the redeemed? Are these realms—and the existences of those in those realms—permanently and eternally fixed?

The Bible has answered some of these questions, but certainly not all of them. This bothers some people. "If God wants us to be with Him in heaven," some will say, "why didn't He tell us more about it?" The best response is: "heaven," as a place or destination, is not the real goal for the believer; *God* is. Jesus said very little about being in heaven, but He spoke often about *life with God*. The apostle Paul, for one, never talked about golden streets, crystal mansions, or other heavenly expectations, but he instead emphasized being "with the Lord" or "with Christ" (2 Cor. 5:8, Phil. 1:23). In the end, it really does not matter what is in heaven as much as it matters *who* is there.

Wherever God dwells *is* "heaven"; the inspiring message of the gospel of Christ is to be where God dwells.

Many people attempt to impose time, physics, and other attributes of our earthly world upon a spiritual one. We try to measure the heavenly realm with an earthly yardstick, so to speak. We ask questions like, "how much?", "how long?", "how many?" or "what kind?" We are uncomfortable with the fact that the afterlife cannot be calibrated, weighed out, or quantified by a standard with which we are already familiar. We like to take Jesus' portrayal of the rich man and Lazarus in their hereafter states of being (Luke 16:19–31) and literalize all the features, even diagram the two realms of which He speaks. We literalize a lot of things in Revelation (that were never meant to be taken literally) because we want to make sense of the spiritual realm. This implies that if *we* can't make sense of it, then it doesn't make sense *at all*, and a person is a *fool* to believe in it.[38] On this point, Paul rightly said, "But a natural [lit., unspiritual or worldly-minded[39]] man does not accept the things of the Spirit of God, for they are foolishness to him; and he cannot understand them, because they are spiritually appraised" (1 Cor. 2:14). There is nothing *natural* about the afterlife; it is, quite literally, a *super*natural existence.

When God created the physical (or material) world, He also created the natural laws and physics that govern this world. He created the concept of time by having this world conform to a necessary sequence of events or life cycles. Energy is a constant component of this world, but the material universe itself is winding down, cooling off, and running out of usable resources. Never mind how long it will take for all this to happen; the fact that it *is* happening is what determines the finite life of the universe as we know it. God also created time by giving us physical markers *of* time—in our case, the relationship between the earth, moon, and sun. One revolution of our spinning earth is one day; one orbit of the earth around the sun is one year; and one complete cycle of the moon's phases is one lunar month. This time is further broken down into seasons, months, weeks, hours, minutes, and seconds—all based ultimately on the physical motion of our planet.

God, having *created* all these things—the earth, moon, sun, material of the universe, natural laws, and time itself—necessarily proves His superiority *over* them. He is self-existent: He does not need us, our world, or a contribution from anything or anyone outside of Himself in order to be fully, completely, and eternally "God." This is what is implied in God's statement to Moses when He said, "I AM WHO I AM" (Exod. 3:14). God is a perpetual, unchanging, self-sustaining, and indestructible Being. He exists as an ever-present reality ("I AM"), without reference to age, future or past, before or after, or any other time-based attributes. "'I am the Alpha and the Omega,' says the Lord God, 'who is and who was and who is to come, the Almighty'" (Rev. 1:8). Alpha and omega are the first and last letters of the Greek alphabet. God says, in essence, "Just as there is no letter before 'A' and none after 'Z,' so *nothing exists in any context apart from Me, and I am the summing up of all that does* exist."[40] "Is there any God besides Me?" God Himself rhetorically asked Israel. He then answered the question Himself: "I know of none" (Isa. 44:8).

God, being superior to the material universe in which we have our physical and conscious existence, is transcendent of our world. This means He is above us in every respect; likewise, we are below Him in every respect.[41] He is in His spiritual heaven—a world of which we have no personal experience. In contrast, we dwell in a world that is affected by but not interchangeable with the spiritual world. God can enter our world in whatever manner He chooses—i.e., through His angels, His Spirit, miraculous intervention, and especially the bodily manifestation of Jesus Christ—but we cannot enter His world except through prayer, spiritual communion, and our own imagination.[42] He can intervene in our world because He made it, owns it, and thus has sovereign authority over it (Eph. 1:19b–23, Col. 1:17, Heb. 1:3a). He is the God of heaven *and* earth; there are no other actual gods but Him (Deut. 4:39, Isa. 45:21, 1 Cor. 8:4–6, etc.).[43] This is why Jesus, being the Son of God, was able to stop a raging storm, walk on water, and raise the dead: He had absolute mastery over our world and everything in it. There is nothing He could not have done while He was here, had it been necessary to fulfill His Father's will.[44]

What all this means: God possesses the power, authority, and sovereignty necessary not only to create and sustain the physical universe, but also the spiritual realm. We do not have to wonder about the how, who, when, or what of the afterlife, since He is already and will forever be in full control of it. This is comforting to those who have a relationship with Him and are prepared to spend eternity in His fellowship. But this can be very disturbing for those who thought otherwise, who perhaps wanted it otherwise, and who do not have any fellowship with Him.

Summary Thoughts

Discussions about the afterlife are admittedly difficult simply because of the lack of specific information available. For His own reasons, God has seen fit to withhold much of this information, forcing us to trust in Him rather than for us to think that we are in control of that situation. Even so, what He *has* revealed—especially about the heavenly realm in which He dwells—is beautiful beyond description, awe-inspiring, and speaks to the deepest longings of the human soul.

Yet, just as beautiful and majestic as heaven is, hell still remains for those who refuse to trust in God and His Son. Nearly every person wants to visualize himself (or herself) in heaven; hardly anyone chooses to contemplate the awful horror of hell—either for himself or his loved ones. Yet, the Bible is unnervingly clear: more souls will be cast into hell than will be ushered into heaven. This grim reality ought to force us to see what must be done to *guarantee* an entrance into heaven—really, an eternal life with God Himself—rather than to simply cross one's fingers and hope for the best. This latter course of action guarantees nothing but failure.

Meanwhile, people try to relate to heaven with earthly measurements, values, and expectations. Or, they try to cram heaven into an earthly context—the one being a mere glorified extension of the other. Such attempts are neither successful nor necessary. God is in full control of His world, just as He commands sovereign authority over our world. If we have a right relationship with God as we leave this world, we shall certainly be well taken care of in His world—He has promised this, and we have every good reason to believe in Him.

There is really nothing on earth (or in the earthly existence) to compare to a life with God in the eternity to come. We taste, sample, nibble, and barely touch the very fringe of what that glorious existence will be like, but there can be no way to experience it in full until we literally stand before Him and see all of His divine splendor. Even so, the tastes, rituals, and samplings that we have here all point forward to something "far more abundantly beyond all that we ask or think" (Eph. 3:20), and we can look forward to such things with great anticipation.

Our faith in God and His world is a human response to all that God has revealed to us. God did not give us our faith, but He has provided the basis *for* it. In other words, we do not exercise blind faith when we believe the words of the Bible and trust in God's redemption of our souls, since He has given us every reason to believe that these things are real. By faith, "we look not at the things which are seen, but at the things which are not seen; for the things which are seen are temporal, but the things which are not seen are eternal" (2 Cor. 4:18). By faith, we can "see" God in His glory and we visualize ourselves in His presence. By faith, we can put our trust—yes, and even our souls—in the hands of the only One who has the desire and ability to help us. By faith in His transformation of our souls, we can know that we shall one day be with Him.

Yet, as good as that message of life and hope is, we have not yet arrived in that new existence. And, until we do, the possibility of the *failure* of our faith remains. This reality demands our most serious attention to the need for a solid, healthy, and enduring faith in the Savior of the world.

Chapter Four: As Heaven Is Real, So Is Hell

C. S. Lewis wrote: "And here is the real problem: so much mercy, and yet there is hell."[45] As joyous as God's gospel message is to all who obey it, there is still that ominous and deeply disturbing hell lurking in the background of it all. All the wrangling over words, disputes over terminology, accusations about God's alleged "unfairness," and other protests cannot get rid of the simple fact that there will literally be *hell to pay* for those who sin against God and do nothing about it. The "problem" is not that hell exists, but that many will *choose* it—inexplicably, unnecessarily, and to their own hurt.

No one wants to hear all this. It's hard even to *write* it. But it is true, all the same. The driving force behind the gospel of Christ, besides God's love for us and His desire for our fellowship, is His plan to save us from hell. We should never forget or lose sight of this. Lewis also said, "If a game is played, it must be possible to lose it."[46] While human life is not a "game," it does have the same attributes: participation, rules, strategy, competition, and a goal. While God can intervene (by our request, through His grace) to change its outcome, the possibility of *losing everything* does exist.

"For God so loved the world, that He gave His only begotten Son, that whoever believes in Him shall not perish, but have eternal life" (John 3:16). This is literally one of the most popular and oft-quoted verses in the Bible. Yet, many people only hear in this verse what they want to hear. What they *hear* is, "Just believe that Jesus died for you, and you will have eternal life!" Yet, what John 3:16 really *says* is: unless you believe and obey Jesus as Lord and Savior, you will most certainly perish. "Perish," in this context, has nothing to do with one's physical death. Everyone will experience an earthly death whether or not they believe in Jesus. Rather, it has to do with the destruction of the soul—something only the unrighteous will experience.[47] This is why it is referred elsewhere in Scripture as the "second death" (Rev. 2:11 and 20:14).

People love to talk about heaven, but hell—even the *idea* of hell—is so dark, unsettling, and jarring to the human experience that many will try to avoid it in any way possible. Some deny its existence, as if it simply evaporates by doing so, like waking up from a nightmare. Some deny *God's* existence, since getting rid of God seems a convenient way also to get rid of hell. Others believe in hell, but that it is only for seriously wicked people, like pedophiles or serial killers—not for their spouses, family members, friends, or people they care about—*especially* not for themselves. Such people may not be saints, they reason, but they are certainly not deserving of hell. Still others will indifferently admit that they are probably going to hell, but they have refused to accept the full implications of this. To them, hell is an uncomfortable place with depressing décor and warm beer, but at least their friends and drinking buddies will be there to share it with them. After all, misery loves company.

A person can believe what he wants about the afterlife, but such beliefs cannot *change* what is there or *customize* it to one's liking. If there is a God, then you have a soul: the same source material from which we factually draw the one conclusion is the source from which we draw the other. If there is a God and you have a soul, then there is an afterlife comprised of both a heaven *and* a hell. The same Bible that confirms the first of these points also confirms the second one. If there is an afterlife—and we have every good reason to believe this—then the destination for your soul will most certainly be either heaven *or* hell. While this may be disagreeable to some—possibly even yourself—it is true nonetheless. There is no other alternative.

Trying to Get Rid of Hell

Many people today—modernists, revisionists, universalists, and liberal theologians in general—claim to love God but are anxious to rub hell out of existence. They assume that God's divine love is incapable of (or, unwilling to exercise) divine wrath against sinners. The idea of a loving God bringing torment and inconsolable weeping upon *anyone* is abhorrent to many, despite all that the NT says on the subject. This begs the question: who is qualified to declare what a "loving God" can or cannot do? Yet, it does not stop people from brazenly doing just that. For example, popular evangelical author Rob Bell completely dismisses the idea of an eternal hell because it does not fit with his view of God or divine love. In what he calls the "ultimate reconciliation," Bell claims that there will be endless opportunities in an endless amount of time for people to say yes to God. As long as it takes, in other words. At the heart of this perspective is the belief that, given enough time, everybody will turn to God and find themselves in the joy and peace of God's presence. The love of God will melt every hard heart, and even the most "depraved sinners" will eventually give up their resistance and turn to God.[48]

Yet, God's revealed word says otherwise.[49] As great as is God's love for us, so is His wrath toward sin. The grace of God, as offered through the sin offering of His Son, Jesus Christ, intensifies the fact that refusal of this grace is an offense of the highest order.[50] God's wrath is appeased only through the atoning blood of His Son. The technical term here for "appeasement" or the satisfaction of God's wrath is propitiation (Rom. 3:25 and 1 John 2:2). God will *lovingly* forgive the one who calls upon Him for His Son's blood to be applied to his soul. Yet, He will *wrathfully* exercise divine justice against the one who, for any reason, refuses to do this. In fact, He promises to send that person "into the eternal fire which has been prepared for the devil and his angels" (Mat. 25:41).[51] Love and wrath, salvation and condemnation, and mercy and justice all come from the same God. "He who believes in the Son has eternal life; but he who does not obey the Son will not see life, but the wrath of God abides on him" (John 3:36).

"If God does not want us to go to hell," someone will say, "why didn't He tell us more about it?" Apparently just *telling* us that hell exists is not enough; we need (and are entitled to?) a full and detailed description of it. Allegedly, the more information we have on this subject, the more people would turn to God to avoid it. But how much does God need to say on the subject? Who is qualified to tell God when more information is needed, or when He has said enough? God has said a great deal about *salvation* in the NT, yet this has not convinced most of the world to pursue it. Perhaps if someone came back from the afterlife to explain it all to us, *then* we would believe. Yet, Jesus already confronted that idea. He said that, in effect, if people will not listen to God's word, they also will not listen to someone who came back from the dead (Luke 16:31). Ironically, Jesus

Himself *did* come back from the dead, and most of the world shrugs and turns away from Him in disinterest or contempt.

Throughout the Old *and* New Testaments of the Bible, God has warned people not to worship false gods, believe in false religion, practice unrighteousness, or reject His word. Perilous consequences have befallen people (and entire nations) who resisted His warnings in *this* life; what makes us think that they will be spared in the life to come? In the Law of Moses, God described nothing short of a hellish punishment for the nation of Israel if they forsook Him (Deut. 28:15–68); what makes us think that such people will face anything less than this in the life to come? Jesus Himself spoke plainly enough: "Do not fear those who kill the body but are unable to kill the soul; but rather fear Him who is able to destroy both soul and body in hell" (Mat. 10:28). His promise of eternal life to believers is as real as His promise of eternal ruin to unbelievers.

Modern revisionists say that the word "hell" as used in Mat. 10:28 (and Luke 12:5) simply refers to a valley outside of Jerusalem which was, in Jesus' day, a continually-burning rubbish heap. Waste, animal carcasses, and even human corpses were thrown there to be slowly consumed by its smoldering fires. Thus, we are told, Jesus spoke only *figuratively* about "hell," not literally. Apparently, He meant (in Mat. 10:28, for example), "Do not fear those who kill the body but are unable to kill the soul; but rather fear Him who is able to destroy both soul and body in the fiery garbage dump outside of Jerusalem." Or, "...Him who is able to destroy both soul and body *as if* you were thrown in the fiery garbage dump outside Jerusalem." While creative, this is not what Jesus said. He said that people can kill your body, but God can destroy not only your body but also *your soul* in the hell of the afterlife. Jesus did not use the word "hell"—this English word had not yet been invented—but *gehenna*.[52] As for the word "hell," consider this insightful history:

> At the time the KJV [King James Version of the Bible] was first introduced [in 1611] the liberties taken by the translators in using the word "hell" so freely was not necessarily as confusing as it proves to be today. Back then the word had a much wider meaning. Actually it was the Old English

equivalent of our modern world "hole." Like its modern counterpart it carried a number of different meanings. Most of them related in some way to a cavern, pit or other dark and foreboding place. Just as one who deals in furs is called a furrier and one dealing in coal was called a collier, a man who patched "hells" in a roof after a "hell" storm was called a "hellier."

Therefore some three hundred years or so ago the word "hell" was commonly used to refer to any dark or foreboding place. A grave could be referred to by that term without readers or hearers automatically envisioning "the lake of fire which is the second death" (Rev. 20:15). The hole dug in the ground to receive the body of a deceased loved one is certainly a foreboding place. A prison, dungeon, lunatic asylum, or a valley such as the valley of Hinnom outside of Jerusalem with equal propriety could be spoken of a "hell" three or four hundred years ago. That is no longer so.

In the intervening years the word has come to have a much more restricted connotation. Aside from being a handy curse word..., in our time "hell" has a fairly settled meaning. When used seriously rather than profanely, its use conjures up visions of the awesome lake of fire judgment reserved for sinners (and the devil that deceived them) in the last day.

In the interest of clarity and more exacting usage, only the Greek word *gehenna* should be translated hell [in the New Testament]. *Sheol* and its Greek counterpart, *hades*, refer to the temporary abode of the dead, both of the righteous and the unrighteous, partitioned by the great gulf fixed between them.[53]

While the fiery garbage dump provided a graphic visual for the people Jesus spoke to (and, hopefully, to us), it does not reduce the reality of hell to a mere figure of speech. It is real; souls really will be sent there; souls really will weep and suffer there; and no one who is sent there ever comes *out* of there. As eternal as is eternal life, so is eternal punishment (Mat. 25:46).

Someone says, "That's your belief, but I choose to believe otherwise." This is an interesting and (sadly) common scenario: someone like myself provides biblical, authoritative, and relevant evidence—outside and regardless of my own opinion on the matter—and someone else dismisses this with a wave of the hand or shift in the conversation. He assumes that his belief is all that matters, not the facts. We should wonder why God said anything at all, since whatever He *did* say can apparently be overruled by private beliefs. Yet, on which would you rather stake your future: someone's unwarranted dismissal of the afterlife, or what Jesus, Paul, Peter, and God Himself said about it? Would you rather listen to someone who has never seen or experienced the spiritual realm, or the testimony of one (Jesus) who has come from that realm and reigns over it? People think that we are simply sparring with personal opinions here, as if everyone gets to choose what his or her afterlife will be like (or not). But divinely-revealed truth does not work this way. God has told us what is real, what is true, and what we are expected to believe. Refusing to accept these things does not change any of them.

It is also interesting that no one seems to have a problem with souls going to heaven (something none of us who have sinned against God deserve) but are upset about souls being sent to hell (something we *all* deserve). God is not making an arbitrary decision about the final disposition of our souls; it is *our* decision, not His.[54] Of all of God's earthly creatures, human beings alone have the moral freedom to choose to obey or disobey our Creator. Our disobedience (sin) constitutes a rebellion, and forfeits our ability to dwell with God in the afterlife on our own merit. Thankfully, we do have recourse for our sin through the atoning blood of Christ—His blood alone redeems us from ruin (Eph. 1:7)—but relatively few people take advantage of this.[55] It is not God's fault when people sin against Him and then refuse His offer of salvation through His Son. Thus, it is not God's fault when people, in effect, *choose hell* over heaven.[56] The Final Judgment, in which all of humanity will be presented before the Father and His Son, simply finalizes the decisions we already made here on earth (Rev. 20:11–15).

The Picture of Hell

Hell—whatever exactly "hell" looks like—is as real as heaven—whatever *that* looks like. Hell is portrayed as both a "lake of fire" (Rev. 20:14) and an "outer darkness" (Mat. 22:13), which appears contradictory when both are measured by earthly or natural standards. Fire creates light, not darkness, so how can the two coexist? "Fire" is God's symbolic term for judgment, whether literally (as in the destruction of Sodom and Gomorrah in Gen. 19) or figuratively (Luke 12:49). It is also His term for refinement (Rev. 3:18) or purification through trials (1 Peter 1:7). The "eternal fire" or "lake of fire" is clearly not for refinement or purification, however, but is an expression of God's *wrath*.[57] It is significant to note that Jesus did not say that eternal punishment will be *like* an "eternal fire," but that it *will be* this. How this "fire" will actually be manifested in the spiritual realm is beyond our comprehension, but literal fire is the closest means of understanding it in human terms.

The fact that God *has* wrath toward sin and sinners should be enough to make any listener sit up and take notice. God is not passive about sin; He has a fierce anger toward it. His divine wrath

> is to be regarded as the natural expression of the divine nature, which is absolute holiness, manifesting itself against the willful, high-handed, deliberate, inexcusable sin and iniquity of mankind. God's wrath is always regarded in the Scripture as the just, proper, and natural expression of His holiness and righteousness which must always, under all circumstances, and at all costs be maintained.[58]

Consider several passages from the NT that underscore this:

- "He who believes in the Son has eternal life; but he who does not obey the Son will not see life, but the wrath of God abides on him." (John 3:36)
- "For the wrath of God is revealed from heaven against all ungodliness and unrighteousness of men who suppress the truth in unrighteousness…" (Rom. 1:18)

- "But because of your stubbornness and unrepentant heart you are storing up wrath for yourself in the day of wrath and revelation of the righteous judgment of God..." (Rom. 2:5)
- "...to those who are selfishly ambitious and do not obey the truth, but obey unrighteousness, [there will be] wrath and indignation." (Rom. 2:8, bracketed words added)
- "Much more then, having now been justified by His blood, we shall be saved from the wrath of God through Him." (Rom. 5:9)
- "Never take your own revenge, beloved, but leave room for the wrath of God, for it is written, 'Vengeance is Mine, I will repay,' says the Lord." (Rom. 12:19)
- "Let no one deceive you with empty words, for because of these things the wrath of God comes upon the sons of disobedience." (Eph. 5:6)
- "For it is because of these things that the wrath of God will come upon the sons of disobedience..." (Col. 3:6)
- "...wait for His Son from heaven, whom He raised from the dead, that is Jesus, who rescues us from the wrath to come." (1 Thess. 1:10)

God is willing to forgive all sinners who come to Him in obedient faith, but this does not mean He is soft on sin. Sin is an open defiance of His divine nature, His authority, and His holiness. Such defiance cannot be excused with a mere human apology. Even those who *once* tasted of God's kindness and received His forgiveness but *then* returned to their sinful ways will no longer experience God's grace, but will feel the full effect of God's wrath. In fact, the gospel of Christ teaches that it is even *worse* for one to accept God's grace and then reject it than to have never accepted it at all (Heb. 6:4–8, 10:25–31, and 2 Peter 2:20–22). "Behold then the kindness and severity of God," Paul wrote, "to those who fell, severity, but to you, God's kindness, if you continue in His kindness; otherwise you also will be cut off" (Rom. 11:22). God's "kindness" (salvation) is conditional, not automatic and not assumed. It can be revoked in the case of impenitent unfaithfulness (unbelief).

The biblical picture of hell is very disturbing. Those who will be forever separated from God do not cease to exist, but enter into a state of eternal darkness and suffering. Separation from God and suffering go hand in hand. Not only are these souls separated from God, but they are also separated from all those who *belong* to God. "To enter heaven," Lewis wrote, "is to become more human than you ever succeeded in being in earth; to enter hell, is to be banished from humanity."[59]

Even in this life, those who remain alienated from God because of sin experience a spiritual suffering, even though this suffering is often anesthetized by pleasures, narcotics, alcohol, and the manifold cares and distractions of this world. Once all these things are removed, however, such people will be confronted with their spiritual suffering in full strength with nothing to medicate, alleviate, or distract them from it. There are several reasons for this suffering:

- They no longer enjoy the benevolent blessings of their Creator. All the pleasures of earthly life, human fellowship, and the physical beauty of this world and the cosmos will no longer be available to them. Their good health, strong bodies, and ability to participate in the earthly context will have ended. They will no longer be able to make decisions, have mobility, or enjoy human fellowship. They will be nameless, hopeless, and forgotten souls cast into an "outer darkness" (Mat. 8:12, etc.). The deprivation of all these things is, in itself, a suffering much like what solitary confinement is for the most dangerous convicts—except this imprisonment will never end.
- They will never experience meaningful fellowship with God. They will know that *others* are experiencing it—and that those people are immeasurably happy—but they themselves will remain permanently cut off from any opportunity to partake of it. In life, they chose to be "excluded from the life of God because of the ignorance that is in them, because of the hardness of their heart," and thus "[gave] themselves over to sensuality for the practice of every kind of impurity with greediness" (Eph. 4:18–19). But once they are swallowed up in darkness, they will no longer have sensuality to medicate them; they will be enlightened by the truth, but unable to benefit from that enlightenment. They will be wretched and miserable with no one and nothing to comfort them.

- They will be filled with an inconsolable regret that will haunt and torment them forever. They will realize that they *chose* this existence by failing to be morally responsible to God when they had opportunity to do so. Whether they rejected God outright or simply neglected to seek Him when they knew in their heart that He existed (Rom. 1:18–20) does not matter. The end result will be the same: they had a priceless and most important opportunity, and they foolishly and carelessly forfeited it. This realization—and the fact that it cannot be resolved—will produce an unimaginable mental anguish that we have never experienced here on earth.
- They will be *punished*. The "wrath of God" (John 3:36, Rom. 2:5, Eph. 5:6, etc.) is not merely God's anger, but also His divine judgment. Read the Old Testament: when God's wrath was unleashed upon various nations, those people did not just *hear* His judgment pronounced, they *felt* it. They personally and physically *suffered* from it. The "penalty of eternal destruction" (2 Thess. 1:9) does not refer to an annihilation of the soul—this concept is foreign to the Bible—but a never-ending *suffering* of the soul as a direct result of divine punishment.[60] What this punishment is, whether it will be different for some souls than others, etc., are questions that do not have to be answered. They do not change what we do know: people who are separated from God will fearfully, perpetually, and painfully *suffer* in that separation. "[I]n that place there will be weeping and gnashing of teeth" (Mat. 25:30, etc.). This is not a picture of being snuffed out of existence; it is the picture of unrelenting pain, fear, and despair.

Such is the ultimate end for those who are separated from God. It is an awful, wretched scenario. But for now, we are simply recognizing this is one *possible* end for the human soul, not the inevitable end. It doesn't have to be this way. It can and ought to be avoided at all costs.

Summary Thoughts
Hell is real, and souls really will be sent there who defy their Creator here on earth. Since this is true, it is in our best interest to live in such a way that draws us near to God rather than court a self-inflicted

disaster. In the afterlife there will be no occasion for repentance; there will be no throwing yourself on the mercy of the court; there will be no "anyway" forgiveness (as in God saying, "I know you sinned against Me and then rejected My gospel, but since you were a relatively good person, I'm going to *forgive you anyway*"). Being with God in His heaven is a powerful incentive to *pull* us forward; hell is also a powerful incentive to *push* us forward. We need both, since the temptation to be absorbed with this life and ignore God can be very strong.

It is disturbing to think about the horrors of hell. The prospect of being in a "lake of fire" *and* "outer darkness" all at once strikes a stabbing fear into the heart of the human psyche. The combination of separation and punishment awaits the human soul that sinned against God yet refused to take responsibility for this. Perhaps if everyone took the time to read the Bible and listen to what Jesus (and others) said about hell, God's wrath, and the Judgment to come, there might be far more people who would do whatever was necessary to avoid it. No sinner deserves heaven, but God provides a means to obtaining it; every sinner deserves hell, but few make any serious effort to avoid it. "For the wages of sin is death, but the free gift of God is eternal life in Christ Jesus our Lord" (Rom. 6:23). God is a just God, and demands justice for every soul that sins against Him. Yet, this justice can be satisfied through His Son—a priceless but limited offer.

Avoiding hell—and, more significantly, *seeking heaven*—are the reasons why God provided His gospel of salvation in the first place. "'Do I have any pleasure in the death of the wicked,' declares the Lord God, 'rather than that he should turn from his ways and live?'" (Ezek. 18:23). This quote is from the Old Testament, but proves that it has always been on God's mind to provide for the *salvation* of human souls rather than their *destruction*. God has not been silent about His intention: "[He] desires all men to be saved and to come to the knowledge of the truth" (1 Tim. 2:4). But, as much as God desires our salvation, He leaves the decision up to us to pursue it or not. This means: while heaven waits expectantly for those who choose to listen to God and do His will, hell also waits eagerly to devour those who continue to resist Him.

Since this world is not your home, one of these destinations is in *your* future. You are the one who decides which it will be; God merely finalizes your decision. If you were to die today, in which destination would your soul be tomorrow?

Chapter Five: What the "Rich Man" Wants You to Know

If God, your soul, and the afterlife did not exist—and if we could prove this beyond a reasonable doubt—then we have nothing *moral* or *spiritual* to worry about. In that case, there would be no truth or error, right or wrong, good or evil, or heaven or hell. We could all just live however we choose—selfishly, aimlessly, hopelessly, and (often) desperately—and then we would all just cease to *be* upon our death. Once the memory of us was forgotten by those who knew us (as they also die and disappear), it would be as if we had never existed.

But this is not the case, and this fact changes everything. God does exist. Your soul does exist. The afterlife does exist. Now, moral responsibility determines our future existence. Truth is something to which we must tenaciously cling; error must be rejected. Righteousness is real, and so is wickedness. Heaven awaits those who are faithful to God, and hell awaits everyone else. Furthermore, your soul is your most important, most valuable, and most enduring possession. It is uniquely yours, remains under your control, and is your responsibility to manage and nurture. Whatever is "seen" is passing away; whatever remains yet "unseen" or invisible is eternal (2 Cor. 4:18).

These are not popular conclusions. Many people today do not regard human *or* spiritual life in such absolutes, or with such clarity or finality. Yet, God gives each person a sufficient *reason to believe* in Him, allowing him (or her) to make responsible choices regarding the hereafter. God has provided numerous success stories of souls that believed in His truth, decided to live for Him, endured this life, and overcame the spiritual challenges to their faith. Most notably, God's own Son, Jesus Christ, overcame the entire world—including Satan and *his* world (John 16:33)—and now reigns in glory at the right hand of the Father (Phil. 2:5–11).

Satan, on the other hand, wants nothing more than for you to forfeit your soul for a few moments' pleasure, self-indulgence, and the delusion of peace and happiness (all founded upon lies and assumptions). Satan does not offer a single "success story" of someone who lived a morally irresponsible life, disobeyed God, and followed his heart rather than the truth *without* any negative consequences in the hereafter. This is because no such scenarios exist.

The Bible does, however, offer a particularly chilling account of one man who ignored his moral responsibility to God and his fellow man, swallowed the world's lies, and sold his soul for a few moments of the "good life." Instead of waking up in the afterlife in a "better place," as mourners tend to say at the funerals of such people, this man woke up in torment with no hope of escaping it. Instead of reflecting fondly upon his earthly life as he revels in eternal bliss, he will spend the rest of his existence—which will never end and never change—filled with pain and regret.

This man's account is told in Luke 16:19–31, and he is simply known to us as the "rich man." He was rich with earthly wealth and pleasures, but he failed to be "rich toward God" (Luke 12:21). His story contradicts everything the world promises those who listen to it. It proves that God is serious about you spending your life here on earth in preparation for the life to come, not being indifferent or oblivious to it. This rich man cannot talk to us—so much for communications from the dead—but we *do* have a conversation between him and Abraham that Jesus has disclosed to us. What the rich man said are things the satanic world will never tell you, and things most people never take time to consider seriously. But we would do well to take that time right now.

The Background of This Account

Before we get into the rich man's story, it is helpful to understand the context in which Jesus told it, *why* He told it, and to *whom* He told it. People in Jesus' day were very much like those today: greedy for money and status; equating success with the accumulation of toys and possessions; focusing on the here and now; sacrificing their spiritual future for peer approval and immediate gratification. Many of the ruling class of the Jews (chief priests, Sadducees, Pharisees, scribes, and elders) were rich men. They (and others) considered their wealth to be a sign of God's approval: they were rich only because God was pleased with them—a belief that underlies the disciples' shock at Jesus' statement in Mat. 19:23–25. Yet, these men did not trust in God, but "trusted in themselves that they were righteous, and viewed others with contempt" (Luke 18:9).

Someone says, "But I'm not rich, so I don't see how this applies to my situation." The truth is: you do not have to be rich to have the attitude of rich men. All you have to do is what most rich men do: put your trust in money, status, and this life, rather than in God. The real issue here is not literal riches but what you worship. Or, we could say: it is the potential misplacement of your worship. Only God deserves to be worshiped; yet many people choose to worship someone or something else, and anything else is inferior to Him. Anyone who trusts in anyone or anything more than they trust in God shares the attitude and unfounded confidence of a typical rich man.[61] Most rich men may give a token nod to God, but they bow to a false god. They will not let go of this world so as to receive the grace of heaven. They will not empty themselves in order to be filled with God. And you do not have to be literally rich to have this attitude. In fact, you can be dirt poor and live under a bridge and still think and act like a godless rich man.

To "believe" in Jesus (as in John 3:16) means far more than acknowledging His existence, sitting through a church service, or dropping a check in the offering plate. It means putting your soul in Jesus' care—whatever this takes and whatever this costs you. Some of the rich men who listened to Jesus did believe He was the Messiah (Christ), but they believed in their wealth and status even more, and "loved the approval of men rather than the approval of God" (John 12:42–43). It is the "rather than" distinction that is condemnable here. Again, one certainly does not have to be rich to succumb to this hopeless endeavor. The world is filled with those who seek human approval *rather than* (or, at the expense of, and even regardless of) divine approval.

Just prior to relating the account of the rich man, Jesus told the Jews that if they could not exercise moral responsibility toward earthly things (like money and material possessions), they were hardly prepared to be spiritually responsible to God (Luke 16:10–11). "And if you have not been faithful in the use of that which is another's [i.e., God's], who will give you that which is your own?" (Luke 16:12, bracketed word added). These men tried to serve two gods at once—"mammon" (wealth) and God—even though Jesus assured them that this was impossible (Luke 16:13). To "serve" here means to *worship*, which includes giving one's allegiance, faith, trust, time, and sacrifice to the object of their worship.

"Now the Pharisees, who were lovers of money, were listening to all these things and were scoffing at Him" (Luke 16:14). No doubt they believed Jesus to be wrong on every point. After all, they were skilled with money *and* knowledgeable of the Scriptures *and* faithfully observed the habits of righteous men (see Luke 18:9–12). They regarded themselves as very religious and pious men, and so did many others. They thought, in so many words, "We not only *do* serve God *and* mammon but are doing it quite well, thank you very much." Additionally, there were no lightning strikes from heaven, the ground did not open up and swallow them, and they enjoyed the approval of their peers. How could hundreds of rich men all be wrong? Therefore, they must all be *right*—and it is this Jesus fellow who is wrong.

But Jesus did not retract His accusations. He did not soften His words or modify His message. He did not apologize in the least, because He knew He was right and that these men were terribly wrong, having been blinded by Satan (2 Cor. 4:3–4). "And He said to them, 'You are those who justify yourselves in the sight of men, but God knows your hearts; for that which is highly esteemed among men is detestable in the sight of God'" (Luke 16:15). These men were not only blind, they were arrogant and filled with themselves. Instead of refusing to expose them any further, Jesus pulled back the curtain to the afterlife to show them just how hopeless (and devastating) their clutch on this world really was. He introduced them to one of their own—a "rich man"—and, like Jacob Marely did for Ebenezer Scrooge in *A Christmas Carol*—showed them their awful future if they did not repent.

Exposition of the Account

"Now there was a certain rich man…" (Luke 16:19). Many consider this to be simply a parable constructed to fit the occasion rather than an actual account of two men. Yet, Jesus does not introduce it as he does His parables ("The kingdom of heaven is like" or "can be compared to"). He says, "There *was* a certain rich man" (emphasis added). This man was a Jew (as was Lazarus), understood by his appeals to "father Abraham" later. Thus, he was covenant-bound to

God through the nation of Israel, and was expected to fulfill the terms and conditions of that covenant.

This rich man lived an unremarkable but comfortable life. He was a sociable person; he was not charged with any particular violation of the Law of Moses. His problem was not even that he was rich, since this is not a crime in itself. Rather, his problem was that he worshiped his riches, and did so at the expense of his fellow countryman (Lazarus) who was in desperate need of his help and compassion. So then, Jesus presented the rich Jews of His day with a rich man who was very much like themselves—a man who did not take his moral responsibility very seriously, thrived on the approval of others, and lavished himself with excessive feasting and comfort.

Lazarus, by sharp contrast, was a poor Jew who was afflicted with disease and thus "covered with sores" (Luke 16:20). We assume he had been faithful to honor the responsibilities of God's covenant when he was in better health and circumstances. Or, he had *always* been in dire straits, having been born with poor health and a family that could not take care of him. Incidentally, a man with weeping sores was not allowed to participate in any of the holy assemblies of Israel; see Lev. 13:42–46 and 21:17–21 (in principle). Lazarus was incapacitated by his sickness, and his inability to earn a living because of this led to his poverty, and thus his need to beg for food to survive. The dogs "licking at his sores" (Luke 16:21) only magnifies his great helplessness, hopelessness, and humiliation. This was not a man resting comfortably in a modern hospital bed surrounded by family, friends, and flowers. Instead, he was a man abandoned by virtually everyone, destitute of every amenity, and suffering terribly through (apparently) no fault of his own.

These two men's lives intersected when Lazarus "was laid" at the rich man's gate (Luke 16:20).[62] His presence at the rich man's gate meant that the rich man (and his rich friends) could not have possibly missed him, yet they simply walked past and ignored his pathetic situation. Meanwhile, as a fellow Jew lay dying at his gate, the rich man and his peers "habitually dressed in purple and fine linen"—comfortable and elegant clothing—and were "joyously living in splendor *every day*" (Luke 16:19, emphasis added). The rich man's life was immersed in wealth, comfort, ease, and all the hallmarks of a carefree life. The contrast of the two men is most striking; the rich man's failure to address Lazarus' condition is appalling and inexcusable.

Yet, despite men's circumstances in this life—whether they be favorable or deplorable—they will soon go "the way of all the earth" (1 Kings 2:2) and die. Upon leaving this physical world, all people enter into a conscious awareness of the afterlife. Having left behind their earthly circumstances, they will then be faced with the consequences (whether good or bad) of the moral choices they had made while they were here. Thus, both Lazarus and the rich man died, and both found themselves in the afterlife. There is nothing said about the grand funeral that the rich man's family and friends no doubt gave him; Jesus simply said that he "was buried" (Luke 16:22). Lazarus' body, on the other hand, was likely unceremoniously thrown into a common grave and covered with lime, but his spirit was conveyed "by the angels" to the "bosom" (or, close and privileged proximity—figuratively or otherwise) of Abraham (Luke 16:22). It was the great anticipation of every Jew to be received on the other side by "father Abraham"—one of their greatest heroes (see Mat. 3:9 and John 8:39, for example).

The rich man, however, enjoyed no such honor. He found himself "in Hades"[63] and "in torment." Whatever his torment was, it included a "flame" or fire-like experience (Luke 16:24). This does not appear to be the "eternal fire" mentioned elsewhere (as in Mat. 25:41), but likely a precursor to it. Nonetheless, it represents the same awful destination of one accursed of God.

Many have tried to explain Jesus' depiction of this account in very literal or even physical terms. For example, some say: there are two literal "compartments" or abodes of the dead; the "chasm" (or "gulf") between the two compartments is literal; the fire is literal; the water (requested by the rich man) is literal; Abraham is easily identified; etc. But such explanations do not honor the context of what is being described. Jesus is not talking about a literal or physical place, or any circumstance that earth-bound humans could comprehend. Jesus clearly indicated that these men are (now) in a *spiritual* realm, not a physical one. No doubt He simplified (or dumbed-down) the explanation so we could even grasp what He was talking about.

Furthermore, Jesus' message was *not* to provide clear, solid, or even doctrinal details about the realm of departed souls, but to magnify the results of the two men's life choices. In other words, the "great chasm" between the two companies of souls did not require further explanation; but the great chasm between those who are known by God (2 Tim. 2:19) and those who were morally irresponsible on earth *needs* to be understood by all. The Jews were supposed to be "sons of the kingdom" (Mat. 8:11–12)—not only waiting for it, but *fully prepared* to enter into it—yet many found themselves in the afterlife *excluded* from this privilege because of the very poor choices they made while here on earth. Those whom they ignored, despised, or even hated might be the very ones who took their place with the patriarchs in the hereafter.

In his awful predicament, the rich man, "lifted up his eyes" (Luke 16:23)—an idiomatic expression meaning: he looked far off and fixed his gaze on something beyond his close proximity. In the distance, he "saw Abraham far away and Lazarus in his bosom." While he suffered "torment" and "flame" (Luke 16:23–24), he watched painfully as Lazarus enjoyed the comfort and company of Abraham and other faithful souls. While on earth, the rich man treated life as though it were one grand and endless party. He thought little of the condition of his soul; he thought even less of his responsibility toward his fellow man (like Lazarus). Now he has no wealth, no fine clothing, no excellent food or drink, no parties, and no friends. He has no joy, no comfort, and—worst of all—no opportunity to re-decide, repent, or have his circumstances changed. Lazarus' torment is now over; the rich man's torment has just begun—and will never end (Luke 16:25). This is, indeed, the ultimate reversal of fortune. The rich man is no longer rich, but will forevermore be destitute of anything good.

Even in this miserable condition, the rich man still thought about himself—again, at Lazarus' expense. "If Lazarus could just help me out, then I could be relieved of some of my suffering!" (paraphrase of Luke 16:24). Yet, the rich man had failed—even purposely *refused*—to relieve Lazarus' own suffering when he had been laid at his gate. Abraham said, in so many words, "You made your choice; now you will have to live with it. Nothing is going to change just because you desire a different outcome" (paraphrase of Luke 16:25–26). The separation between the two men cannot be breached; furthermore, it is permanent.

Suddenly—but *too late*—the rich man started thinking about someone other than himself (Luke 16:27–31). He begged Abraham to send Lazarus back from the dead to warn his five brothers who apparently were just as wealthy, uncompassionate, and morally irresponsible as he himself had been. Abraham quickly dismissed the request; "They have Moses and the Prophets; let them hear them." The rich man persisted: if Lazarus were to come back from the dead, then *surely* this would convince them to repent and avoid the rich man's demise. Abraham responded, in essence, "If they will not listen to God's word, then a miraculous sign from God will not change their hearts."[64]

Lessons to Be Learned

There are a number of lessons that come from this account that Jesus gave of the rich man and Lazarus. One of the striking things to think about is this: if the dead *could* communicate with us, they would all say the same thing: "Listen to God!" If the soul of a dead man woke up in torment like the rich man did, he would warn anyone else from coming to where he is. If he woke up in glory like Lazarus did, he would encourage everyone to be faithful to God's word so that they also would be where he is. In either case, the message from the dead would be united and consistent.

The rich man had no way to inform his "five brothers" of their awful future (if they remained on their present course), but he does have several messages for us. There are some things the rich man wants you to know—regardless of whatever you think of God, your soul, or the afterlife. These things include:

- **Everyone dies.** It does not matter who you are, your status in life, or even your moral disposition. Your gender, ethnicity, language, culture, economic situation, the number of friends (or enemies) you have, your accomplishments, your belief system, and all your opinions—none of these will keep you from your appointment with death (Heb. 9:27). Look around you—all that you see will end *for you*. In this way, you are not exceptional or unique; you

cannot claim exceptional or unique circumstances to avoid your death.
- **This world is not your home.** You are not staying here on earth forever. Difficult as it is to imagine yourself in a different context, realm, and surrounding than what you presently know, this earthly life is not the sum of your existence. In fact, it is a very small—but extremely important—part of it.
- **You *do* have a soul.** The rich man found this out (for certain) the hard way. Jesus, in narrating the account, confirmed it. A person can pretend that he does not have a soul (like atheists claim), or that he's not sure (like agnostics claim), or that it really doesn't matter to him (like irreligious people claim, in effect), but the fact remains: everyone has a soul. This soul will outlast one's earthly life, and will ultimately be presented before God. There are no atheists or agnostics in the hereafter; once there, *all* will believe that God exists, for they will most certainly face Him in the Judgment.
- **Your soul will not die with your body.** You will have a conscious existence long after your funeral. This existence will either be very good (like Lazarus') or horrifying (like the rich man's). Your soul will not "sleep" until Christ calls all men from the grave; it will continue to see, feel, remember, be comforted, and even suffer. Take a walk through a cemetery: all the bodies laid to rest there remain on earth, but the *souls* of those bodies are still alive, conscious, and experiencing either joy or torment—nothing in-between.
- **Wealth, prosperity, popularity, earthly success, earthly privilege, academic honors, celebrity status—none of these carry over into the afterlife.** None of these can secure or guarantee a good "place" in the afterlife. On the other hand, the righteous deeds of righteous people will "follow after them" and be remembered by God (Rev. 14:13; see 1 Cor. 15:58).
- **Decisions made here on earth concerning your moral responsibility toward God will be finalized upon your death.** There will be no changes to this in the afterlife. If your soul is saved, it will never again be in danger of being lost. Times of trials, temptations, adversity, and coexistence with wicked people will be over—

forever. If your soul is lost, it will never again be given an opportunity to be saved. Lost souls in the hereafter will not be able to repent, beg forgiveness, or throw themselves on the mercy of the court, so to speak. Once you have died and your soul wakes up in the spiritual realm, you will either have prepared for that experience or you will have entered it unprepared. There are no second chances once this life is over.

- **If your soul is *saved*, it will only be because you *chose* to be saved when given the opportunity here on earth.** You read the word of God; you listened to His instruction; you were touched by His love, moved by His entreaty, and inspired by His grace. You surrendered your soul to God; He forgave you of your sins. You trusted in His ability to perform; He credited you with righteousness for your faith (Rom. 4:3–8). You remained "faithful until death" (Rev. 2:10); He remained faithful to you as well, since He cannot be *un*faithful, no matter what (2 Tim. 2:12–13). In other words, no one is saved by accident; no one stumbles into heaven any more than he can stumble into hell. Both are choices, and death finalizes this choice.

- **If your soul is lost, you will not be able to go back and warn ungodly spouses, family, friends, or anyone else of the horror that you will experience.** Despite claims of Hollywood movies (like *What Dreams May Come* [1998]), claims of paranormal experiences, tales of communication with the dead, seances, etc., you will be in a realm entirely separated from the living. Those you left behind will continue to make their choices just as you had opportunity to make your own choices. They may well ultimately join you in your suffering, but do not expect it to be a happy reunion. Watching your loved ones suffering horribly will only intensify your own. Or, if you are cast out into the outer darkness, never to see (literally) another human soul for eternity, you will still be overwhelmed with sorrow, fear, pain, and regret—and you will know that your lost loved ones are experiencing all of this as well.

- **Just as the rich man's five brothers were given the Law (of Moses) and the writings of the prophets, so you have the record of the gospel of Christ.** You will either listen to this gospel or you will not; you will either be obedient to it or you will not. There is no middle ground; there is no sitting on the fence—and besides, *the devil owns the fence*. There will be no preaching of or obeying the gospel in the afterlife, and you already know far too much to claim ignorance.

- **If you choose to listen and obey God, then you can look forward to what He has promised the faithful (1 Peter 1:3–5).** He offers faithful believers a priceless and otherworldly inheritance that cannot fail ("imperishable"), cannot be corrupted ("undefiled"), and will never lose its glory ("will not fade away"). Nothing and no one on earth can make such a guarantee, but God *can* and *does* for all those who remain "faithful until death" (Rev. 2:10). And, nothing on earth—except your own unbelief—can stop *you* from being a faithful believer and thus an heir to these promises.

- **If you choose not to listen or obey—for any reason—then you will most certainly receive what God has promised the disobedient (Rom. 2:5–11).** God will not make a special concession for you; Christ will not perform a special miracle just for you; angels will not make a special appearance for you. You have the gospel of Christ; if you will not listen to that, then neither will you listen to anything else. You do not *need* anything else—not even a visit from beyond the grave.

- **Just as the Law of Moses was inaugurated with signs and wonders, so the gospel was accompanied by numerous signs and wonders (Heb. 2:3–4).** The greatest of these, ironically, was *a Man coming back from the dead* to convince us of His power and authority. The resurrection of Jesus was meant not only to inspire us to believe in Him, but also to warn us of what is coming (Acts 17:30–31). Since God has revealed His gospel, He expects all people to repent. Since His Son has risen from the dead, everyone will one day be resurrected from *their* deaths to stand before Him (John 5:28–29, Acts 24:14–15, Rom. 8:11, etc.). Since Christ has been exalted to the right hand of God, there most certainly will be a Day of Judgment in which all will answer for how they chose to live on earth (2 Cor. 5:10).

Summary Thoughts

If you find the account of the rich man a bit unnerving, it is supposed to be. Jesus provided this account to those who were rich with wealth, comfort, and confidence in this life, but not rich toward God (Luke 12:21). These men needed a wakeup call, and—since it is so easy to imitate them—perhaps we need one as well. They worshiped the things of this world, but "the world is passing away, and also its lusts; but the one who does the will of God lives forever" (1 John 2:17).[65]

Jesus' intention was not merely to frighten us, but far more so to *warn* and *protect* us. First, He warned us that our soul does exist, continues to exist after death, and will receive the reward or consequence for decisions made in this life. Since all these things are true—and are confirmed by the highest authority that exists—we would be wise to prepare for that future. Second, He does not want to lose those who have already become Christians. Our belief in God, the soul, and the afterlife does not *by itself* make us immune to succumbing to the same errors of false worship that the Jews of Jesus' day committed. We are warned that God has "no pleasure" in those who go back on their original promise to Him. But, hopefully, "we are not of those who shrink back to destruction, but of those who have faith to the preserving of the soul" (Heb. 10:38–39).

The rich man's soul still exists in the hereafter, but he is no longer rich. He not only lost all of his wealth and comforts, but *he himself* is forever lost. He has been tormented since his physical death, and his awful regret for what might have been, lost opportunities, and the impossibility of any recourse only intensifies this suffering. Anyone who lives like the rich man lived—carelessly, morally irresponsibly, and uncompassionately—will join this wretched man. On the other hand, anyone who has faith like that of Abraham, "being fully assured that what God has promised, He was able to perform" (Rom. 4:21), will not have to fear the afterlife. He will be not only with Abraham forever, but with Someone infinitely greater—Jesus Christ.

Losing your soul is the very *worst* thing that could ever happen—yet this loss is entirely avoidable. The rich man wanted to warn his five brothers of where he had ended up. He was prevented from doing this. Jesus used this man's pathetic situation to warn all who read of his account. Hopefully, we are all listening to His message.

Part Two: Satan's World and How It Affects You
Chapter Six: The World of the Darkness

God's world is filled with light, love, joy, redemption, and salvation. This should be extremely attractive to us. We should be magnetically and gratefully drawn to it. Thankfully, there are some of us who *are* drawn to it. Yet, even as we find God's world so beneficial and attractive, we are always being strongly enticed by another world—one that seeks to gratify our carnal lusts, not the longings of our God-given soul. This other world is ominously referred to in the NT as "the darkness."

"[T]he Light has come into the world, and men loved the darkness rather than the Light, for their deeds were evil" (John 3:19). God sent His Son into the world to help us—to connect with, redeem, and enlighten us—but (sadly) this "Light" must compete with "the darkness." One of the most disturbing phrases here is "rather than": people are given a choice between God's light, love, joy, redemption, and salvation—and most people choose darkness *rather than* what He offers. This "rather than" expression does not present two comparable things of equal worth or value. Instead, it presents a superior thing being rejected or forfeited for an infinitely inferior one (so it is with all "rather than" statements in the NT).

The decision to reject the Light and embrace the darkness is both foolish and pathetic. It does not make sense; there is no rational justification for it; it contradicts every human instinct for survival. Yet, even those of us who once pledged to love the Light rather than the darkness are still being lured *by* the darkness to break faith with our God and plunge headlong into the allegedly blissful depths *of* the darkness. This darkness does not offer any advantage to us, however, but seeks only to destroy us entirely.

"The darkness"—not just "darkness," but *the* darkness—is not some random, unidentifiable stranger to us. Rather, it is that with which we are all too familiar. We *know* this darkness; we have partaken of it before; perhaps we are dabbling in it—harmlessly, we assume—right now. We have spent much time in this darkness, and once we step into it, we know where it will take us because we have been there on many occasions. We also know that the darkness is where we should not be, and yet there is an almost giddy sense of thrill as we course through its pleasure-strewn paths.

Not only do we know this darkness, but it also knows *us*. Not only does it know us in the most general sense, being quite aware of human beings and our human nature, but it knows us *personally*. It knows me by name, just as it knows you by name. In fact, the darkness knows far more about you than you know about it. Thus, when people "[love] the darkness rather than the Light," they unwittingly choose to love something they do not really understand, *cannot* fully understand, and most certainly cannot control.[66] In every human-darkness relationship, it is always the darkness that has the upper hand. The darkness always leads in this morbid dance; the human never leads the darkness, no matter how powerful or knowledgeable he thinks he is.

The purpose of peering into the world of darkness is not to increase our desire for it, or to glamorize, sensationalize, or give unnecessary attention to it. The darkness is an incredibly powerful force, and not something we should spend any more time examining than what is necessary to know the enemy. Many, many souls have been lost in the darkness, never to be found. You cannot afford to become one of those lost souls.

What "the Darkness" Is

The first order of business is to define (to the extent that we are able) what the darkness is. The Bible actually uses "darkness" in four different contexts. First, there is literal darkness (the absence of physical light). This is simply "night" (John 13:30), or the obscuring of the sun during Jesus' crucifixion (Mat. 27:45). Second, there is the darkness of spiritual ignorance (John 12:35) or moral blindness (2 Cor. 4:3–4). People are enveloped in this darkness when they reject God and His truth. Third, there is the "outer darkness"—a term which Jesus introduced in His ministry (Mat. 8:12)—which is the realm of condemned souls who have been forever banished from God's presence.

Finally, there is the domain of wickedness in which Satan and his demons operate. It is also the realm from which human souls are tempted to sin, persuaded to reject divine truth, and afflicted with mental and spiritual anguish. This is not an actual "place"—we are dealing with a spiritual realm, not a physical one—but it is a real *power* nonetheless (1 John 5:19). Satan does not reign over his realm in a visible or literal way, but he does reign; he is no match for the kingdom of God, but he does oversee a kingdom or dominion of his own (Mat. 12:26, Acts 26:18, etc.). He exerts a wicked influence that wants to seduce, possess, imprison, and destroy human souls. In a very real sense, Satan's world—and all demonic activity—operates in "the darkness."

"The power of darkness" (Luke 22:53) indicates a collusion between the human heart and this demonic realm. Just as every person is either on the narrow way that leads to life or the wide path that leads to destruction (Mat. 7:13–14), so every person's heart is either illumined by divine truth or deceived by satanic falsehood (Mat. 6:22–23). When Paul speaks of "world forces of the darkness of this present age" (Eph. 6:12), he refers to the ungodly effect that Satan's realm has upon people. The unconverted world is being guided, deceived, and quietly led to destruction by the wicked influence of moral darkness. This is not an earthly foe, *per se*, and the battle is not a physical one. Yet, the damage, carnage, and casualties of this war are visible everywhere we look: greed, lies, betrayals, unfaithful marriages, broken homes, addiction, self-destructive behaviors, sexual deviancy, corruption, and wickedness of every kind.

The power of darkness is an active corruptive agent that poisons human hearts and thus compels men to be wicked, depraved, and irresponsible. Once people give their hearts to it, the darkness exercises a controlling interest over them. Thus, the darkness—as well as Satan—is parasitic in nature: its falsehoods infect the willing host; it feeds on the power and compliance that host gives to it; the darkness manipulates the host to give it even *more* power; once this has been accomplished, it pushes that soul off a cliff, so to speak, to its own destruction. Meanwhile, the darkness seeks out other souls and feeds off *their* power, so that the darkness becomes so strong that no single human soul can possibly resist it on its own. It has no fear of running out of willing hosts; sadly, the darkness finds many new ones all the time.

Satan and the Darkness

There is something else going on here, however. When we think of darkness and evil, we tend to think that Satan is in absolute *control* of all of this. It is true to say that Satan is a part *of* the darkness, his kingdom operates *in* the darkness, and he is even filled *with* darkness. But there is nothing in the Bible that says he *is* the darkness. Remember that the Bible is our *only* authoritative source of information about the spiritual realm. Nothing in Scripture says Satan is the inventor of sin, the creator of evil, or the prince of darkness. In a very real way (but one that exceeds human comprehension), Satan himself is a prisoner of the darkness much in the same way sinners are made prisoners of Satan (2 Tim. 2:26).

"The god of this world" (2 Cor. 4:3–4) is most certainly Satan, but this does not mean that Satan is the god of all spiritual and moral darkness. The world has willfully (albeit foolishly) chosen Satan to be its god rather than the Creator Himself, much in the same way that Israel chose an inferior human king rather than the kingship of Jehovah (1 Sam. 8:4–8). Now Satan has *billions* of people at any given time on this planet giving him allegiance, and he is drunk with their power, giddy with the excitement of leading them astray, and completely unconcerned with how much pain and misery he will bring upon them.

But just because Satan *operates* in a "domain of darkness" (Col. 1:13) does not mean he is the *origin* of the darkness, only that he uses it to his advantage. This is no different than a wicked person who uses greed to his advantage: he is not the master of greed, but quite the opposite—greed is *his* master. "Do you not know that when you present yourselves to someone as slaves for obedience, you are slaves of the one whom you obey, either of sin resulting in death, or of obedience resulting in righteousness?" (Rom. 6:11). We have assumed that Satan is his own god, that he somehow deified himself. There is some truth to this, of course, but it is not *entirely* true. As a pawn being deceived into thinking he is a king, so Satan has deceived himself into thinking he is the master over that which deceived him. Pawns do have power—anyone who plays chess knows this—but their power is derived from the king, not the other way around.[67]

In Rom. 6:11–14, Paul does not say, "Satan shall not be master over you," but "*sin* shall not be master over you" (emphasis added). When a person gives himself over to sin, it leverages controlling interest over that person's heart. This does not mean Satan is not involved in the process, for most certainly he is. Yet, Satan never overtook sin to become *his* slave; rather, sin overtook Satan to become *its* slave. The implication of all this is more than unnerving—it is frightening beyond words. Whatever filled Satan's heart is presently seeking to fill your heart and my heart. In a real sense, it is not Satan using the darkness to do his bidding, but the darkness is using Satan and his demons to carry out its work—let that sink in for a moment.

The point is: there is a power to the darkness (sin itself) that cannot be removed by mere churchgoing, Bible reading, hymn-singing, prayer-speaking, good works, or good intentions. Many Christians—likely, *most* Christians—have been led to believe things about sin and Satan that did not come from the Bible. Instead, they have been conditioned by traditional thinking, traditional preachers, and personal assumptions. Many will reason, "If I guard against *Satan*, then I will be alright"—often quickly followed up with, "and this is something I can do *myself*, since I know how Satan works." Yet, what we truly must guard against is not only what Satan *is* (a monster, liar, and "roaring lion" seeking to devour us—1 Peter 5:8), but also what Satan is inciting us to do: sin against God.

Sin is the power of the darkness, not Satan. "The sting of death is sin, and the power of sin is the law" (1 Cor. 15:56). What gives sin power over your heart is not Satan having stolen you away from God and imprisoned your soul in some spiritual dungeon. ("You" here means you, me, and every one of us.) Rather, it is your personal violation of God's commandments. Your rebellion against the life-giving Creator is your downfall; Satan is simply there to incite you to *do* this, and to coax you to *continue* doing this, to your own unspeakable hurt. Satan tempts, persuades, lies, deceives, and manipulates, but he has no power of his own to force you to sin against God *or* fill your heart with darkness. This is a decision you make. This is not something that happens to you against your will; this *is* your will choosing to ally itself with Satan's world *rather than* God's. And when you do this, the same darkness that fills Satan's heart will fill *yours*. Just like the ancients enslaved themselves to false gods, so you enslave yourself to Satan. You are no better than they.

The world scoffs at the idea of sin, darkness, and Satan, yet is oblivious to its own spiritual slavery—and the awful consequences that such slavery will bring in due time. Just as Satan and his demons will soon be destroyed, so will all who follow him. When God calls time to an end and summons every human soul before His great tribunal, He will destroy all who chose darkness over "His marvelous light" (1 Peter 2:9). Those who are filled with the Light of this world will enter the glorious light of God's presence, where joy and peace will be theirs forever. Those who "loved the darkness rather than the Light" will find themselves forever engulfed *in* that darkness, and "in that place there will be weeping and gnashing of teeth" (Mat. 22:13).

The Power of the Darkness

The power of the darkness is real, tenacious, and lethal. Since the darkness operates within the spiritual realm, earthly power and human effort cannot defeat it. It is stronger—*immensely* stronger—than what a person is capable of removing once he has allowed the darkness into his heart. It takes time, effort, sacrifice, and moral courage to fight against the darkness (which is why many will not even try), but even these things by themselves cannot overcome its clutch on the human heart. The darkness stands ready to take advantage of every moral weakness, every secret lust, every taboo desire, and every lapse of attention. It does not matter who you are, whether you are a Christian, how long you have been going to church, or how faithful you believe yourself to be. The darkness lies stealthily and patiently in the background, just waiting for you to let your guard down. Its desire for you is *relentless*.

The darkness also knows how to mess with your head. It cannot read *what* you think, but it certainly knows *how* you think, what you like, how you behave, and what you secretly lust after. Thus, it also knows how to feed your doubts about God, the Bible, Christ's redemption, and whether you can ever be forgiven. It discourages every would-be disciple of Christ from believing in saving grace; it prevents such people from taking God or sin too seriously. It seeks to trip up every faithful Christian. Once they have fallen, it then bombards them with shame, guilt, feelings of worthlessness, and debilitating disappointment. What feeds the darkness is the complacency of every idle Christian, the procrastination of every good intention, the compromise of every spiritual commitment, the proud boast of every humble act of kindness, and the spirit of self-reliance in every person who confidently tells God, "I can handle this *myself*."

The apostle Paul said that "all have sinned and fall short of the glory of God" (Rom. 3:23). We should be asking ourselves, "When I am not walking *with* God, what am I falling *into*?" When Peter was not walking *with* Jesus on the sea (see Mat. 14:22–33), he was sinking *into* the water. Peter fell, so to speak, when he gave attention to the storm *rather than* keep his eyes focused on the Master. Similarly, when we give attention to the world, we fall short of God's holiness and fall *into* the darkness. Once we are there, it will take nothing less than the power of God to get us back to where we need to be.[68]

Many have said, in so many words, "The darkness has such a grip on my soul, I don't think even Christ can help me." This is exactly what the power of the darkness wants us to believe. It wants us to see ourselves as filthy, hopeless, and unredeemable. It wants us to believe that God does not care about us anymore—that He is only interested in "clean" people—and that Christ is unable to help us. It wants us to believe that the gospel message is outdated, is out-of-touch, offers no solutions, and has no power. It wants us to curl up in a fetal position, bawl our eyes out in hopeless frustration, curse God, and die. Spiritually-speaking, many people do just that.

Satan—who himself is filled with the darkness—imprisons us not because he is smarter and more powerful than Christ, but because of our own *lack of faith* in Christ. Satan does not seek to penetrate our strongest resistance; he looks for chinks in our armor, points of weakness by which he can gain entry. He does not break down the front door, so to speak; rather, he knocks, offering us all sorts of wicked enticements that we believe we cannot live without, and then we unwittingly—even stupidly—invite him in. This is like having a grotesque monster politely asking if he might have a word with us, and we foolishly welcome him inside. The thing is, he does not look grotesque or ghoulish; he looks seductively *pleasing* and *charismatic*. He makes us believe we will gain some advantage by letting down our guard and bringing the enemy within. The fact is, he remains a vicious monster, and we are naïve to the danger—at least, up front.

Once inside, Satan disarms our resistances, poisons our mind with lies, trivializes all biblical warnings and instructions, and convinces us to gratify our carnal desires. Just as a cult leader slowly breaks the will of his followers and indoctrinates them with a false gospel, so Satan slowly breaks a person's will and makes him pay attention to "deceitful spirits and doctrines of demons" (1 Tim. 4:1). More than anything, he keeps his prisoner from seeing God, believing in Him, searching for Him, or even thinking about Him. Satan is saturated with the darkness—a highly infectious contagion—and he pollutes souls with his own putrid corruption.

People who are addicted to alcohol, nicotine, street drugs, etc. are, in reality, addicted to the darkness.[69] If you imagine the darkness as a haunted, horrifying, and demon-filled castle, addiction is simply the death-filled ballroom in that castle. This is where addicts come to dance with malevolent demons who drain all life and hope from their captives. Addicts think, "If I can just get over this *addiction*, then I will be alright," but they remain in the castle, just in a different room. Some recovering addicts assume that they are now "saved," since they have escaped addiction's clutches. Thus, sobriety and rehabilitation become the gods that they think will rescue them, but those gods cannot deliver them from the power of the dark castle. Those people are still trapped within it, and the situation has really not improved. They may no longer have an active addiction to alcohol, but they are still in the grip of Satan and domain of darkness. Sobriety, by itself, cannot deliver you; drug counselors cannot save you; *you* cannot rescue *yourself* from the darkness. Only God has the power, authority, and willingness to "[rescue] us from the domain of darkness, and [transfer] us to the kingdom of His beloved Son, in whom we have redemption, the forgiveness of sins" (Col. 1:13–14).

Summary Thoughts

No one other than Jesus Christ—the most powerful authority figure to have ever walked on this earth—tells us that many people *love* the darkness and therefore *reject* the Light. In other words, this is not just a religious fable, a Christian talking point, or Jesus' opinion.

This is God's truth, and His truth is just as true today as it was 2,000 years ago. Learning about what the darkness is and how the darkness operates helps us not to fall victim to its lies and seductions. At the same time, learning who the Light is and how He operates should also make Him increasingly attractive to our souls. The darkness cannot harm those who walk in the Light, but those who reject the Light—no matter what the reason—are slowly being engulfed by the darkness.

Satan also has succumbed to the darkness. He is not the master of darkness, but the darkness has mastery over him. But we should not think that, just because Satan is not the "prince of darkness" that Hollywood has made him out to be, he is helpless to utilize the power *of* the darkness to his advantage. Satan and the darkness both want the same thing: to inflict as much pain and damage against God as possible. People's souls are merely a means to that end; we are not the ultimate target.

The darkness is powerful—more powerful than we can even imagine. Since this is true, it is to be avoided at all costs. It is not something we should dabble in, toy with, be ignorant of, or dwell upon. It is not something we should think that we can take on through our own strength, cleverness, or religious status. You and I are not strong enough, smart enough, or big enough to take on the power of the darkness. It operates in a realm that we have only heard of but have never seen, have very little knowledge of, and have virtually no control over. The darkness, on the other hand, knows our world very well, knows *us* very well—knows *you* very well—and has no trouble finding willing souls to carry out its bidding here on earth.

While we are not capable of overcoming the darkness, Christ most certainly is. He has proven His supremacy over demons, Satan, death itself, and the world of darkness. He is the *only One* who can help us—the only One who can help *you*. His help is not a last-ditch effort but is exceedingly capable of doing all that needs to be done. He does not offer general guidance, helpful assistance, or good advice; He promises a clear and decisive victory for every person who puts his or her faith in Him. He is not a morale-boosting cheerleader or a proverb-quoting life coach; He is a proven, battle-tested, and unconquerable warrior. You do not need an effeminate waif of a man who walks around affectionately blessing everyone (as the religious world sometimes depicts Christ); you need a strong, fearless, and virtuous King who can deliver on every promise He makes. Nothing less than this will be able to rescue you from the darkness.

"For the word of the cross is foolishness to those who are perishing, but to us who are being saved it is the power of God" (1 Cor. 1:18). The world sneers at God, shrugs at Christ and His cross, and mercilessly belittles Christians. Yet, it is the world that is perishing, not God, not Christ, and not faithful Christians. The world is perishing not only because it does not have fellowship with God, but also because it *does*—often ignorantly, carelessly, and unconsciously—have fellowship with the darkness. The world stumbles in the darkness, but those who are being saved walk in the Light. In the end, the world will disappear into the darkness forever, while those who walk with God will be "swallowed up by life" (2 Cor. 5:4).

Chapter Seven: The Influence of the Darkness

There is a reason why burglars and thieves often work at night and hate floodlights and security cameras: they prefer to operate in *the darkness*. Darkness offers a cloak of protection from being exposed and identified; light destroys this protection and anonymity.

Sinners—all those who practice sin and live outside of a right relationship with God—are the same way: they love the darkness and hate the Light of the world. When God's truth shines upon them, those who wish to remain sinners scatter like cockroaches, running for cover. But those who allow themselves to be exposed by the Light will hear the truth, accept what it says about them, and do whatever is necessary to draw near to it.

We have much to say about the Light of the world in due time, but for now we would do well to know something about the darkness so as not to be fully ignorant of it. Furthermore, we need to address the reason why so many people are drawn *to* the darkness (despite all of its negative effects) rather than to the Light. At face value, you would think that people would gravitate toward light, life, truth, and all that is good. Sadly, we see just the opposite. Comparatively, only a handful of people choose to walk in the Light for every million that choose to live in darkness.

Manifestations of the Darkness

Our present world—the visible and tangible realm of ungodly human activity—has plunged headlong into the darkness. The world has done so willingly, although it did not consider the consequences of this up front. Human society is reeling from the awful effects of its unwholesome and unhealthy relationship with the darkness. We can blame other things or factors if we want to (politics, economics, racial tensions, etc.), but these are merely symptoms, not the actual disease. This is like choosing to smoke cigarettes all of your life, and then blaming your doctor for the lung cancer that has developed within you.

The disease we are talking about here is far worse than lung cancer. It is our pathological fixation on the darkness *rather than* fixating on the Light (1 Tim. 4:6–11). Faithful Christians are trying hard to warn people of the dangers of this relationship—and how to break free from it—but we are being ridiculed, marginalized, and muzzled. In some places in the world, we are being martyred. *We* are vilified as the enemies rather than *the darkness*, yet it is not us who are destroying many millions of souls at this very moment, but the darkness most certainly is. Much of the world is oblivious as to who or what is the real enemy.

The darkness—and Satan in particular—has always been in our midst, though it has maintained a relatively low profile until recently. The darkness has been working subversively rather than overtly, slowly but steadily undermining the pillars of a value-oriented, virtue-based, and God-fearing society. It is not as though the darkness is more powerful than God's truth, but that it is being far more widely *accepted*. While preachers, statesmen, and other leaders have been promoting core values, patriotic virtues, and the need for moral courage, many politicians and citizens have already been seduced by pride, greed, adultery, and materialism. We are trying to build a grand castle (our nation) on a rotting foundation (our compromised moral system). Such a building project will not end well.

Presently, the darkness is no longer working in the background. It is out front, in our face, and cramming its repugnant agenda down our throats. It no longer sees the need to work subversively, since its many followers are now doing its bidding out in the open. The power of the darkness has not only infiltrated our society, it is now beginning to control it (at least, to the extent that God will allow). Now we are hearing people—preachers, politicians, journalists, corporate leaders, and citizens in general—talking in such a way that *makes no sense.* Logic and reason have been jettisoned; these only interfere with the darkness's agenda. Those whose souls are filled with the darkness openly lie about facts, evidence, and "what happened." They are flagrantly contradictory and hypocritical, yet they show no shame, remorse, or concern for this. They champion the lowest common denominator in society—those who are morally, mentally, or sexually perverse—and demand that the rest of the nation applaud and *advocate for* these people. They prey upon the weak-minded, morally-confused and biblically-ignorant—an increasingly large segment of our society. They demand that we all be "tolerant," non-discriminatory, and open-minded, yet they advocate an agenda that is intolerant of dissent, discriminates against anyone who questions them, and is so narrow-minded that it seeks to silence (or "cancel") those who speak the truth.

What was once unthinkable, unacceptable, and unnatural has now become doable and defendable. Satanic behaviors are not only being practiced; they are being normalized, as though these are part of a progressive, enlightened, and advanced society. Wickedness is not only increasingly common; it has become the new status quo. People are not only being tempted to do evil; they are *expected* to do it, and are stigmatized if they do not. The Bible, like those who believe in it, is painted as an oppressive, outdated, and backward prescription for an allegedly bigoted, intolerant, and racist age. Now we welcome the re-definition of marriage, no matter how irrational or ridiculous the premise. Now we hold up sexually- and gender-confused people (for example) as though they are the paragons of a new world order. Now racism—the favoring of one race over another—is denounced even as we exalt one *particular* race over another. Now we condemn discrimination even as we openly and unapologetically discriminate against Christians.

Satan has no original thought; he cannot come up with anything on his own. He merely takes whatever God has given us and perverts it, "maligns" it (2 Peter 2:3), and corrupts it with lies, deceptions, and misrepresentations. For example, God made humankind "male and female"—not male *or* female—"in His own image" (Gen. 1:27), but Satan has perverted this. God created marriage as the human union of a man and a woman (Gen. 2:22–24), but Satan has perverted this. God has made many nations and ethnicities of people (Acts 17:26–28), and His people are taught to treat *all* people with dignity and respect (Mat. 7:12), but Satan has perverted this. God's people are taught to love *all* people—not just our family and friends, but even our enemies and persecutors (Mat. 5:43–47). But Satan has hijacked the word "love" and turned it into something repulsive. Anyone who does not "love" like the ungodly world has defined the word is automatically a "hater" and deserves all kinds of condemnation, hostility, and, well, *hatred*.

Blame individual people who are spouting Satan's lies if you want to—specific politicians, celebrities, authors, etc. But what you are seeing is the darkness exerting its awful influence upon them. This is not to excuse all such people, for they are without excuse (Rom. 1:18–20). Yet, we are looking past the symptomatic manifestation of the problem and identifying the problem itself. These people have allowed the darkness to control them, and now they are under its spell, blinded to its manipulations, and corrupted in their thinking. They have bought into a "wisdom" that does not come from God, but one that is earthly, unnatural, and demonic (James 3:13–16). They have listened to the "father of lies"—Satan himself (John 8:44)—who also once swallowed the darkness's lie that he could exalt himself against God and get away with it.

Paul talked about Christians being "bewitched" [lit., under a spell] who accepted a perversion of the gospel that came from men rather than the true gospel that came from heaven (Gal. 3:1–3). This is what is happening to our world: people are accepting Satan's lies and rejecting God's truth. In order to turn *toward* what is evil, people must first turn *away* from what is good (2 Tim. 4:3–5). In order to give allegiance to the darkness, people must first turn away from the Light. Look around you, and you will see the darkness at work:

- Broken homes, single-parent families, and out-of-wedlock pregnancies have all dramatically increased in recent decades. So have depression, suicide, theft, assault, rape, domestic violence, vandalism, social irresponsibility, revolts against authority, and a general apathy toward life. While politicians loftily promise unity and equality, their policies are divisive and protect only a small percentage of people. As a result, life is getting harder for everyone. People are not happier; they are being overwhelmed with stress, despair, and hopelessness. Ethics have plummeted as more and more people follow the example of many of their leaders—men and women who are liars, hypocrites, thieves, and self-serving. Now, our schools, local governments, and workforce are permeated with many of these same evils, and we wonder *what went wrong*.

- Atheism, agnosticism, humanism, postmodernism, mysticism, paganism, and Satanism are all on the rise and gaining popularity. This is especially true among younger generations that lack historical perspective, the influence of biblical teaching, and a working moral compass. Witchcraft, sorcery, soothsaying, divination, spiritism, paranormalism, demonism, and occultism are also making great strides—again, both targeting and brainwashing our young people. Followers of these "-isms" indulge in: a quest for immortality; sexual power, seduction, and rape; isolation and alienation; rebellion, violence, and murder; blood-shedding and blood-drinking; drugs, alcohol, and ecstasy-inducing practices; and the outright worship of Satan. People who walk in the Light stay clear away from all these things; people who walk in the darkness seek sensual pleasure, personal gain, or power from them.
- False religion (which may masquerade as "Christianity" but has simply hijacked its basic premise) is poisoning the minds and lives of many millions of people. As a result, many become soured by this grossly-distorted message, or they think they are forgiven, righteous, and "saved" when in fact they are not. People who walk in the Light do not segregate, denominationalize, and contradict His word; people who walk in the darkness, however, do all of these things and call it "good," "holy," and "righteous." This is a lie, but it is being preached as though it were the truth, and many people have swallowed this lie assuming that it *is* the truth.
- Our American society worships the creature rather than the Creator (Rom. 1:25). In other words, we worship the naked human body—particularly, the naked *female* body. Technology has made this easier, more accessible, and more visually-graphic than ever before in all of human history. Our society is addicted to sensuality, eroticism, pornography, and sex. Social media is riddled with erotic images and softcore porn. Movies cannot wait to expose actresses' breasts and steamy sex scenes. We want our young women (in particular) to dress like hookers so we can see their underwear, get aroused from their cleavage, and fantasize about them being naked. Pre-marital sex is considered normal, expected, and strongly encouraged. The major premise of many

TV comedy series involves how quickly and creatively two people can have sex with each other.
- The "sensual conduct of unprincipled men" (2 Peter 2:7) has convinced many that homosexuality is normal, wonderful, and even *godly*. While God says that men fornicating with other men, and women fornicating with other women, is unnatural, unholy, and degrading (Rom. 1:26), our society promotes it as acceptable and progressive. People apparently believe—against all knowledge of biology, genetics, and science in general—that they can arbitrarily choose their sexuality and gender. Or worse: they believe—against any objective proof or evidence—that they are *born* with their unnatural desires and cannot possibly resist them. This rebellion against God, heterosexual marriage, sexual propriety, and the natural order of Creation did not come from people who walk in the Light; this all came from the darkness. Yet, many continue to be seduced and mesmerized by its wicked propaganda.
- We have become a foul-mouthed, irreverent, and sacrilegious nation. We did not used to be this way, but we certainly are now. Profanity is epidemic, from the President on down to the typical fourth-grader. Many award-winning movies, TV shows, and Broadway productions are laced with F-bombs, expletives, and pervasive vulgarity. We have "explicit lyrics" warnings on music recordings, especially the music of the younger generations (even though explicit language is what they have grown up with and seems normal). Comedians cannot wait to unleash their most offensive material, trashing anything and everything that has long been deemed sacred, holy, and reverent. Making fun of religion—and the Christian religion in particular—is a huge source of entertainment and big business. There seems to be a contest among comedians as to who can deliver the raunchiest and most brutally-shocking standup routine—and Americans are enjoying this, paying for it, and applauding it. These are things we never learned from God, the Bible, or those who walk in the Light. Instead, these are things the darkness has led us to believe are harmless and acceptable.

- Modern America has become a drug-dependent culture. This dependence is not just on illegal drugs, but also prescription drugs. It is hard to find a middle-aged person who is not on some "maintenance" drug due to his poor lifestyle choices. (To be clear: I'm speaking of *human* choices here, not congenital situations where a person needs a certain medication to survive, through no fault of his own.) We are a pill-happy, drug-pushing, and over-medicated society. From marijuana to meth, painkillers to Prozac, and physicians to pharmaceuticals—if we can smoke it, put it into our mouth, shoot it into our veins, or dispense it in a plastic amber vial, we'll take it. We allow drugs to control our lives, modify our behavior, and even ruin our souls. Bowing down to the gods of medicine and recreational drugs is not something we learned from the God of heaven. Instead, addiction to the drug culture is the work of the darkness.
- Alcohol is everywhere. In most sporting events, for example, it is both sold and anticipated—and this has become normal and acceptable. The darkness has convinced us that *alcohol* is not the problem, but rather alcohol-*ism*, as if these were two unrelated things. This addiction is now labeled as a "disease"—a disease which, apparently, does not come and attack us against our will, but is invited into the lives of those who drink, and especially those who drink *a lot*. Given this premise, we throw drugs and counselors and therapy at alcoholics, while avoiding saying anything critical of them for fear of "judging" or sounding insensitive.[70] Yet, no one wants to admit (publicly, anyway) that such people chose to dabble in the power of darkness, thinking that they were doing something harmless, socializing with their friends, or trying to "numb the pain." In reality, they opened up a portal into their life that allowed the darkness to find a very comfortable place to live—really, to reign over them. None of this has come from God or is the result of drawing near to God. No Christian who is living faithfully to God has ever become an alcoholic (yet, many alcoholics have, thankfully, become Christians). Instead, all of this deception and damage is from people loving the darkness rather than the Light.

- "Sin" is no longer *sin*. It has lost all moral connection to a fixed, absolute, and transcendent authority. It is no longer regarded as a violation of God's laws or His holy nature. In fact, our society has virtually etched it out of our social vernacular. Now, instead of calling something for what it is—*sin*—we talk about "addiction," "sickness," "mental illness," "medical (or psychological) disorders," or "behavioral disabilities"—all of which, we are told, can be addressed with doctors, drugs, expensive specialists and therapists, treatment centers, and welfare programs.[71] But these are not really the issue; sin is the issue. Of course, no one gets any money or funding for sin treatment, which is at least one reason why our attention is immediately and even forcefully turned away from this. Treating the effects of sin is a huge (and lucrative) business, so it is more financially advantageous to medicate (through whatever means) "disease"-ridden people than it is to seek a cure for the alleged disease itself.

The point is: "the Light has come into the world, and men loved the darkness *rather than* the Light" (John 3:19, emphasis added). We have become a blasphemous, sacrilegious, pornographic, homoerotic, sexually-confused, morally-deviant, profanity-spewing, lying, careless, and morally-irresponsible nation. And this is happening despite our having been founded as a (more or less) "Christian nation," our currency that proclaims "In God We Trust," an abundance of Bibles and churches, the influence of Christian people, and the annual reminder of Jesus' birth (at Christmas) and His resurrection (at Easter).[72]

In other words, *that* is how powerful the darkness is. It is strong enough to convince otherwise intelligent people to take the path of least resistance and champion the lowest common denominator. It is strong enough to destroy marriages, families, communities, and entire nations—even Bible-quoting churches. It is strong enough to ruin the human soul and render it unfit to be in the presence of its Creator. That is a power we should do everything in *our* power to avoid. That is a power to be respected—but also *hated to its core*.

Why People Choose the Darkness over the Light

Yet, if the darkness is so ruinous, why are so many people—in some ways, *all* of us—drawn to it? Why does it pose such a strong attraction? What could we possibly hope to gain from something that God has told us explicitly will destroy us? Why are we doing this to ourselves? One might argue, "Not everyone *knows* what God has said about the darkness's wicked agenda," and this is true—at least to some extent. Many people—both within and without the church—are simply unaware of what the Bible teaches. Even so, God has given all of us a conscience to let us know what we are doing is *right* or *wrong* (Rom. 2:14–15). We may not be aware up front of how much damage our trespass into forbidden territory will cost us, but we *should* know that it is wrong to go there in the first place.

Besides our conscience warning us when we choose to violate it, there is the lure of the darkness itself. It does not just sit off to the side, hoping we will notice it over time. Instead, it offers a tantalizing and seductive attraction to us. A man will likely not be drawn to an old, wrinkled, and disheveled hag, but he might well put himself at great risk to spend some time with a gorgeous, curvaceous, and perfumed young lady. In a sense, it's all in the packaging. Anyone who has gone fishing knows this: technique is part of it, but your first impression upon the fish is your *lure* and *bait*. The darkness lures us in with a fine package—something we already want, do not want to miss out on, and (likely) have experienced before with great pleasure. When we bite into the bait, the hook pierces deeply into our soul and the darkness begins reeling us further into its grasp. In the end, all such people—apart from divine help—will be fully consumed by the darkness.

In some respect, we do not only want what the darkness *offers*, we want *the darkness*. We may never put it in those words, but this is how it translates. Jesus said that the reason people turn away from the Light is because they "loved the darkness"—not just what is in it, but the darkness itself. This does not speak of a casual or harmless fling. There is something about the darkness that the proud, self-serving, and pleasure-seeking human spirit craves, pursues, and worships. The darkness is provocative, mesmerizing, and captivating; we have a strange and giddy attraction to it. Entering into the world of the taboo is *exciting*—every one of us has experienced this. For some of us, our desire for the darkness lies just below the thin veneer of our everyday personality. For others, it is buried deep beneath thick strata of spiritual training, biblical instruction, and self-discipline. But it has not gone away, no matter who we are or how long we have been Christians.

I do not have to tell you all this, for you know it already. Maybe you are unwilling to admit it, or maybe you are slowly nodding with appreciation for what I am saying. Left to ourselves, we are all pleasure-seekers by nature, and *pleasure*—in one form or another—is the darkness's shiny lure that attracts us the most. Our carnal nature is not so concerned about God, our responsibility to our fellow man, or our spiritual needs.[73] All spiritual training aside, we want to relax, have fun, and cruise through life on the path of least resistance. Many people may dabble in Christianity and call it "discipleship" (which is like sticking your toe in the pool and calling it "swimming"), but their strongest desire is for the darkness, not God. They actually nurture a certain fondness, affection, and affinity for the darkness; their brain literally begins to re-wire itself to desperately crave it. Jesus said, "No one can serve two masters; for either he will hate the one and love the other..." (Mat. 6:24). There is *no way in the world* a person can walk in the Light if he has a love affair with the darkness. There have been many Christians who thought they would be the exception to what Jesus said, and they were always wrong.

People continue to love the darkness because they become very comfortable with it. They become very *familiar* with it. They know their way around, where the "sweet spots" are, and how to squeeze from it the most intense pleasure. Imagine a man sitting in front of his computer, allowing himself just a moment of indulgence in the darkness. He has learned how to bypass all the restrictions, navigate the websites, and arrive exactly where he wants to be: his favorite porn pictures. He has developed an emotional attachment to this procedure—it excites him and makes him feel warm and comfortable. He knows this routine, and its familiarity brings him a euphoric sense of completion that he fails to achieve from his otherwise mundane, ordinary, and responsible life.

You do not have to be addicted to pornography in order to understand this. It is the same experience for the man who craves a drink at his favorite bar, a woman who flirtatiously courts a man who is not her husband, and those who love to destroy others anonymously with their online criticism. We are all creatures of habit, and our habits are generated from behaviors we have come to know very well and thus we feel very comfortable engaging in them. For example, bring me to a coffee shop, set me in front of a chessboard, or invite me into a racquetball court, and I know exactly what to do. I am very comfortable and familiar with all of these contexts. So it is with the darkness: people know exactly what to do once they allow the darkness to lead them into a context that, from trained experience, they know all too well.

When these people sit through a church service and hear a preacher say "you need to get your life right," or, "you need to honor Christ as your Lord and Savior," they cringe inside. They do so *not* because they disagree with the message or disapprove of the one saying it. Rather, they are so entrenched in the ways of the darkness that a walk in the Light seems distant, unachievable, and unfamiliar to them. They know that walking the "straight and narrow path" is the right thing to do, but they have trained themselves to feel far more at home with the wide, meandering, and pleasure-strewn path of least resistance. These may say to the ones trying to encourage them to walk with the Lord, "You don't know what I'm talking about!" The fact is, it is the people in *the darkness* who do not know what the people walking in *the Light* are talking about. We all know what it is like to partake of the darkness; relatively few know what it means to genuinely commune with God in the Light.

People choose the darkness because it provides a place to *hide*. Those who are living in contradiction to God's will or in violation of their conscience want concealment, not exposure. The darkness (allegedly) offers protection, secrecy, and evasion. It offers a chance for people to live unrealistically and irresponsibly, yet undetected all the same. It allows people a "place" to do what they really want to do rather than what they ought to be doing. People who walk in the darkness rarely accuse one another of anything, either. There is a kind of unspoken solidarity and support group—in essence, an unholy fellowship—among partakers of the darkness. Such people do not worry about being morally responsible to God or accountable to one another since their fellowship in the darkness removes the need for these. The apostle Paul speaks of such people: "although they know the ordinance of God, that those who practice such things are worthy of death, they not only do the same, but also give hearty approval to those who practice them" (Rom. 1:32).

People are drawn to the darkness because it promises them much but (seemingly) demands little or nothing in return. The darkness does not ask you to give up anything that you want to do. It accommodates your heart's desires, your masquerades and deceptions, your bad habits and addictions, and all of your excuses and crutches. In the darkness, you can be whatever you want to be—however *self-serving* you want to be. The darkness welcomes your self-pity, your victimhood status, and your sad story of "what happened" that you want to unload on everyone who shows any interest in you. The darkness applauds one's perverse desire to indulge in fornication, gender confusion, or even his legalistic quest to aggressively justify himself to those who would dare challenge his unholy lifestyle.

The darkness is all about tolerance, diversity, and non-discrimination—all the buzzwords of our seemingly "progressive" society. It tolerates every evil and godless way. It wants you to diversify your wickedness to include whatever pleasure turns you on. And it will not discriminate against anyone who does its bidding. You do not have to give up your pleasures, complacency, or procrastination. On the contrary, the darkness encourages you to be lazy, distracted, self-absorbed, and careless. "Don't judge!" is the bumper sticker philosophy of the darkness. Fill your belly, indulge in your secret sin, tell your little white lies—the darkness will always be there to support and encourage you in this. Don't take God so seriously—a token nod to heaven every now and then is all that is needed. Don't let the gospel of Christ constrict your plans—you have a life, right? It is permissible to forsake moral responsibility, the church, or God Himself, because there are others who will pay attention to those things.

As long as you are a good person—whatever that means to *you* ("God knows my heart!")—then the darkness stands behind you, smiling, nodding in approval, and patting you on the back. "I'm there for you," the darkness seductively whispers in your heart. "You know that you are right, no matter what God says otherwise. Don't feel that you have to change *anything* for me—I love you just the way you are." The darkness tells you to "follow your heart"—something you crave anyway—because it knows that it already *owns* your heart, if indeed you have been listening to its soothing persuasion.

Those Who Have Been Deceived by the Darkness

The darkness has lied to and deceived every person who has listened to it. They are not "free" and "independent" and their "own person," as they assume; they are its helpless prisoners. The darkness wants such people to remain what they are *not* because they are safe and protected, but because they are corrupted and perishing, and the darkness does not want them to be rescued. They are like moths fluttering around an artificial light, intoxicated with its attraction. The darkness makes it seem as though a person really can live life on his own terms, but the fact is that *all people who refuse the Light will die in their sins* (John 8:24).

The darkness sounds supportive, understanding, and even reassuring. It pretends to validate your skewed beliefs, justify your sinful behavior, and accept your irrational worldview. Yet, it is purposely creating moral confusion within your mind so that you will believe truth to be lies and lies to be truth (Isa. 5:20–21, 2 Thess. 2:10–12). The darkness does not really *care* about you—not one bit. It does not care about *anyone*. Its objective is to deceive, divide, and destroy. Those who fellowship with the darkness, no matter who they think they are or claim to be, have no fellowship with God (2 Cor. 6:14). Thinking oneself to be a "good person," calling oneself a Christian, or being active in a congregation will not change this.

Jesus said that in order to follow *Him*, you must give up everything—your pride, your personal agenda, your self-will, and even your *life* (Mat. 16:24). His objective is not to make you comfortable, but to bring you into holy fellowship with Him. By examining your heart in the light of His word, He seeks to reveal what needs to be removed in order for that fellowship to happen. He does not want you to live life on your terms—this will be the spiritual *death* of you—but on His terms, since He offers you eternal life (John 6:40). The darkness promises much but cannot deliver on any of it. Jesus promises you a place in heaven—and He has proven to possess the power and authority to *deliver fully on that promise* (John 10:27–29, 2 Peter 1:2–4).

Think about this in another context: Suppose you invite a huge monster of man into your house, even though he is a known rapist, pedophile, murderer, and pathological liar. You give him room and board, pay for all of his expenses, allow him to eat dinner with you, and let him baby sit your children while you are gone—but you think *nothing of this*. You trust him implicitly and give him full access to all of your private information, even the combination to your safe—but you think *nothing of this*. Then suppose someone comes along and says, "You need to get out of your house because you and your family are in *perilous danger*! There is a well-armed, incredibly resourceful, and honorably decorated Navy Seal outside your home waiting to escort you to safety!" And imagine that you say, "I can't leave everything I own behind—that's a lot to ask. Besides, how do I know I can *trust* that Navy Seal not to take advantage of me and my loved ones?" This is how ridiculous and completely illogical it is to commune with the darkness and resist Christ's help. Yet, most people reason this way.

Summary Thoughts

America may have once been characterized rightly as a God-fearing nation—not truly "Christian" (because only *people* become Christians, not nations), but at least God-fearing. We once had some respect for God, and we held the Bible and authentic preachers *of* the Bible in high regard. We used to have a collective desire to do what is right, seek what is good, and make sacrifices to achieve these things. Such noble attitudes and aspirations are quickly evaporating. The darkness, like a thick, menacing, and almost palpable fog, has stealthily enveloped our country. This spiritual fog has blinded our eyes, stopped up our ears, and brainwashed our minds. It has intoxicated our senses, making us numb to the presence of evil and the dangers of sin. Many Americans accuse Christians of stupidly believing in an "imaginary god in the sky," yet those who do so are oblivious to their own spiritual ignorance as they are dragged unwittingly deeper and deeper into their own ruin. While "professing to be wise" in their own eyes, their foolish hearts have become "darkened" (Rom. 1:21–22).

We do not stumble accidentally into the darkness. Rather, we are drawn to it, entangled in it, and imprisoned by it. The darkness is not a passive danger; it is a menacing predator. In order to ensnare us, the darkness offers different things to different people. To many, it is an intoxicating alternate reality; to others, it is the bewitching lure of material wealth and possessions; to others, it is a powerful sexual or emotional seduction; and to others still, it is the rush of power, greed, and status. While all of us are drawn to the darkness for what we *think* it is, few ever realize what it *really* is.

People have a certain fondness for the darkness; they find it familiar and seemingly navigable; they are allowed to hide in its folds and shadows while they live life on their own terms. Even so, they profit from none of this. "For the wages of sin is death, but the free gift of God is eternal life in Christ Jesus our Lord" (Rom. 6:23). The darkness does not offer mercy, grace, or forgiveness—only God can do this—but only spiritual "death." In essence, the one who follows the darkness is ultimately engulfed completely by it—swallowed whole, never to escape, and yet never to lose consciousness.

What God offers is not just the opposite of the darkness, but infinitely greater. "Eternal life" is not just an escape from eternal darkness, but a full, completely satisfying, absolutely thrilling, and *wonderful* existence in the presence of a benevolent God in His unfathomable world. His world is one of light, love, joy, warmth, fellowship, and incomprehensible beauty. Millions of souls that "have been purchased from among men as first fruits to God and to the Lamb" (Rev. 14:4) will be there. Instead of being swallowed up by darkness, those who are in God's world have been "swallowed up by life" (2 Cor. 5:4)—not forever lost, but forever *found* without any fear of ever being lost again.

To which world are you presently heading?

Chapter Eight: Satan May Not Be Who You Think He Is

Nearly every scary story has its boogeyman—some wicked, malicious character that has no other agenda but to seduce and destroy as many people as he can. This predator may come disguised as a friend, a familiar face, or someone to be trusted. Yet, he remains a predator nonetheless, and predators are never friendly or trustworthy. In other cases, the boogeyman is not disguised as much as he is hidden or obscured from view. He lurks in the shadows, prowls in the darkness, and conceals himself in a crowd of otherwise harmless people. He does not attack by gaining your trust, but through the element of surprise. Just when your attention is diverted elsewhere, he strikes—and his intent is not merely to inflict a superficial wound but to destroy you.

Thankfully, most scary stories are just that—harmless, fictitious, and fanciful stories meant only to entertain. It's weird that being scared can be entertaining, but—and I speak from experience—it is. This means that the boogeyman in those stories is also harmless, fictitious, and the fanciful projection of someone's imagination. Pretend boogeymen cannot hurt you; thus, you have no reason to fear them.

But there is one boogeyman—a purely evil, sinister, and malicious character—that is very real. He is often lampooned, marginalized, and dismissed as harmless, but he is an extremely cunning enemy and a force to be reckoned with. He is predatory by nature, which means no matter what he says, does, or pretends to be, his goal is to seduce and destroy as many people as he can. He comes disguised as a friend, a familiar face, and someone to be trusted. Or, he lurks in the shadows, just outside of your periphery, but is simply waiting for an opportune time to attack you by surprise. Since he is not pretend, he can and will hurt you, if given the chance.

I am talking, of course, about that age-old character known to us as Satan. But just because he has been known to us for a long time does not mean we know him or his tactics very well. In fact, Satan may not at all be who you think he is, and he capitalizes on your ignorance, false understanding, or sheer indifference to his true identity. The less you know about him—even if you choose to dismiss him altogether—just plays into his hand and makes his seduction of your soul easier.[74]

The Origin of "Satan"

The word "satan"—whether used as a proper name or a generic noun—is transliterated from the Hebrew word *satan* (pronounced saw-*tawn'*) which means "adversary."[75] Transliteration is when a word is carried over from an original source language into another language without being changed. "Satan," as used in the Bible (and especially the Old Testament [OT]), is literally *an* adversary, not always *the* adversary. *The* adversary is an actual and singular personage that is known to us by many descriptors: dragon, deceiver, accuser, tempter, Belial, Beelzebub, prince of the power of the air, god of this world, wicked one, evil one, strong man, serpent of old, father of lies, enemy, murderer, and sinner. His proper names include Abaddon, Apollyon (Rev. 9:11), Beelzebul (Mat. 12:27), Belial (2 Cor. 6:15), and, most commonly, Satan. In the NT, his most common descriptor is "the devil," which is translated from the Greek word *diabolos* (from which we get our English word "diabolical" which means *satanic*).[76]

Satan is inseparably linked to the world of darkness. In a sense, this is *his* world—not because he owns it, or created it on his own power, but this is the domain in which he operates and has built his kingdom. Many people think Satan is the personification of evil but do not believe he is a real or individual entity. He is "indispensable to our understanding of the Christian past," to the point that "it is hard to imagine Christianity without him."[77] In more superstitious times, Satan was greatly feared, and he was personally blamed for much of the evil in the world. The modern world, however, does not take him so seriously. As far back as the early 19th century, Friedrich Schleiermacher (*The Christian Faith*) wrote, "The idea of the Devil, as developed among us, is so unstable that we cannot expect anyone to be convinced of its truth."[78] In more modern times:

> The devil has been largely dismissed in the modern world. Most scientists and doctors advance the idea that all phenomena can be explained and understood by natural

principles. ... Scientists [have] denied the presence of any demons, devils, or unknown, unseen spirit world whatsoever. The modern world, in the view of science, was an improved world where superstition was fleeing and witchcraft took its rightful place in medieval history and fairy tales. Everything in this new and improved would could be explained in terms of natural forces, which could be touched, smelled, seen, heard, and understood through logic, deduction, and reasoning. Few people, either inside or outside of the [Roman] church, challenged the growing skepticism surrounding the devil. ... [Even those who still believe in God, Jesus Christ, and the afterlife] have trouble believing in the devil or hell.[79]

This seems to sum up the general consensus of the humanistic and mechanical worldview. Satan has no place in the Age of Technology, any more than God does. Satan has been reduced to a harmless caricature—nothing more harmful than a man with plastic horns on his head, wearing a red costume, and carrying a toy pitchfork.

Yet, despite all attempts to deny his influence, diminish his power, or eradicate his existence, Jesus and the NT writers all claim that he is alive, active, powerful, and *real*. As stated earlier, the Bible is the only source of *factual* information on the unseen spiritual realm and all those who operate within it. Everything we know factually about God, Satan, angels, demons, heaven, hell, the soul, sin, and the afterlife comes to us from the Bible. Unless the Bible itself is completely fictitious—something no one has proved—there is no reason to discount what it says about Satan simply on the grounds of "I choose not to believe he is real" or "the biblical account does not fit my worldview." You cannot just opt out of something that God says is true, unless you can prove that God does not exist—another thing that no one has done.

While the Bible repeatedly and consistently affirms Satan's existence, it still offers little in the way of explanation of who he is or how he came to be the "adversary." The word *satan* is barely used in the OT. When it is used, it is nearly always in a general sense or with the definite article (i.e., "*the* satan"). In this way, it is not used to describe a specific entity, but anyone or anything that serves as an "adversary" to someone else. For example, Hadad the Edomite was a *satan* ("adversary") to King Solomon of Israel, as was a man named Rezon (1 Kings 11:14, 23). Thirteen times various men—not the devil—are called *satan* in the OT. In fact, the angel of the Lord is called a *satan* ("adversary") to Balaam as the prophet went to prophesy for Barak (Num. 22:22, 32). Only *once* in the OT is "Satan" used without the definite article: "Then Satan stood up against Israel and moved David to number Israel" in a census (1 Chron. 21:1). If we compare this with its parallel passage in 2 Samuel 24:1, however, we see that it is *God's anger* that serves as the "adversary" to David, not the devil as we know him now.

In establishing a history of Satan, many people run to the book of Job. In chapters 1 and 2, it appears that Satan—as *the devil*—presents himself before God and tries his best to get Job to abandon his faith. While on the surface this seems to be a conclusive portrayal of Satan, closer examination does not support this. The Hebrew text does not give the antagonist a proper name, but refers to him only as "the adversary" or "the satan." We tend to read these ancient passages with knowledge that we have of Satan in Jesus' day, and assume that the two "Satan" entities must be one and the same.[80]

Similarly, we see "the adversary"—often subjectively translated as a proper name ("Satan") by some Bible translators—accusing Joshua the high priest in Zech. 3:1. We assume, because we have been conditioned to believe so, that this must be the devil known to us from the NT who is doing the tempting, but the text does not demand this. While the devil that Jesus spoke of certainly was an accuser (the very meaning *of* "devil"), it does not stand to reason that every spiritual entity that accuses God's people must be *this* devil. Just as there are many angels, and even multiple archangels, there may as well be many devils, and (at least at one time) multiple arch-accusers. By the time when Jesus entered the world—over 500 years after Zechariah's vision—Satan had become the foremost accuser and a self-declared rival of the Son of God.

Our first *assumed* introduction to Satan is, of course, in the Garden of Eden—or so we have all been conditioned to believe. Yet, nowhere in the text (particularly Gen. 3) does it mention Satan personally. It does mention "the serpent" several times, and we have all assumed that Satan was the one manipulating and giving voice to that creature—"possessing" it, we will say—but the serpent clearly is depicted as an earthly creature that acts on its own volition. It is the serpent that is cursed for what *the serpent* said and did, not Satan. It is *the literal serpent* that once walked and talked but now is forced to crawl on its belly in the literal dust of the literal earth. If Satan *is* the serpent—as in, the two being one and the same—then we should expect him (a spiritual being) to be manifested as a literal serpent (a physical creature).

There is nothing fanciful, allegorical, or mythological about the account of the serpent in Gen. 3. The apostle Paul, for one, takes it at face value. In fact, Paul admits that Eve was deceived by "the serpent," not personally by Satan (2 Cor. 11:3). We are quick to cite Gen. 3:14–15, where it is prophesied that "the seed" of the woman will "bruise" the serpent's seed on the head, and that the serpent's seed will "bruise" her seed on the heel. Many believe that God is talking *to* Satan, but clearly the text says that He is talking *directly* to the serpent.

It seems far more accurate, in light of a later confrontation between Satan and Christ, that while God was indeed talking (literally) *to* the serpent, He was talking (prophetically) *about* Satan. Thus, the serpent serves as a "type" (or, foreshadow) of Satan, and the future conflict between the two "seeds" as a type of what would later happen. It also seems far more accurate to say that the serpent itself—acting alone, as far as the temptation of Eve was concerned—was itself tempted by Satan to say what he said. In other words, it was not Satan taking the form of a serpent, but the serpent had been already seduced by Satan to speak evil of God. Thus, the first corruption in the new world was not the fall of Man but the infiltration of Satan into the natural world as a means to *cause* the fall of Man. The serpent never would have lied to Eve if it had not itself been lied to. The darkness, having caused the fall of Satan (whenever that was), then caused the fall of nature, which led to the fall of Man. Thus, the whole of Creation—angelic, natural, and human—has been corrupted by the darkness. In light of this, think about what Paul said in Rom. 8:19–23:

> For the anxious longing of the creation waits eagerly for the revealing of the sons of God. For the creation was subjected to futility, not willingly, but because of Him who subjected it, in hope that the creation itself also will be set free from its slavery to corruption into the freedom of the glory of the children of God. For we know that the whole creation groans and suffers the pains of childbirth together until now. And not only this, but also we ourselves, having the first fruits of the Spirit, even we ourselves groan within ourselves, waiting eagerly for our adoption as sons, the redemption of our body.

It is not just the human race that has suffered from sin, but "the whole creation." It is true that the fall of Man brought pain and suffering into the world. Yet, the serpent—a creature "of the field" which God had made (Gen. 3:1)—had already defied its Creator when it lied to the Creator's greatest creation—that which was made "in His own image" (Gen. 1:27). Instead of listening to the voice of the Creator, Eve listened to the voice of the creature, which is the essence of idolatry (Rom. 1:25). Thus, Eve followed the wisdom from *below* rather than the wisdom from *above* (cf. James 3:13–17).

In Rev. 12:9 and 20:2, Satan is clearly defined as "the serpent of old"—undoubtedly, it seems, an allusion to the serpent in the Garden. But this becomes problematic when we remember that "the serpent" in Gen. 3 was an earthly creature and Satan is a spiritual being. Taken at face value, we are forced to say that Satan once *was* a literal serpent, that he *was* created as such among all the other beasts of the field, and that *he*—not merely "the serpent"—was forced to crawl on his belly in the dust. Then, we assume (with nothing to go on but this unexplained reference in Rev. 12:9 and 20:2), *somehow* the serpent remained a serpent while Satan morphed into a wicked spiritual being. This is not a consistent or satisfying explanation.

The Biblical Role of Satan

You do not have to believe all that I have just proposed. The important point so far is this: in nearly every case—if not in *all* cases—people assume that Satan in the NT is automatically the "Satan" of the OT. This assumption also maintains that a single personage has been the primary agent of evil for all of human history. Yet, there is nothing in the OT that identifies Satan as the "prince of darkness," the source of all evil, or the tempter of all men. Israel was confronted by numerous "adversaries" (both spiritual and human)—including God Himself—but nothing leads us to believe that the NT personage of Satan always *was* that adversary.

In Gen. 4:7, God told Cain that *sin* was crouching at his door, not Satan. Paul later says essentially the same thing: it is *sin* that seeks to master us, not Satan (Rom. 6:16, 20). It is true that Satan ensnares people and thus they are "held captive" by him "to do his will" (2 Tim. 2:26), but it is *sin* that is Satan's power, not Satan himself. Remember that Satan himself was once seduced by the darkness and thus rebelled against his Creator. Satan may be regarded as the accuser of men—and oppressive guilt and fear of judgment are two of his favorite instruments of torture—but this is not the same as saying he is evil personified, the inventor of sin, or the creator of the darkness.

All this does not mean Satan did not yet exist in the OT, however, but that he was not yet personally identified and his role was not yet clarified. I am not suggesting that the Satan we know today in the NT was not involved in any way in the *satan* passages we have just discussed. Rather, I am suggesting that it does not have to be him, and we should not blindly assume that it is him. The OT Scripture speaks of evil spirits other than Satan (see 1 Kings 22:19–22 and Dan. 10:13, 21, for example). Furthermore, I am suggesting that even if it *was* Satan (the devil himself), he was *then* in a far different role than the one he played in the NT.

In Rev. 12:1–9—the scene is symbolic and visionary, but *true* nonetheless—we see Satan ("a great red dragon") preying upon the "woman" (Israelites who kept the promises of God alive through their faithfulness to Him) and her "Child" (Jesus). The tail of the dragon "swept away a third of the stars of heaven and threw them to the earth"—a likely reference to the great host of angels that joined Satan in his rebellion against God (compare Dan. 8:10 and Rev. 1:20).[81] We have assumed that this mass rebellion—and the fall of Satan himself—occurred before the creation of the world, but there is nothing in Scripture to prove this.[82]

Satan's rise to power—if not his subsequent fall from heaven—coincides with the advent of demonic activity and demon possession during the time of Christ. (Can you think of a single OT account of demon possession resembling anything like what Jesus faced?) Satan plummeted the world into the darkness just as Jesus manifested Himself as the Light of the world; "The Light shines in the darkness, and the darkness did not comprehend [or, overpower] it" (John 1:5). Christ, the "Light of the world" (John 8:12), was made even more brilliant against the blackened backdrop of demonic activity like what the world had never seen. Satan was "the strong man" in Mat. 12:28-29 (see Luke 11:20-22), but Christ is *stronger than Satan* in every respect. In other words, if God needed a formidable villain to confront His Son in His earthly ministry, then Satan—blinded by pride and drunk with power—unwittingly accepted the challenge.

What Satan Was Created to Be versus What He Became

The questions everyone wants answered, of course, are these: Who was Satan and what was his role prior to his fall? *How* did he fall? What exactly was his sin? And why did God allow him to sin? Much of this we do not know—actually, *cannot* know—because God did not tell us. Remember: all we know about the spiritual realm is what God has revealed to us. This has not stopped a lot of people from making stuff up, and over time many of these imaginative speculations have morphed into "church tradition," now masquerading as "gospel truth."

Theologically—that is, by studying the doctrines God has revealed to us in His word—we cannot reconcile any *agreement* between God and Satan.[83] In other words, it is impossible to reconcile the God of light, love, righteousness, and holiness intentionally creating a wicked creature to serve His need for a strong but inferior rival to His Son. In the Medieval Era, some saw Satan as God's so-called hatchet man, hangman, or executioner—i.e., God needed someone to carry out His dirty work, so He created Satan.[84] It seems that many people today still cling to this idea. Yet, any explanation which lays the responsibility for Satan at God's feet is blasphemous to the incorruptible, absolutely pure, and perfectly holy Being that He is. "The Son of God appeared for this purpose, to destroy the works of the devil" (1 John 3:8), not the works of God. If we make Satan a work of God, then this pits Christ *against* God. Jesus Himself said, "If Satan casts out Satan, he is divided against himself; how then will his kingdom stand?" (Mat. 12:26). This would be true about God as well, if indeed He was divided against Himself (!).

Thus, any theory, tradition, or religious doctrine that makes God morally responsible for what Satan has become or what he does is unbiblical and therefore *untrue*. "God cannot be tempted by evil, and He Himself does not tempt anyone [to sin against Him]" (James 1:13, bracketed words are mine). This has to mean: God did not create an evil being to tempt people to sin against Himself. And yet, there is nothing wrong with God *allowing* a created being to choose to *become* evil and then letting that being—by its own volition—fulfill what God needed to be done.[85] This is exactly what we see in the case of Judas: this disciple of Jesus, by his own volition, turned against his Master and thus "turned aside to go to his own place" (Acts 1:25). Judas' *role* was predicted in prophesy (Psalm 41:9, John 13:8, 17:12, Acts 1:20, etc.), but Judas *himself* made his own choice to fulfill that role. As I understand it, this parallels what happened with Satan.

God did not make Satan what he is now. Rather, He created a heavenly angel—likely of high rank and authority—to a position of great responsibility. In *his* beginning, this angel's name was not "Satan" ("adversary"), but was likely something incomprehensible to us (see Judges 13:17–18, for example). At some point, this beautiful and powerful angel chose to sin against God and thus lost his innocence, lost his favored position, and sealed his ultimate doom. Thus, Satan made himself what he is now: an enemy of God and an adversary to Christ and His church. Having been seduced *by* the darkness, his heart was filled *with* the darkness, and now operates in the realm *of* the darkness. Satan, by his own volition, became the awful monster that we now know him to be. Such is the intoxicating, overwhelming, and malicious power of sin, that it can take even one of the strongest angels of heaven captive to its will.

This ought to frighten us to the core. If *we* choose evil, if *we* choose to oppose God, and if *we* embrace the darkness rather than the Light, what will become of *us*? The answer is clear: we will also become unholy, wicked, and hell-bound monsters. Just because we do not yet see ourselves this way does not improve our situation. Just because we have not yet experienced our spiritual ruin does not mean it is not real and will not happen. If we choose the same course of action that Satan chose long ago, then we shall join him in his awful punishment (Mat. 25:41). God will not destroy those who are made righteous and innocent, but He most certainly will destroy those whose hearts are filled with the darkness.

But *why* did Satan choose to exalt himself against God? The answer to this has not been revealed to us. The closest we are given may be in 1 Tim. 3:6, where Paul says that "the condemnation of the devil" is directly linked to pride that a new convert might experience if he allowed his position in the church go to his head.[86] The traditional view (which may be the best that we have) claims that Satan was either jealous of God's glory *or* envious that God made human beings in His image rather than doing this for His own angels.[87]

We do know this: Satan *had to have fallen* from what God had created him to be. All who sin—including angels themselves—*fall* from the perfect, innocent, and virtuous beings that God had created them to be (Rom. 3:23; see 2 Peter 2:4 and Jude 1:6). Sin marks not only the reason *for* this fall, but also the historical occasion *of* it. When Satan sinned against God, he fell into condemnation.[88] As a result, he was ultimately banished altogether from God's presence—but not from the world.

Separating Fact from Fiction Concerning Satan

Satan is a real, identifiable, and (like all spiritual beings) masculine personage—always identified with "he," "him," or "his," never as an "it." He is not: fictitious; a figment of our collective imagination; or the product of ancient myth (who evaporates in the face of science and reason). Jesus never used air quotes with reference to Satan; He always spoke of him as an actual entity. He never said, in so many words, "*I know he's not real, but you people think he is, so I'll just play along with your small-minded beliefs.*"

Likewise, the gospel writers never treated Satan as a fictitious character, but as one that is real and definable. They spoke of him in real terms and as having real action and real effect on people. The apostle Paul (especially) referred a number of times to Satan, but never in a "wink, wink" manner, and always in a factual context. Peter spoke of Satan as "your adversary, the devil" (1 Peter 5:8), and he is not warning us against a mythical boogeyman.

Modern science, modern psychology, and even contemporary religion have reduced Satan to a virtual fairy-tale status. The idea that Satan exists is regarded as outrageous, outdated, and unconventional. The modern person is (allegedly) too enlightened, too sophisticated, and too pragmatic to accept this notion. But many modern people also deny the existence of God, divinity of Jesus, heavenly authority of Scripture, and reality of sin. They offer no proof about what they claim; it simply does not fit their secular paradigm. Particularly, it does not agree with what they have been indoctrinated to believe otherwise. The modern narrative is overflowing with assumptions, opinions, and contradictions that render it *unfit* for intelligent consideration.[89] Satan is a spirit, and the only factual information we have about the spirit world is from the Bible, not from those who have never seen the spirit world and have no personal knowledge of it.

While Satan is a spiritual being, he is only a *created* being and not a divine personage. He has power and authority—even as a fallen angel—but not *divine* power and authority. Only the divine Persons of the Godhead—God the Father, God the Son, and God the Holy Spirit—can exercise divine ability. This means that Satan can only do what God *allows* him to do, and no more. While God gives him latitude to act within a certain boundary, He also constrains his power and can interrupt that power whenever He chooses.

Whether "the satan" in Job's account is the same Satan that Jesus encountered in His wilderness trials (Mat. 4:1–11) cannot be known for certain. However, in both accounts, we see a created being asking God permission to do certain things, not a being that equals or surpasses His own authority. God says, in essence, "I will allow you to do *this much*, but no more," and the adversary (whoever it is) cannot argue this or go beyond it. Likewise, Jesus said to Simon Peter, "Simon, Simon, behold Satan has demanded permission to sift you like wheat" (Luke 22:31). This speaks of Satan's subordination to Jesus: he could not do anything more or different than what Jesus allowed him to do. This did not make Jesus responsible for Satan's evil, any more than He is responsible for *your* evil. But it does reveal that evil itself—the power of the darkness—cannot overstep its God-given boundary.

In Rev. 20:1–3, John is shown a vision of Satan being subdued, bound with a great chain, and incarcerated in "the abyss" for "a thousand years." All the elements here are symbolic, but do point to real truths. Otherwise, the interpretation becomes highly subjective (i.e., each person decides when the elements are literal or figurative), and even ridiculous. The angel, "Satan," the binding, the chain, and the pit all give us a *picture* of what is happening, not the literal *details* of it. In other words, the angel is not necessarily *one* angel, but indicates the exercise of God's spiritual power and authority. "Satan" is not only Satan himself, but also all the demons that have joined his rebellion—his kingdom. The "chain" simply illustrates the constraint or limitation of Satan's power.[90] And the "abyss" illustrates a place—not a literal hole in the ground, but a confined state of being—from which Satan and his demons cannot escape. However, they *will* be freed at some point in the future (Rev. 20:7).

All this to say: Satan is spiritual, he is powerful, and he has a domain in which he operates. But while God does not directly control what goes on in that domain, He certainly limits the *effect* and *extent* of it. Satan can and does sin against God—God is not controlling *that*—but he cannot exceed the limitations imposed upon him. He defies God with insolent railings and accusations, but he cannot rival, threaten, or overthrow Him. So it is with us: God has given us the ability—not the permission, but the *freedom*—to sin against Him, but we cannot remove ourselves from His authority. We, like Satan, will stand before Him in judgment, and we will give an account for our actions. We will answer to *Him*, but He does not have to answer (as in, be judged by) *us*.

Because Satan is a created being and not a divine personage, he cannot do what only the Personages of the Godhead (the Father, Son, and Holy Spirit) can do. For example, Satan cannot create something out of nothing—only God has this ability. Satan can tweak, corrupt, and malign what God has made (if God allows it), but he cannot bring a thing into existence that did not previously exist. Only God can "make all things new" (Rev. 21:5); Satan cannot make anything new.[91] The book of Revelation, if nothing else, unmasks Satan as the great imposter and deceiver that he is. For everything God revealed to us—His Son, His church (the "bride"), His sealing of those who follow Him, and His heavenly truth—Satan reveals a grotesque distortion of these same things—his "beast," his "harlot," his "mark of the beast," and his river of lies and deceptions.

Jesus Christ has supreme power over Satan and his demons, but these have no power over Him. In the gospel accounts, Jesus cast out demons (Luke 4:36), predicted His binding of the "strong man" (Luke 11:17–22), and told Satan to "be gone"—and he had no choice but to leave (Mat. 4:10–11). But we never see Satan or his demons casting *the Holy Spirit* out of anyone, binding Jesus against His will, or telling Jesus to "be gone." This is because Satan, a fallen angel, is no match for Jesus, the Son of God. Jesus' authority is infinitely greater than whatever Satan possesses. Likewise, Satan cannot force you away from God, but you—if you *submit* to God—can "resist the devil and he will flee from you" (James 4:7).

Nowhere in Scripture does it say that Satan can read a person's mind, know his thoughts, or communicate to him in a dream or vision.[92] These are things that only a divine Personage can do, and Satan is not divine—he is not deity. No one can know a person's thoughts except that person himself and God (1 Cor. 2:11). Thus, Jesus *did* know the hearts of men (John 2:24–25), and the Holy Spirit *does* know the thoughts and intentions of every person (Heb. 4:12–13). The only way Satan can know what is in your heart is when you *show* him this by your actions. Yet, while Satan cannot know what is *in* your heart, he certainly can *speak* to your heart by enticing you with what he knows will cause you to stumble. We will return to this thought later.

God alone can condemn the unredeemed human soul to its final destination—the outer darkness of the spiritual world. Satan, despite popular belief, cannot do this. In fact, he himself stands under condemnation by God and in due time God will give him his well-deserved punishment. This means that Satan cannot take possession of your soul and then make God redeem it from Satan with His Son's blood. To maintain otherwise is *blasphemy*. God does not negotiate with Satan; He does not make ransom payments of any kind to this monster.[93] Christ's blood is not provided for Satan, but for *God*: it is

God's condemnation that must be satisfied, not Satan's (Col. 1:19–22). The best that Satan can do (as he sees it) is to convince you that he *does* have God-like power over your soul so that you will feel helpless and remain captive in his deception. Sadly, he is very good at what he does.

Jesus speaks to Satan's true personality and character in John 8:44: "[The devil] was a murderer from the beginning, and does not stand in the truth because there is no truth in him. Whenever he speaks a lie, he speaks from his own nature, for he is a liar and the father of lies." Jesus is not speaking of a metaphorical "Satan" here, but a real and identifiable one. Furthermore, He is not *likening* him to a liar and murderer, but states he *is* a liar and a murderer. Satan is not confused, the victim of circumstances, or simply misunderstood; his heart is filled with pure evil. This is not Jesus' "take" on Satan, but is the absolute truth *about* him.

When Satan speaks, he is not to be trusted. Even if he made true *statements* (like demons sometimes did; see Mark 1:24–25), they are made with a false or ulterior motive. Even if he quotes Scripture (like he did to Jesus; see Mat. 4:6), it is with the intent to misapply, misinform, and misdirect. He is a liar, which means that all human lies are merely an imitation of Satan's own lying character. *This* means that all forms of human lying—cheating, deception, misdirection, evasion, falsifying evidence, etc.—are satanic and demonic.

God cannot be destroyed: one of the fundamental attributes of His holiness is His indestructibility.[94] Satan, however, is a created being and not a divine being: he *can* be destroyed, and God promises *to* destroy him. However, God also promises to destroy every human soul that follows him. This means there is no profit, advantage, or positive outcome for anyone who listens to, serves, or imitates Satan's wicked character.

Summary Thoughts

While Satan has been dismissed as an ancient tradition, a mythological boogeyman, or a reflection of our own fear and guilt, the Bible regards him as a very real and capable entity. He is not only the Christians' adversary (which is what his name means), but he is also the adversary of God, Christ, and every human soul that is in need of divine redemption. While there are many things about Satan that remain mysterious to us, what we *do* know is sufficient—and unnerving. We are not dealing with a neighborhood bully here; we are dealing with a predatory monster of impressive strength, ability, and knowledge.

Because he is a spiritual being (and has an army of other spiritual beings to carry out his bidding), Satan has an incredible advantage over mere people who are limited in understanding of the spiritual world and limited to the confines of our material, three-dimensional existence. Thus, Satan can freely move about in our world, because he understands it (and our human nature) better than we do. And, when we make ourselves slaves of sin, we give ourselves over to Satan's world—and the power of the darkness. Satan knows what he has gotten himself into; we, however, are often naïve and even oblivious to our sinful predicament.

Powerful as he is, Satan is not *all*-powerful. He cannot hold a candle to Christ's power and authority. He cannot harm us beyond what God allows him to do for His own purposes. He may kill the body, but he cannot destroy the soul—God alone is capable of this. Yet, while Satan is not all-powerful, we should not underestimate him and his cunning. Just because we know *about* Satan does not mean that we are masters over him. While we should "not [be] ignorant of his schemes" (2 Cor. 2:11), this does not mean that we *know* all of his schemes—or that we will not succumb to them from time to time.

Our brief glimpse of Satan and his world is not for the purpose of mere curiosity and intrigue. Instead, we are seeking a better understanding of what and who we are up against. We are repeatedly warned in Scripture concerning this very thing. If the possibility remains for any of us to share in Satan's own awful demise, then we should do everything possible to avoid this. Learning about who Satan is, how he operates, and how he deceives us is part of this. Learning about Christ, and what He offers, and how His power is *infinitely superior* to Satan's is another way. "And this we will do, if God permits" (Heb. 6:3).

Chapter Nine: Satan Wants to Destroy You

Every one of us, at some time or another, turned away from the Light and turned toward the darkness instead. While we were thinking that we sought something *in* the darkness—and once we obtained it, then we would be satisfied—we became ensnared *by* the darkness instead. Once we became ensnared, we could not extract ourselves. Like a man sinking in quicksand, it was only a matter of time before we would succumb to a horrifying, painful, and unending death.

Satan operates in the world of darkness. When we invited the darkness into our hearts, we invited Satan in as well. We turned to Satan as a friend rather than a foe, and in the process, we made ourselves enemies of God rather than enjoy His fellowship (Rom. 8:6–8, James 4:4). We accepted Satan's lies instead of honoring God's truth. We made Satan the lord of our heart instead of Christ (1 Peter 3:15). Against all better judgment and everything that is good and holy, we gave control of our lives over to a lying, wicked, perverted, and malicious entity that seeks nothing less than to destroy every person who does this.

This is a sad and bleak picture. Even so, it is *our* picture—not just mine or yours, but *ours collectively*, as an entire race of adult human beings. We were once innocent children, but then we fell—and the hardest part to accept (and even understand) is that we *chose* to fall. If someone chooses to jump off a cliff to kill himself, we call that suicide—in essence, a self-murder. But if someone chooses to sin against God and ally himself instead with Satan, we call that a "lapse of judgment," a "minor indiscretion," or simply "a mistake." Some people do not even acknowledge it. The reality is that this is just another form of jumping off a cliff—only the consequences in this case are far worse than literal suicide. One's leap into the darkness is nothing less than making a pact with death and thus committing *spiritual* suicide. Satan nods with approval whenever someone does this. That person has made the devil his (or her) master; he has given the darkness controlling interest over his soul.

We need to understand—to the degree that we can and is necessary to understand—what Satan is up to. He does not want to help us. He has zero sympathy, mercy, or compassion for us. He does not care how much you lose, hurt, suffer, or cry with regret—he just wants to *destroy* you. And destroy you he will, unless you listen to and obey the One who is infinitely more powerful than both you *and* Satan: Jesus Christ.

Toying with Disaster

"The devil made me do it." Many of us have thought this or said this. We might have said this humorously, making light of the fact that we sided with Satan as we sinned against God. Yet, there is nothing funny about sin, or Satan, or defying God's holiness. Many seem to believe, however, that the devil really can make you do something against your will. Many probably want to believe that, if the *devil* made them "do it," then they did not "do it" themselves and are therefore not responsible for what happened.

All this gives Satan (the devil) far more credit than he deserves. It is true that you can let Satan into your heart and give him control, but that is something *you* did, not him. In other words, *you* invite him in, *you* give him permissions, *you* allow him access to your world, and *you* resist all godly influence in the process. That is hardly Satan making you "do" anything. What Satan does from that point forward is the result of you allowing him to enter your heart and wreak havoc on your soul. To blame him for taking over is like giving a known reckless driver the keys to your very expensive car, inviting him to drive it however he wants to, and then *blaming* him for driving recklessly and destroying it. That just does not make sense; it is irrational; sin is *always* irrational. If justification for sin does not work now, it most certainly will not work in the future Judgment.

Many people may cite NT examples of demon possession at this point. Such possession may seem to indicate that people were just minding their own business when suddenly a demon—or many of them—invaded their minds, causing them to sin against God, go into violent fits, etc. Yet, the NT description of demon possession is not necessarily what Hollywood has described in its theatrical, sensational, and typically misrepresentative way. Of course, Hollywood is not interested in honoring the biblical text; it is interested in making movies and money. Demons in the NT took control of people's *bodies* (as in Mark 9:17-22), but there is no indication that they took uninvited control of people's *minds*. In cases where they *did* control a person's mind (as in Mark 5:1-15), there is no reason to assume that this control could not have been resisted if that person had sought God's help in the matter. It is more than conspicuous that we see no faithful Jews *or* faithful Christians having any personal trouble with demon possession.

So it is today. We do not see men and women who are genuinely faithful—as *God* defines "faithful"—being overtaken by demonic activity. Satan "flees" from those who submit to God (James 4:7); he does not possess them and inhabit their bodies. Demons—like Satan himself—do not have the power to do whatever they want, possess whomever they want, or exercise god-like authority. Christians do not have to lay awake at night wondering if demons are going to overtake them. Those who "draw near to God" (James 4:8) will have *God* draw near to them, not Satan.

But this does not mean that evil entities no longer exist or cannot afflict people. We see no evidence of demonic possession today on the scale that Jesus encountered in His ministry. Even so, those today who wish to dabble in demonology, occultism, witchcraft, so-called paranormal activity, or outright satanism should not be surprised by the power and wicked influence that demons can still exert over them. Demons are still masters of deceit, fraud, and manipulation. They take full advantage of human weaknesses, gullibility, and ignorance. They let people who invoke their power think that they have the demons on a leash, but it is quite the opposite. Those who do not belong to God obviously belong to someone or something else. Whomever we choose to serve becomes our master (Rom. 6:16)—and Jesus Himself said that we cannot serve two masters at once or equally (Mat. 6:24).

Satan does not have merely a passive interest in your downfall. Demons are not mild and timid creatures that attack only when provoked. Satan and his demons—the wicked army of the darkness—are not only aggressively opposed to your salvation, but they can be very effective at *destroying* it if you do not "[fix] your hope on the living God" (1 Tim. 4:10). Satan is a fool to think that he could take on God's Son and overcome Him, but he is still extremely intelligent, cunning, and tenacious in going after those made in God's image.

"Be of sober spirit, be on the alert," Peter strongly warns us. "Your adversary, the devil, prowls around like a roaring lion, seeking someone to devour" (1 Peter 5:8). "Devour" here comes from a Greek word which means "drowned," "overwhelmed," "entirely swallowed," or fully destroyed.[95] It takes a formidable and intelligent enemy to do that to so many people, and Satan is such an enemy.

How Satan Destroys People

Satan dwells in the spiritual realm, whereas we are only *aware* of that realm. We cannot peer into it literally, which puts us at a great disadvantage to know how Satan—or any spiritual being—operates *in* that world.[96] Thus, none of us can say with firsthand knowledge, "This is *exactly* what Satan is doing to overcome people!" Yet, the NT does provide sufficient insight into his activity, giving us a fairly good idea of what he does. We should begin by recognizing that "Satan" and "devil" are used collectively some 70 times in the NT, which means he is not an insignificant or random subject. Indeed, there is far more than meets the eye upon first glance.

Satan *personally* is introduced in the Bible as the "tempter" (Mat. 4:1–11). His first order of business was to tempt Jesus to use His divine power for His own purposes rather than to carry out the will of His Father. If Satan will be so bold and daring as to tempt the Son of God to His face, we can be certain that he will be no less bold to come after us as well. Satan did not tempt Jesus with what He could *not* do; he tempted Him with something that He *could* have done if He so chose. Likewise, Satan does not tempt you and me with what we *cannot* do, but always with what is within our power *to* do. You and I are unable to turn stones into bread, but Jesus did have that ability—and Satan knew it and preyed upon it.

Yet, Jesus never once succumbed to Satan's invitations to use His power for self-exaltation, and finally told Satan to leave Him alone. "When the devil had finished every temptation, he left Him until an opportune time" (Luke 4:13)—in other words, Satan did not give up quickly or easily. He was relentless with Jesus, tempting Him throughout His ministry in different ways, often through the suggestions of other people (e.g., Mat. 16:1, 21–23, John 6:15, 7:3–5, etc.). Likewise, just because Satan flees from us on one occasion does not mean he is done with us altogether. You can be sure that he is simply waiting for "an opportune time" to re-attack.

In His parable of the sower (Mark 4:1–9), Jesus said that some of the "seed" (word of God) is cast upon "the road" (the places where people travel), and yet "Satan comes and takes away the word which has been sown in them" (Mark 4:15). Jesus did not explain to us *how* Satan "takes away" the word of God, but he cannot do it by force. He cannot *make* someone disbelieve in God—the Bible provides no evidence for this—but he *can* surround people with doubters, skeptics, godless friends and family members, "bad company" (1 Cor. 15:33), and other negative influences that can persuade or convince people to disbelieve in God. All we have to do is read the book of Acts and see how often Paul and others confronted disbelief and blasphemy against God even among those who claimed to be His people. Today, it is increasingly popular to be filled with disbelief in God, contempt for the Bible, and hatred toward Christians. This mindset is where most of the world travels, so to speak; it is "the road" (or wide path) in which most people choose to remain. The world listens to its own (1 John 4:5) and, with modern technology, creates a giant echo chamber in which to propagate and reinforce its own satanic agenda.

In the parable of the weeds and tares (Mat. 13:24–30), Jesus identified the "enemy" of God as "the devil" (Mat. 13:39). The devil sows weeds among the wheat, infiltrating and compromising the crop. In other words, he sows false believers among the earthly church in an attempt to corrupt the brotherhood. He sows discord, jealously, strife, self-serving ambition, lies, deceptions, heresies, false teaching, and evil desires within Christians who are deliberately weak or those who pose as Christians but are impostors. Satan is evil, but not stupid. He knows what he is doing, and (sadly) is very good at doing it.

In some cases, the Bible record says that Satan "filled" the heart of one person or another (see John 13:27 and Acts 5:3, for example). We wonder, "how can Satan 'fill' a person's heart?"—but this is really not so difficult to understand. Satan does not enter your heart uninvited, but when you give him control over you, he will most certainly take advantage of this. Once he gets a foothold, he will worm his way further and further into your mind and your life until he has complete mastery over you. Satan is not the initial problem; rather, it is our own carnal lusts (James 1:13–16). If you fill your heart with evil thoughts, then evil actions are what come out of you (Mat. 15:17–20). If you fill your heart with Satan, then it is not surprising that you become his worker and disciple. In other words, when you lust after and fill your heart with the same things that Satan lusts after and fills his heart, then he "fills" your heart, fills your mind, fills your thoughts, and corrupts your conscience.[97]

Those who are "filled with the [Holy] Spirit" (Eph. 5:18) actively desire God and pursue fellowship with Him. Those who are filled with Satan actively desire what Satan desires and therefore—consciously or not—pursue fellowship with *him*. Christians ought to imagine every temptation to sin as a demonic entity whispering in our ear, "Feed me so that I can *destroy* you!" Instead, many see their temptation and wonder, "How close can I get to sin without actually *sinning*?" Such people are practically begging Satan to enter their house, so to speak, and have his way with them.

Satan is not merely in disagreement with the gospel of Christ; he actively interferes with its preaching and reception. Those who actively oppose Christ's gospel (especially by persuading others not to obey it) make themselves followers of Satan by serving his will. On the island of Cyprus, the apostle Paul rebuked a man named Elymas because he obstructed the preaching of the gospel. He said to him, "You who are full of all deceit and fraud, you son of the devil, you enemy of all righteousness, will you not cease to make crooked the straight ways of the Lord?" (Acts 13:10). This is an accurate depiction of what such men make themselves. Satan does not have to provide all the opposition himself; he recruits many people to join him, whether or not they are even consciously aware of this. On the contrary, those who are baptized into Christ are "sons of God by faith" through their active submission and obedience to God's will (Gal. 3:26–27).

We have already recognized that "Satan disguises himself as an angel of light" (2 Cor. 11:14). We should not ask, "Does Satan disguise himself?" because he most certainly does, but, "*Why* does Satan disguise himself?" The basic answer is: he wants to trick you, deceive you, and blindside you. He wants to conceal his true identity from you in order to get closer to you. He wants you to believe that he is harmless, friendly, and trustworthy so that you will not hesitate to welcome him into your inner circle, your home, and your heart. The NT says over and over, "Do not be deceived," yet it is never Christ who seeks to deceive us, nor faithful believers, but Satan and those who identify with him.

If the one we know as "Satan" was once an angel of light, he is now an angel of the darkness—an angel that is drunk with the power of the darkness, raging with contempt for God, and filled with jealousy toward men. He is an enemy of Christ, and therefore is an enemy of all who identify with Him. The best way to for an enemy to infiltrate the camp, so to speak, is to look, dress, talk, and act like someone to be trusted. For example, a strong and healthy tree can withstand all kinds of external forces of nature, but internal rot makes it weak and vulnerable. So it is with people (and churches): it is seldom the external forces that compromise us, but the internal rot. If Satan can implant that rot—if we *allow* him to do so—then he most certainly will. Those who cause this moral rot—like Satan himself—come disguised in "sheep's clothing" but are in fact "ravenous wolves" (Mat. 7:15). Jesus said so Himself.

Paul says that many people are caught in "the snare of the devil, having been held captive by him to do his will" (2 Tim. 2:26). We wonder, "How does Satan 'ensnare' people?" He does so through false teaching, to mislead us and fill our heads with lies, errors, and half-truths. He ensnares through false hope, letting people think that they are "saved" through means different than what the NT actually teaches, or that everything is going to be "all right" even though they have not obeyed God's commandments. He ensnares people through their own guilt, making them believe that they are unforgiveable and unworthy of God's love, and so "what's the use in trying?" He ensnares people by distracting them with entertainment, idolatry (in all of its forms), wealth, materialism, greed, and sensual pleasures.

All of these tactics worked in Paul's day, and they still work today because human nature has not changed. In fact, most of the world is ensnared and held captive by Satan's lies and deceptions; "The whole world lies in the power of the evil one" (1 John 5:19). The gospel teaches that "the one who practices sin is of the devil; for the devil has sinned from the beginning. The Son of God appeared for this purpose, to destroy the works of the devil" (1 John 3:8). Satan's strategy is to convince Christians that we can "practice sin" and not get hurt—that we can somehow create a holy union of wickedness and righteousness. Yet, Jesus did not "appear" in our world to perpetuate satanic behavior, but to put an end to it. By following Christ, we "destroy the works of the devil." In the end, Christ will destroy the devil himself. But He will also destroy all those who allowed themselves to be ensnared by him.

Satan does not have to come after us with a huge army of demons; he only needs to find the weakest point of entry into our heart. Sadly, we often provide this for him. We "give the devil an opportunity" (Eph. 4:27) when we purposely let our guard down, fail to suit up with the "full armor of God" (Eph. 6:13–17), allow ourselves to be deceived, etc. Thus, what we may regard as personal weaknesses or points of vulnerability are often self-inflicted or self-created. We choose to be weak by refusing to do what it takes to be strong. Someone has said, "What you allow will continue." This is so true: when we *allow* ourselves to be weak, then (not surprisingly) we *continue* to be weak. Satan knows this—and he preys upon our weaknesses.

Satan is no different than people in that he chooses to take the path of least resistance. Instead of trying to pierce your hardened, tested armor, he will go after the soft flesh (so to speak) of whatever you have left exposed for him. He is very crafty, devious, and malicious in what he does. If you only put on a "helmet of salvation," he will throw a spear at your chest. If all you wear is a "breastplate of righteousness," he will take a swing at your head. And even when you have your helmet and breastplate on, he will make a sweeping kick at your legs. In other words, when you think you are smart, clever, perceptive, and resourceful, Satan is far more so. He will outsmart and outmaneuver you. He is stronger and smarter than you. This is why you should *never* be without God's protection.

Paul wrote, "Put on the *full* armor of God, so that you will be able to stand firm against the schemes of the devil" (Eph. 6:11, emphasis added). God never told you to wear only partial armor because you need *everything* He provides. The "full armor" is not some custom-designed armor that you come up with; it is *God's* armor for you. He gives it to you to wear, but it is your responsibility to put it on.

Satan's plan, in part, is to convince you that you do not need this armor—after all, you are wise, strong, and capable on your own. You (in my continued editorial usage of "you") trust in calling yourself a "Christian," years of churchgoing, and active participation in church work. You say prayers, sing hymns, and partake of communion. You think that these things keep you safe from attack.

Satan is not deterred by any of these things. He knows that many of us are filled with pride, overconfidence, and a false sense of security—he banks on this. Satan hurls "flaming arrows" at us (Eph. 6:16), and we think that we can protect ourselves with church attendance, charitable deeds, and memorized Bible verses. Paul urges us to "take up the full armor of God, so that you will be able to resist in the evil day, and having done everything, to stand firm" (Eph. 6:13), but many of us believe that we can "stand firm" on our own, and that the "full armor" is merely a religious metaphor. Satan knows that as long as we remain unprepared, vulnerable, and ineffective, he will overcome us in due time. He knows that *all* who do not suit up with the "full armor of God" will indeed fall—it is just a matter of time.

The Ultimate Stalker

Someone says, "I don't believe Satan can really hurt me." But you do not *have* to believe this in order for it to be true. Things are not right, real, or true only when you believe them. Truth exists—even the truth about Satan and his schemes—regardless of your or my beliefs. Ironically, the more you disbelieve him, the more ignorant you remain of his "schemes," then the more susceptible you remain to the power of sin and darkness, and the more vulnerable you make yourself to wicked influences. In fact, it works to Satan's advantage when you dismiss him as an empty threat, a mythological boogeyman, or a mere cultural scare tactic designed to keep people from doing bad things. People think they are *too smart* to believe in Satan, when in fact they are among those who are constantly doing his bidding: "Professing to be wise" apart from God, people become "fools" who are puppets of the darkness (Rom. 1:22).

One reason why Satan can be so successful at overwhelming you is because he knows you far better than you know him. Left to yourself, he will always have the upper hand, the psychological edge, and the element of surprise. You and I know very little specific detail about the world of darkness, the activity of demons, Satan's true methods, and the invisible spiritual realm in general. But this is Satan's playground, he knows it well, and he takes full advantage of our ignorance of it. Satan has a kingdom (Mat. 12:26), and thus he is organized, methodical, and has many wicked spirits to do his bidding. He is not coming at us in an awkward or clumsy manner, swinging blindly and stumbling badly, but he attacks us like a skillful boxer and a resourceful antagonist.

Satan is a meticulous observer of human nature. He has both intuitive and experienced knowledge of all people because he has been watching them for thousands of years. He cannot know precisely what you are thinking, but (given your human nature) he certainly knows *how* you think, your typical *pattern* of thought, and how to attack you effectively and efficiently based upon this knowledge. He has been watching you personally since you were old enough to sin against God. Thus, he knows:

- What you like, what catches your eye, and how you react to different situations.
- What distracts you, captures your attention, and draws you away from God.
- What causes you to doubt God, and what you are afraid of (in every respect).
- What you read, what you watch on TV, where you surf on the Internet, and what you do for entertainment.
- Who you keep company with (and what kind of people they are), and whether or not such people will be instrumental in leading you astray or filling your head with false ideas.
- Everything you say—he listens to all of your conversations, no matter how private or secretive they are.
- How you rationalize wrongful behavior, justify your "indiscretions," and spin your stories.
- Your strengths as well as your weaknesses.
- What interests you because of how you spend your time, how you spend your money, and what you give your effort toward.

- What excites you and—because of this—how you most likely will be tempted.

He knows you so well because you have been showing him everything about yourself all along. Someone once described "character" as who you are when no one is looking.[98] But God is always looking—and so is Satan. Armed with all of this private, personal, and inside information about you, Satan knows how best to attack you. He knows what will violate your conscience and compromise your integrity. He knows what will undermine your marriage and divide your family. He knows that if your marriage is weak and dysfunctional, it will be just a matter of time before your children are negatively affected by this. He knows that if your faith is weak, undernourished, and compromised by wicked thoughts and sinful behavior, it is just a matter of time before you will forsake God and lose your soul. He knows that if you lack commitment, you will be an undisciplined and ineffective servant of the church. He knows that if you claim to "know" God but will not keep His commandments, you will be a *liar* just like he is (1 John 2:3–6). He *knows* all these things not because he is a divine being, but because he is an excellent observer of all that you and all humankind have been showing him for millennia.

Things Satan Does Not Want You to Know

But there are some other things Satan knows—things he does not want *you* to know (because knowledge is power, and he wants to keep you ignorant and weak). For example: he knows Jesus Christ is infinitely more powerful than he is, but he depends upon you *not* knowing this or not *believing* it. He knows that the gospel of Christ is "the power of God for salvation to everyone who believes" (Rom. 1:16), but he banks on most people *not* believing, or remaining distracted, indifferent, or apathetic. He knows if you draw near to God, he cannot hurt you (James 4:7), but he relies on the fact that most *Christians* will "draw near" to lesser and unimportant things instead. He knows Christians will "overwhelmingly conquer" him, his demons, and the power of sin by putting their full confidence in God's ability to perform, putting on the "full armor of God," and seeking atonement through the blood of Christ. He knows all this, but he does not want *you* to know it—or, at least, he does not want you to *believe* it. He would rather keep you in the dark—better yet, as he sees it, he would rather keep you in *the darkness*.

So often I have heard, in so many words, "I just can't *help* but to sin against God!"—as if sinning was a bodily illness, genetic trait, or birth defect. This is a lie. You *can* resist temptation and you do *not* have to sin—but you will not do this on your own power. Paul said: "No temptation has overtaken you but such as is common to man; and God is faithful, who will not allow you to be tempted beyond what you are able, but with the temptation will provide the way of escape also, so that you will be able to endure it" (1 Cor. 10:13). You either believe this or you do not. This is *right*, *true*, and *real* regardless of your belief. If sin can be resisted and there always is a "way of escape" from it, then sin is a choice, not an irresistible compulsion.[99]

Temptation to sin is not a sin in itself. If it was, then Jesus sinned every time Satan tempted Him—and if He *did* sin (even once!), He could not be our Lord or Savior. Rather, temptation should be regarded as *decision time*—the fork in the road, so to speak, that requires a person to choose one direction over the other. In being tempted, you are being asked, in essence, to give power and controlling interest to sin or to God. Sin is always "crouching at the door" (Gen. 4:7), waiting to exercise dominion over your heart, but God is waiting for you to prove your faithfulness to Him instead. One who rejects God's offer to help him ends up fighting Satan on his own. Whoever enters into a dance with the devil should know that the devil is always leading, is in full control, and knows exactly where this dance is heading.

Summary Thoughts

Repeatedly, the NT warns, "Do not be deceived, do not be deceived, do not be deceived." God will never deceive us; in fact, He is incapable of doing so. The one who seeks to deceive us above all others is Satan. He is not a harmless caricature of evil; he is not an out-of-touch, bumbling, ineffective foe; he is not stupid, inattentive, or lazy. Rather, he is a daunting, formidable, and *relentless* enemy. He wants you destroyed—and, quite frankly, he *will* destroy you unless or until you seek the right kind of help in resisting his assault.

We have spent a good deal of time talking about Satan. This is *not* to give him any praise, undue attention, or even the slightest hint of admiration. Rather, we have done this so we can know our enemy and how he operates. The NT offers quite a bit of information on Satan—not as much as we may want to know, but all we *need* to know. Jesus warns us against knowing "the deep things of Satan" (Rev. 2:24)—i.e., dwelling upon him in order to tap into his power and use it (we think) to our advantage. But the Holy Spirit saw fit to provide certain information about Satan so we can avoid being taken advantage by him and not be "ignorant of his schemes" (2 Cor. 2:11).

Satan is the tempter, the enemy of God, the enemy of God's Son, and the sower of wickedness among God's people. He disguises himself as an angel of light, but he is in fact an angel of the darkness. He cannot "possess" us if we are walking in the Light, but when we give him unlimited access to our minds, our hearts, and our lives, he most certainly will take full advantage of this. It appears that he ensnares people and holds them captive, but the fact is that we far too easily make ourselves his prisoners. He weighs us down with troubles, fears, paralyzing guilt, and petty distractions, but we should not be ignorant of what is really going on. Satan's "schemes" are many—and, sadly, they are often very effective—but, if we are grounded in the truth and cling to our Savior, we can be wise to all of them.

Satan cannot know your exact thoughts, but he has been watching your pattern of behavior for all of your life. He not only knows everything about you, but he knows how to use that knowledge against you, to cripple and ultimately ruin you if he can. On the other hand, there are a number of things he does not want you to know about *him*. Just as he can learn of and exploit your weaknesses (if you let him), so you can learn of and exploit *his* weaknesses—and there is nothing he can do to stop you.

Sin is a choice, not a disease. Sin is what *people* pursue, whereas diseases pursue *us*. Just as you can choose to be faithful to God, so you can choose to sin against Him; just as you can choose to put on the "full armor of God," so you can choose to succumb to wicked temptations; and just as you can choose to walk with the Savior on the narrow path that leads to life, so you can choose to join the huge throng of those deceived by Satan on the wide path that leads to destruction (Mat. 7:13–14).

This world is not your home, because you are not staying here forever. However, if you make yourself at home *in* this world, then you should remember that "the whole world lies in the power of the evil one" (1 John 5:19). On the other hand, you have opportunity to ally yourself with the One who has overcome this world (John 16:33) and is more powerful than death, Satan, and the darkness: Jesus Christ. It is to Him that we will now turn our attention.

Part Three: Christ Has Overcome the World
Chapter Ten: Christ, the Light of the World

The information in the previous section is admittedly unpopular and disturbing. We do not like to hear about Satan, the darkness, and the ruin of human souls. Some of those ruined human souls will be people we know on earth who, for whatever reason, are choosing to remain captivated by the darkness until they die. After this, they have no recourse: having chosen the darkness over the Light on earth, they will be cast into the "outer darkness" (Mat. 8:11–12) in the world to come.

Unnerving and unspeakably sad as that is to hear, it is necessary for all of us to take seriously the full implications of what is at stake. If you or I embrace the darkness in this life, then *we too* will be cast into that "outer darkness." If *we* allow Satan to deceive us in the here and now, then *we too* will join him in his eternal misery in the hereafter (Mat. 25:41, 46). While we grieve—deeply, painfully, and even inconsolably—over those who have been lost, we need to pay careful attention to our own souls so that we will not share their same awful end.

Thankfully, *no one still alive has to lose their soul*. God has given us a "way of escape" (1 Cor. 10:13) from our self-inflicted problem—our sinful decisions. We do not have to be swallowed up in darkness, but we can instead have fellowship with God and walk in His light. Regardless of what others do or have chosen, *we* can choose to be saved from God's wrath against us because of our sins.

What is *your* choice?

The One to Whom You Should Listen

Sin is not just *a* problem; it is *your* problem. This is true no matter who you are. No one shoved you into the darkness—you voluntarily chose to go there. The darkness did not snatch you into it—you could have resisted, but some part of you secretly craved what it offered. Satan did not cause your problem—*you* did. Satan may have tempted you to sin, but you are the one who actually did sin. Put another way: Satan may have put bullets in the gun chamber and handed you the gun, but you are the one who held it to your head and pulled the trigger. As was said earlier, sin is a form of spiritual suicide, inasmuch as no one else is responsible for your spiritual death other than you, the one who caused it.

Satan also knows what will save you from this spiritual death—and he is doing (and will continue to do) everything in his power to keep you from being saved. It does not matter if you are a Christian or a serial killer—Satan wants nothing more than to see you lose your soul because of the lies, deceptions, and "flaming arrows" that he repeatedly hurls against your soul (Eph. 6:16). His objective—until he himself is destroyed—is your and my destruction. He wants the darkness that fills his heart to fill our hearts.

Who is *able* and *willing* to save you from your own ruin? Well, it is not me, nor is it you. It is not your best friend or your favorite family member. It is not your minister, pastor, priest, pope, reverend, rabbi, imam, witch doctor, shaman, guru, Dalai Lama, or life coach. All these people may be *willing*, but they are not *able*. It is not your congregation, your elders, the board of directors of any denomination, a religious synod, a decree from some religious council, or any other group of men, however well-intentioned. People cannot save *you* from the same problem to which *they* have succumbed. It is not an angel, patron saint, the so-called Virgin Mary, or any other alleged spiritual intermediary.

There is only one person who is capable of saving you from your own spiritual ruin, and that is Jesus Christ. He loves you more than does anyone else on this earth—and He has already proven it. If you are seeking to be "saved" by anyone other than Christ, you have succumbed to the wicked spell with which Satan has bewitched you. But if you want the truth—the *gospel* truth—then here it is: there is only one Savior in all of time and history, and He wants to be *your* Savior if you will but listen to and obey Him.

The Huge Contrast between Christ and Satan

In sharp contrast to the inferior and pathetic position from which Satan speaks, Jesus Christ speaks from a position of superiority, victory, and glory. Satan is merely an angelic being; Christ is a divine Personage of the Godhead. Both dwell in the spiritual realm, but only Christ has full and sovereign authority *over* that realm. Satan cannot do anything that Christ does not allow him to do; Christ never asks Satan permission for anything.

Christ has created all that exists (John 1:3, 1 Cor. 8:4–6, Col. 1:5–17, and Heb. 1:1–3). Satan has not created anything, but only tweaks, distorts, and mimics whatever Christ has created. Satan is a pathetic illusionist, while Christ is the Absolute Truth and is the Prime Mover of all things (Eph. 4:20–21). Satan tells you only what you want to hear, so as to lead you astray with your own carnal lusts; Christ tells you what you need to hear, and thus provides illumination, guidance, truth, and love. Satan tempts you to sin in order to destroy you; Christ provides (in Himself) a perfect example of how to walk rightly with God because He wants you to succeed, grow, flourish, and live. Satan incites you to corrupt your heart (James 1:13–15); Christ warns against *having* a corrupted heart, and repeatedly calls you to get your heart *right* (Mat. 15:18–20, Luke 11:34–36, etc.).

Satan says, "Follow your heart!"—and when people do, their self-serving heart leads them into error and self-delusion. Christ says, "Follow Me!"—and all those who do so are led directly to the Father in eternal life (John 14:6). He offers wisdom and truth because He is the wisest of all and "cannot lie" (Titus 1:2). His words, teaching, and example are timeless, unchangeable, infallible, and universal (i.e., they apply to all people, regardless of who they are or their circumstances). Satan speaks from a position of repeated and utter failure; Christ speaks from the highest position in the universe (Mat. 28:18) and has never failed at *anything*. Satan is a thief that comes only "to steal and kill and destroy"; Jesus came to give us life, and to give it "abundantly" (John 10:10).

Satan is the enemy of Christ and His church, but Christ is the Shepherd and Savior of His church. Christ came to us "in the flesh," not to deceive us (as the serpent did Eve) but to identify with us, sympathize with our plight, and then save us through His own self-sacrifice.

> For the grace of God has appeared, bringing salvation to all men, instructing us to deny ungodliness and worldly desires and to live sensibly, righteously and godly in the present age, looking for the blessed hope and the appearing of the glory

of our great God and Savior, Christ Jesus, who gave Himself for us to redeem us from every lawless deed, and to purify for Himself a people for His own possession, zealous for good deeds. (Titus 2:11–14)

Despite the accusations of unbelievers, condemnation of critics, and scorn of atheists, Christ has done us no wrong. Throughout His earthly ministry, everything He did was meant to open our eyes to *the truth*, regardless of what it revealed to us. He pulled back the curtain, so to speak, in order for us to see God the Father, the spiritual realm, and the great conflict between good and evil that has been going on since the beginning. He does not coerce, manipulate, or mislead; instead, He simply lays out the truth, proves His authority to reveal this truth, and then leaves it to each person to decide how he will respond to it. He wants all people "to come to the knowledge of the truth" (1 Tim. 2:4), which means "the truth" does not accommodate *us*. Instead, we must leave *our* "truth" behind in order to come to *His*.

As powerful as the Father is—there is no one greater than Him—He could not save us from our sins apart from the mediatory work of His Son. Since God the Father is the source of all life, He cannot die. Since God the Spirit is the giver of all life, He also cannot die. God the Son, however, *could* die—and He most certainly *did* die in order to provide what the Father's perfect justice required in response to our sin. But He also showed His mastery *over* death in His bodily resurrection, proving once and for all that even God the Son cannot die—not permanently. And, through His death *and* resurrection, we are offered life (salvation) in His name. "For it was the Father's good pleasure for all the fullness to dwell in [His Son], and through Him to reconcile all things to Himself, having made peace through the blood of His cross" (Col. 1:19–20).

"It is a trustworthy statement, deserving full acceptance," the apostle Paul proudly proclaimed, "that Christ Jesus came into the world to save sinners" (1 Tim. 1:15). He did not come into the world to save churches, man-made religion, those who do not need saving (i.e., innocent children), or those who *cannot* be saved (i.e., fallen angels—Heb. 2:16). He came into the world to save you and me—people who have sinned against our own Creator and have thus incurred His condemnation. "For while we were still helpless, at the right time Christ died for the ungodly" (Rom. 5:6). We are helpless to save ourselves because the problem of our sin is humanly insurmountable: we lack the authority and ability to overcome it on our own.

There is no good reason to believe that Christ would have come into the world at all, much less die a horrible death, if we could save ourselves. Christ would not have "emptied Himself" of His heavenly glory (Phil. 2:5–8) to offer one of many "salvations" to choose from. Instead, there is only one salvation, one Savior, one route that leads to life, and one opportunity—this life—to choose all of this. While it is popular today to believe that Christ's gospel is merely an alternative "path" to heaven (among many others), this is unbiblical and offensive to God *and* His Son.

The Light of the World

"In the beginning," God called the world ("the heavens and the earth") out of darkness and into His marvelous light (Gen.1:1–5). When the world was still shrouded *in* darkness, it was "formless and void"—literally, a waste place and empty of His divine influence. But He did not create the world to remain this way (Isa. 45:18); He created it to be a haven for His greatest creation of all—human beings made "in His own image" (Gen. 1:27). So then, He bathed the world in *light* and filled it with an amazing diversity of *life*. Having created a perfect world, He created a beautiful sanctuary *in* that world—the Garden of Eden. He then "formed man of dust from the ground, and breathed into his nostrils the breath of life; and man became a living being" (Gen. 2:7). The Garden provided everything needed for life and godliness.

So far, so good. Sadly, it did not last for long. Having given Man (both male *and* female—Gen. 5:2) the freewill to obey Him or not, it was only a matter of time before His greatest creation would turn against its own Creator, which is exactly what happened.[100] Adam and Eve rejected the Light in order to listen to the seductive words of the darkness. As a result, they were both banished from the Garden and sent out into a world that would be filled with toil, sweat, and pain in order to survive.

This story is literally as old as time. Darkness and chaos are the result of turning away from the Light of God's fellowship. The ancient Israelites found this out the hard way when they indulged in idolatry and paganism for many years. God took away their blessings, creature comforts, and general welfare, leaving them with curses, devastation, and misery. Their land became "formless and void" (Jer. 4:21-26)—the exact same language as when the earth was still in darkness and chaos. Such disorder is the result of selfish ambition and demonic influences (James 3:16). This is not the world God created, but it becomes the world of those who purposely turn away from Him in sin and rebellion. The world of darkness promises everything, but offers nothing but death. This world did not come from God, and He does not want this for you—or anyone.

When Jesus came into the world—not merely "was born," but *came of His own pre-existent volition*—He entered a world shrouded with darkness. The Jews (God's people by covenant) had largely abandoned their covenant responsibilities to God and suffered dearly as a result. They groped through spiritual ignorance, suffered with numerous diseases and sicknesses, and many were afflicted by demons.

Jesus' entrance was foretold in Isa. 9:2: "The people who walk in darkness will see a great light; those who live in a dark land, the light will shine on them" (see Mat. 4:12–17). This is confirmed in John's account of the gospel of Christ: "There was the true Light which, coming into the world, enlightens every man. He was in the world, and the world was made through Him, and the world did not know Him" (John 1:9–10). Jesus came as the "Light of the world" (John 8:12) into a world filled with hopelessness and despair. Yet, He did not come merely to expose the darkness for what it was—the realm of Satan and demonic activity. He came also to show the great and superior power of the Light.

"This is the message we have heard from Him and announce to you, that God is Light, and in Him there is no darkness at all" (1 John 1:5). God is not merely "enlightening"; He is not merely filled with light; and "light" is not merely one of His divine attributes. More than all of this, *God is Light*—this is who He is, what He is, and therefore what He gives. When God said in the beginning, "Let there be light" (Gen. 1:3), He was not merely saying, "Let light appear in the place of darkness." In reality, He was saying, "Let this formless and void world be immersed in *My Presence*." This first "light" was not a physical light, since that would not be produced until He created the luminaries in the sky (i.e., the sun by day, and the moon and stars by night—Gen. 1:14–19). The first light the world experienced was God's Presence—His glorious, brilliant, and life-giving *Light*.

Millennia later, Jesus came into a world that had sunk deep into the ignorant, depraved, and demon-filled world of darkness. He did not merely "enlighten" us—although He does this, too—but *He Himself* was the Light, the Presence of God in the midst of His own people who had largely forsaken Him. "In Him was life, and the life was the Light of men. The Light shines in the darkness, and the darkness did not comprehend [or, overpower] it" (John 1:4–5). His light brought not only truth, wisdom, and hope; He brought *life* to those who were dying in their own sins. He said this Himself:

- "I am the Light of the world; he who follows Me will not walk in the darkness, but will have the Light of life" (John 8:12).
- "I am the resurrection and the life" (John 11:25).
- "I am the way, and the truth, and the life; no one comes to the Father but through Me" (John 14:6).

"The Light shines in the darkness, and the darkness did not comprehend it." Darkness is the *absence* of light; it has no objective reality of its own.[101] When the Light came into the world, the darkness could not maintain its power, since it was being *overpowered*—really, displaced or dispelled—by the Light. Wherever the Light went, the darkness was forced to yield to Him. Sickness, disease, deformities, disabilities, and even demonic possession could not continue their afflictions in the presence of the Light (Mat. 4:23-24, 8:16, 15:30, Luke 4:40, 7:21, etc.). At His command they disappeared, just as the darkness disappeared when God commanded, "'Let there be light'" (2 Cor. 4:6).

Restoration of the Natural Order

While the darkness produces chaos, disorder, and fear in the realm of humankind, Jesus came to restore the natural order of the world that God had created long ago. This is not to say that Jesus came to *eradicate* all earthly problems or *end* all human suffering. His miracles of healing and restoration were to demonstrate His power *over* these things, but He had a much greater objective in mind. His mission was not to return the world to the natural beauty and comfort of the Garden of Eden. Rather, it was to bring us into a *spiritual* world in which there is always beauty, comfort, and joy, because this transcendent world is where God dwells. Wherever God is, there is order, structure, security, and peace, because "God is Light." Jesus' miracles proved His ability *not* to reduce God's transcendent world to the lower realm of humankind, but to bring *us* into His transcendent world of Light.

While a person remains outside of Christ—in a state of alienation from God, or simply, *lost*—he remains in darkness. The "domain of darkness" (Col. 1:13) is the realm of the unconverted, the unbelieving, and those who are "dead" to God (Eph. 2:1–3). Such people have made sin their master; they gave it authority over their souls. This malevolent master always seeks the destruction of all who surrender to it. This results in the spiritual "death" of that person (Rom. 6:16, 21, and 23). This "death" begins as God's judgment of condemnation against that person, but it ultimately leads to the actual and irrevocable ruin of that person's soul.

Jesus, "the Light of the world," did not come into our world to rub our face in our condemnation. Satan does that in his accusations against us. We also do our share of self-deprecation through our feelings of shame, guilt, and unworthiness. Instead, Jesus came to *rescue* us from the domain of darkness. He did not come to give us church services and religion; He came as a rescue mission to save us from the darkness, God's condemnation, and *ourselves*.[102] "But as many as received Him, to them He gave the right to become children of God, even to those who believe in His name, who were born, not of blood nor of the will of the flesh nor of the will of man, but of God" (John 1:12–13). In order to be born again to live to a new Master, we first have to die to that to which we once gave our allegiance—the *old* master. Dying to sin is necessary in order to live "in Christ."[103]

Once we are "in Christ"—a phrase Paul uses repeatedly to describe one's covenant relationship with God *through* Christ's intercession—we are no longer "sons of disobedience," but "children of light" (Eph. 5:6–8). While the physical world most certainly does benefit from the Christian influence of His people, it is Christians themselves who are given a newness of life that alludes to the natural order of Creation. In other words, just as God brought light, order, structure, and life to a world that was "formless and void," so He brings all these things to the mind, heart, and soul of the believer. *Our* world—our personal and spiritual existence—is also "formless and void," being shrouded in darkness and ignorance (see Eph. 4:17–19), until Christ rescues us from it.

Just as "God is Light, and in Him there is no darkness at all" (1 John 1:5), so there is no darkness in Jesus Christ. He came as "the radiance of [God's] glory and the exact representation of His nature" (Heb. 1:3)—brimming with love, light, and life. If we have "seen" Him (through the eyes of faith), then we have "seen" the Father (John 14:7–11). His incomprehensible power rescues us from the darkness and brings us into the light of His glory. Once rescued, we are not left to ourselves; we are made part of "God's household" (Eph. 2:19) and thus heirs of salvation (Gal. 3:29). The apostle Peter says of those who are rescued (1 Peter 2:9–10):

> But you are a chosen race, a royal priesthood, a holy nation, a people for God's own possession, so that you may proclaim the excellencies of Him who has called you out of darkness into His marvelous light; for you once were not a people, but now you are the people of God; you had not received mercy, but now you have received mercy.

Out of the chaos and suffering of the darkness, Christ brings us into the order and comfort of God's divine Light. In this realm of light and prosperity, we are blessed with "every spiritual blessing" (Eph. 1:3) and "everything pertaining to life and godliness" (2 Peter 1:3).

Summary Thoughts

Satan *seems* alive and well, but in fact he is very close to his own eternal destruction, and he is anxious to take as many human souls with him as he can. He is a dead man walking—a phrase used to describe a death-row inmate who is literally walking to the execution chamber. Yet, Christ is alive and well, and He is patiently holding off the destruction of all things—including Satan's own destruction—so that more and more people will turn to Him with repentance and obedient faith (2 Peter 3:9). Satan's hatred for you, which is an extension of his hatred for God, drives his desire to devour your soul. Christ's immense love for you, which is an extension of His unfathomable love for His Father, is the driving force behind all that He does to bring you into the fellowship of the Father's love.

The world is drowning in moral confusion and spiritual darkness. Unfortunately, we tend to dwell far too much on what is wrong with *the world* and too little time on what is right *with God*. We tend to give far too much attention to what Satan is doing in the world and far too little on what God has already done, is doing now, and promises to do for those who believe in Him. Satan rules over a failed and pathetic kingdom, yet we worry about what he might do to us and our way of life. Christ, however, is a living Savior who rules over *all that exists*, and yet we do not always trust in His ability and authority. Do you?

This world is not your home, since your soul will go on to experience another world after your physical death. The choices you make here will determine where that eternal home will be. If you choose to live in fear, indulge in the pleasures of your heart, or simply fail to give urgent attention to your spiritual life because of disinterest, laziness, or procrastination, then you will be with Satan in the "outer darkness." But if you choose to live by faith in Christ, serve His will (which always serves *your* best interest), and "Strive to enter through the narrow door" of life (Luke 13:24), then Christ will share His inheritance with you in the life to come. In that glorified and ethereal existence, you will experience only love, peace, joy, and absolute contentment.

Which choice sounds best to you?

Chapter Eleven: The Finest Man to Have Ever Lived

Jesus Christ is the finest, humblest, and most extraordinary person to ever walk the face of the earth. He has had an incalculable effect on religion, moral philosophy, ethics, and human behavior in general. The destruction of ancient idolatry, the elevation of women (from mere property to dignified persons), and the abolition of slavery in America are all rightly attributed to His divine influence. An untold number of books, songs, and sermons have been written about Him. He single-handedly turned the world upside-down, and yet...

...and yet He never wrote a book, a psalm, or even a theological treatise. He never married, raised a family, or received a college degree. He was born to a young peasant couple of no particular distinction (in the eyes of their peers), and He led a simple and lowly existence. He had no home of His own, "nowhere to lay His head" (Luke 9:58), and traveled on foot nearly everywhere He went. He never held a government position, never commanded an army, and never served in the Levitical priesthood. If He had written a résumé, it would appear most unimpressive. Given the basic human expectations for employment, it is unlikely that He would be hired by any reputable business today. And yet...

...and yet Jesus did things that no other man has ever done. He spoke words that shook the foundations of all that had been assumed to be true. He spoke with authority—not merely *authoritatively*, as one who has obtained his credentials from other men, but as though possessing in Himself *divine* authority (Mat. 7:28–29). There was something otherworldly, transcendent, and ageless about His teaching. He did not merely repeat what men already knew; He did not merely regurgitate what He had heard from others. Instead, He spoke with such eloquence, such timeless truth, and such *command* that it was like hearing God Himself speaking.

Unprecedented In Every Way

Jesus did not try to mimic the lofty, purposely-complicated, and often pretentious rhetoric of the rabbinic professors of His day. Instead, He spoke of simple things—rocks, soils, seeds, plants, trees, birds, etc.—

basic, fundamental, and everyday realities that anyone could relate to. Yet, He used these simple word pictures to reveal the profound truths of the most sublime and powerful organization that has ever existed: God's kingdom. His words exposed human hearts, unmasked human hypocrisies, and pierced human souls. He spoke principles, parables, and prophecies, and He did so with such ease and expertise that they never came out as though scripted, rehearsed, or phony. Truly, "Never has a man spoken the way this man speaks" (John 7:46).

Jesus *healed* people—with His own hands, His own words, and sometimes only with His own *mind*. His healing was unlimited, unparalleled, and immediate. There was no problem, disease, malady, or sickness that He could not cure (Mat. 4:23–24, 9:35, 15:30, Luke 4:40, 7:21, etc.). His healings transcended all human expectations, all medical treatment, and distance: He could heal from afar as easily as with His literal human touch (Mat. 8:1–13). He did not have stage hands weed out the really difficult cases (like modern "faith healers" do); He did not perform His healings on a stage with lights, a choir in the background, and a great deal of pompous "God talk" (again, like modern "faith healers" do). He healed out of compassion (Mat. 14:14), not out of mere obligation. He healed in order to prove who He really was: the Son of God. As Nicodemus said, "Rabbi, we know that You have come from God as a teacher; for no one can do these signs that You do unless God is with him" (John 3:2).

Jesus' healing was not limited to physical sickness, but extended to *spiritual* maladies as well. He exorcised demons from people's bodies and lives—powerful entities that could do nothing but submit in the presence of His power. He forgave people of their sins—not with the permission of the Jewish rabbis, and not with an over-the-top theatrical performance, either. He did what only God alone is capable of doing, thus proving Himself to be a divine being. (Mark 2:1–12). He even forgave the criminal who was crucified alongside of Him, promising that he would be "in Paradise" with Him before the day was over (Luke 23:39–43). Thus, while He had been falsely arrested, fully humiliated, beaten, spit upon, severely whipped, and then His lacerated body brutally nailed to a cross, Jesus took time to deal gently with a man who came to his senses and begged Him for mercy. Being the Son of God, He graciously responded.

Jesus performed more miracles than any man of God had ever done before Him, and more than any man since. It may well be that He performed more miracles than *all* other men had ever done *combined* (John 20:30 and 21:25). He turned many gallons of water into excellent-tasting wine (John 2:1–11); on more than one occasion, He fed thousands of hungry people by multiplying a few loaves of bread and a couple of fish (Mat. 14:13–21, 15:32–39). He walked on water (Mat. 14:22–27); He commanded a fierce storm to "be still," and it obeyed Him (Mark 4:35–39). He called a dead man out of his coffin, and he sat up and came back to life (Luke 7:11–17); He called another man out of his tomb who had been dead for four days, and that man obeyed Him (John 11:1–44). He fulfilled literally hundreds of prophecies about Himself that had been written many hundreds of years before—a miracle in itself that often receives little acknowledgment.

Jesus did all these things *not* with the assistance or consent of other people, but by His own authority as the Son of God. His apostles performed miracles in *His* name (or, by the authority He imparted to them—see Acts 3:6), but He needed no human authority to do what God alone is capable of doing. These many miracles were not for show, merely to amaze and entertain His audience, or to raise money. He provided these signs to prove irrefutably who He was: the Son of God. He even challenged His listeners *not* to listen to His words unless they *were* accompanied by the "works" that could only come from God (John 10:37–38). His miraculous works served as an undeniable and factual testimony to His claim of having come from the Father (John 5:36).

Yet, Amazingly Unappreciated

Again, Jesus Christ is the finest, humblest, and most extraordinary person to ever walk the face of the earth. And yet, with all that He has done, all that He has taught, and the many millions of souls that He has helped, *most of the world* refuses to listen to Him, much less follow Him. He is often reduced to being a "good man," a "religious teacher," or a lightning rod for controversy. He has been denied—for no good reason—the attention, praise, and allegiance that He so rightly deserves. His profound, life-altering, and transcendent message of *saving us from ourselves* is often eclipsed by the godless, self-promoting, and arrogant celebrity-of-the-moment. He is often ridiculed by comics, trashed by late-night talk shows, and outright blasphemed by atheists and others. It is a wonder, in light of all this, that He has not already unleashed divine judgment against the entire world.

Meanwhile Satan has done *absolutely nothing* to warrant the attention, praise, or loyalty of *anyone.* He has provided no profound teaching, but lies to everyone about everything he says (John 8:44). He has not helped a single person out of his or her misery, but gleefully contributes to it. He is "full of deceit and fraud," an "enemy of all righteousness," and does "not cease to make crooked the straight ways of the Lord" (Acts 13:10), and yet many millions of people foolishly give him controlling interest over their souls. He has no original thought, but only twists, perverts, and maligns whatever good things Christ has done or created. His demons have tormented many people through the ages, all without his apology or concern.

Satan is evil, malicious, exploitative, and seething with contempt for all people. He does not care how many people he hurts, how many marriages and families he destroys, or much damage he causes. He seeks the destruction of all people, but targets Christians—especially new converts. While having done absolutely nothing good *for* the world, he nonetheless receives the attention *of* the world (1 John 5:19). Instead of extolling the virtues of Christ, admiring His great love, and humbly acknowledging His great sacrifice to save the world, *most people* pay Him little mind, regard Him with great contempt, or ignore Him altogether. Meanwhile, Satan gains followers every day—people who think themselves incredibly wise and think that giving glory to Christ is simply beneath them.

How can so many otherwise intelligent people think this way?

A Perfect and Unparalleled Man

Jesus—a humble Jew who lived an austere but phenomenal life as the Christ—was not the first to perform miracles, nor even the last. Many of His own countrymen thought Himself to be a prophet, but not many were willing to admit that He was *the* Prophet—especially, an even *greater* Prophet than Moses. He was a righteous Man, to be sure, but it is hard sometimes to understand Him as a *perfect* Man. After all, Noah was called a "righteous man" (Gen. 6:9), and so was Abraham (Gen. 15:6), John the Baptist (Mark 6:20), and even Joseph of Arimathea (Luke 23:50). But none of these other men were *perfectly* righteous, and thus none of them can truly be compared to Jesus. In fact, Jesus has no equal; He was not only an extraordinary Man, but He was unique in all of human history.

A *perfect* Man—one who has never had an evil thought, never made a spiteful remark, and never committed a single sin—is hard to wrap our heads around. We do not know any perfect people in our lives. Everyone we know (including ourselves) is riddled with flaws, defects, a troubled past, or some moral blemish. These imperfections may be relatively small, few, or rare, but they exist—and, *because* they exist, they have lost all claim to innocence. In God's eyes, until our souls are cleansed in our conversion to Christ, we are all damaged goods. Thus, a perfect, sinless, flawless Man that has risen above all of this seems almost unbelievable. Yet, this is exactly what all the evidence in Scripture says of Him (Isa. 53:9, 2 Cor. 5:21, 1 Peter 2:21, etc.).

While it is hard enough to acknowledge Jesus' moral perfection in such a dark and sinful world, we have barely scratched the surface of who He really is. When we consider also His *divine nature*, this becomes even more challenging. A Divine Being is one who has never been created, but is transcendent *of* Creation and therefore not bound to the limitations of time, space, and natural laws. The Divine Being who became known to us as "Jesus" is a Personage of the Godhead, and has been with God the Father in the eternal past (John 1:1–2, 17:1–5). Thus, before the foundation of the world—before all time and history—He lived fully, completely, and majestically in the midst of God the Father (John 8:58, 17:24, Phil. 2:6–7, 1 Peter 1:20–21, etc.). In becoming a Man (John 1:14), He did not cease to be the Son of God, which is like saying an apple became an orange without ceasing to be an apple. In a more natural explanation, it is like a married man who becomes a father without ceasing to be a husband. His identity does not change, only the role that he has taken on. Thus, the eternal Son of God took on the human role of "Jesus" while still maintaining His divine nature (Col. 1:19, 2:9).

Despite this, much of the Jewish leadership of Jesus' day took issue with His intimate association with God (John 5:18, 10:30-33, 19:7, etc.). They considered it blasphemy—an act of profaning God—even though three years' worth of teaching, unprecedented miracles, and other irrefutable evidence proved His association with God to be legitimate. The Jewish Council's final determinant in finding Jesus allegedly guilty was His own admission, made under oath, that He was indeed the Son of God (Mat. 26:63-65, Mark 14:61-64, and Luke 22:70). Like us, those Jews had a hard time wrapping their heads around the idea that this Man *Jesus* and the *Son of God* were one and the same Person. Yet, instead of objectively weighing the evidence and admitting the truth, they simply chose to execute Him in order to justify themselves.

So then, this Jesus was not only a Man who was morally perfect, He was also a Divine Being whose essential nature and intimate relationship with God the Father puts Him above all of Creation. This means that whatever *has* been created—which is *everything that exists* in the visible and invisible realm aside from the Godhead itself—is in subjection to Him. As the apostle Paul says, "He is before [i.e., pre-eminent to—MY WORDS] all things, and in Him all things hold together" (Col. 1:17). This means that whatever exists that is not "God" is below Him in authority, power, and nature. It also means that all such things (rulers, authorities, powers, dominions, and people) will be held accountable to Him (Eph. 1:19b-23). This *also* means that *you*—whoever you are—will answer to Him in due time (2 Cor. 5:10).

After resurrecting from the dead and presenting Himself before His disciples, Jesus confirmed to them, "All authority has been given to Me in heaven and on earth" (Mat. 28:18). This means that no created authority is exempt from or outside the bounds of His own divine authority.[104] Every earthly authority—kings, presidents, all government leaders, all religious leaders, the Dalai Lama, the Pope, et al.—will answer to Jesus Christ. Even those who *do not believe* in Christ (or in God, or in any supernatural being) will answer to Him. In due time, "every knee will bow" and "every tongue will confess that Jesus Christ is Lord" (Phil. 2:9-11). This means *you*—whoever you are, whatever you believe or even refuse to believe—will also answer to Him. To "answer" in this case does not mean to state your case before Him in an attempt to vindicate yourself. Rather, it is to have *Him* evaluate *your* life based on what you did (or, perhaps, failed to do) in connection with the moral responsibility you had as one created in God's own image.

As if all this were not enough, the revealed word of God goes one step further. Jesus is not only a perfect Divine Being who rules above all that exists; He is also the *Creator* of all that exists. Any sincere, objective, and open-minded observation of our world (and the universe) will admit that it did not "just happen" over myriads of fortunate mistakes and eons of time. Everything bears witness of an all-powerful and all-knowing Creator: "The heavens are telling of the glory of God; and their expanse is declaring the work of His hands" (Psalms 19:1). While the Bible is not the sole basis for this conclusion, it does identify who this Creator is (and, to some extent, the manner in which the Creation came to be): "In the beginning God created the heavens and the earth" (Gen. 1:1). It is not until the NT, however, that we learn that "God" here specifically refers to *Jesus Christ* acting on His Father's authority, rather than God the Father acting alone. Several passages explicitly teach this (bracketed words are mine):

- "All things came into being through Him [i.e., Christ, the Word], and apart from Him nothing came into being that has come into being" (John 1:3, bracketed words added).
- "He was in the world, and the world was made through Him..." (John 1:10).
- "[T]here is but one God, the Father, from whom are all things and we exist for Him; and one Lord, Jesus Christ, by whom are all things, and we exist through Him" (1 Cor. 8:6).
- "For by Him all things were created, both in the heavens and on earth, visible and invisible, whether thrones or dominions or rulers or authorities—all things have been created through Him and for Him" (Col. 1:16).
- "[I]n these last days [God] has spoken to us in His Son, whom He appointed heir of all things, through whom also He made the world" (Heb. 1:2).

There are other passages as well that speak of "God" creating the world (Acts 17:24, Rom. 11:36, 1 Cor. 11:12, Eph. 3:9, Heb. 3:4, and Rev. 4:11), but in light of the passages cited above, this can be referring to Jesus as well.

Despite this, many people view Jesus as merely a religious teacher, or perhaps a moralist at best. And, if they do not like what He says or do not follow His "religion" (their word, not mine), they simply dismiss Him altogether, thinking Him to be expendable or ignorable. But if He is the Creator of all that exists, this changes everything. Now, the Creator Himself has come into the world that *He* created to tell those to whom *He* has given life how they can live forever in *His* world and not "perish" (John 3:16). This is not someone to dismiss or ignore. This is also not someone with whom we should feel comfortable negotiating the terms of our own salvation, or thinking that we can choose which of *His* terms to honor. This is Someone with incomprehensible power and authority that has the ability to *save* or *destroy* us.

As the Creator—the One who made *everything* out of *nothing*—Jesus stands above all of His Creation. For a time, He "emptied Himself" of His full, eternal glory as a Divine Being in heaven in order to take on "the form of a bond-servant [i.e., a human being—MY WORDS]" (Phil. 2:7). During the time that He lived among people, He received instruction from His Father only on a need-to-know basis (John 5:19–20, 30, 8:28, 12:49, etc.) in order to serve His Father's will (John 4:34, 6:38, etc.). His relatively brief earthly ministry was not a demotion, but a voluntary withholding of His divine *right* in order to provide a sacrifice for our sins.

> But we do see Him who was made for a little while lower than the angels, namely, Jesus, because of the suffering of death crowned with glory and honor, so that by the grace of God He might taste death for everyone. For it was fitting for Him, for whom are all things, and through whom are all things, in bringing many sons to glory, to perfect the author of their salvation through sufferings. (Heb. 2:9–10)

In order to suffer for men, Jesus had to bear the image of a man (Phil. 2:8). Similarly, in order to identify with sinners, He had to take on the *likeness* of sinners (without *becoming* one) (Rom. 8:3–4). In order to *free* us from death—what we deserve for our crimes against God—He had to "taste death for everyone" and die in our place (1 Peter 2:21–24).

Jesus Christ (the Creator) did all this for two enormous reasons. First, He loved His Father so much that He was willing to do *whatever it took* to obey His will. Second, He loves whomever the Father loves, so that He was willing to do *whatever it took* to rescue those people (all of us!) from our self-inflicted ruin. There is a relationship between the enormity of His love and the massiveness of His Creation. Many have asked, "Why did God make the universe incomprehensibly vast? The enormous cosmos seems unnecessary when all He had to do was create the earth as a dwelling place for humankind." True, the universe is immense beyond words; true, the earth is the only place where human beings exist in it. However, the vastness of the universe symbolizes the vastness of Christ's love for us. He (the Creator) surrounds human beings with an immense universe in the same way that He surrounds all of us with an immense, beautiful, and incalculable love. Just as we will never find the end of the physical universe, so we will never exhaust the Creator's love for His highest creation: *people*.

"But," someone asks, "there is so much pain, suffering, and *darkness* in the world! How can He surround us with such immense love and still allow these things to exist?" These are the huge questions that philosophers, moralists, and theologians have been wrestling with for centuries. No one can answer these questions to *everyone's* satisfaction. (See "Appendix I: The Problem of Evil" for an expanded response to this.) However, in light of all biblical teaching, our fallen world is not meant to be free from problems. This life is a proving ground, not heaven itself; if there were no choices to make or allegiances to honor, there would be nothing to prove. Christ's (or, God's) love for us needed to be proved, and our love for Him—which necessarily implies our *trust* in Him—also needs to be proved.

As for the proof of His love for us, this has been made. "God demonstrates His own love toward us, in that while we were yet sinners, Christ died for us," Paul wrote. "Much more then, having now been justified by His blood, we shall be saved from the wrath of God through Him" (Rom. 5:8–9). The apostle John wrote, "By this the love of God was manifested in us, that God has sent His only begotten Son into the world so that we might live through Him. In this is love, not that we loved God, but that He loved us and sent His Son to be the propitiation [or, appeasement of His wrath—MY WORDS] for our sins" (1 John 4:9–10).

Many people think that the physical universe itself has something to offer us. They look to the positioning of stars, the lining up of planets, or some celestial "sign" to let them know that the universe *cares* for them. They depend upon a mystical, almost magical, convergence of cosmic sights, vibrations, and special knowledge for their enlightenment, advancement, and (in so many words) salvation. This is all useless and hopeless. The physical universe is a cold, mostly dark, and mostly empty cosmic wasteland that has no capacity for thought, mercy, or redemption. The universe does not love you. In fact, it has no ability to love *or* hate, because it is not a living thing or capable of moral decisions. If you leave the earth on a spaceship and step into outer space or onto another planet without essential, life-preserving equipment, you will die a quick but horrible death. The universe is not unkind, because it is unable to *be* kind. It is simply a hostile environment that was never *created* to sustain human life.

To liken Jesus' love for us to the *size* of the universe is one thing. To think that Jesus' love is as cold, hostile, and *apathetic* as the universe is quite another. These are not related analogies. Jesus (the Creator) does love us, and because of this He created a planet designed for optimal human existence. The fact that we have corrupted it with our sins, pollution, and misuse of its resources does not remove this original premise. Because He loves us, He also provided a way to save us from ourselves when we sin against His Father. And, because He loves us, He also does not force Himself upon us but allows each of us to choose for ourselves whether we will love Him in return. Our world's pain, suffering, and darkness are not His fault, but are the collective fault of all of us who have ever lived here. On the contrary, He promises to take those who believe in Him to a world in which none of these awful things exist. He promises such people an entirely *new* existence—a world that is not surrounded by the vast blackness of cold, unmerciful space, but is enveloped in the warm, brilliantly-lit, and thoroughly enjoyable presence of God.

Jesus needed to demonstrate His love for us, and He did so more than sufficiently. But we also have to demonstrate *our* love for *Him*. This love does take time to learn, understand, and put into practice. At the same time, it cannot be reduced to a warm sentiment of our heart, nor a mere intellectual agreement to His words. What Christ seeks is an unconditional surrender of will, chosen obedience, and unswaying devotion. This is what real love looks like. This is also the only kind of love that an all-powerful, all-knowing, and supremely-loving Divine Being deserves.

Summary Thoughts

Jesus was presented to the world as a perfect specimen of what it means to be human. He was morally flawless: He never lied, never succumbed to temptation, never sinned. He "went about doing good...for God was with Him" (Acts 10:38). Indeed, the gospel accounts of His ministry are filled with examples of His kindness, mercy, healing, forgiveness, and restoration of broken human beings. He came speaking, teaching, and exhorting; He also came revealing God to us, performing miracles, and bearing witness to heavenly truth. No one else in all of human history has done what He did. No one else ever *could* do these things.

Jesus disclosed Himself as the Son of God—a Divine Being that is united (or, "one") but not interchangeable with the Father (John 10:30). He did this privately and discreetly at first, but by the end of His ministry, He held nothing back. He also disclosed Himself as the One who will raise the dead and judge all souls in the end of time (John 5:25–32). This is both the *responsibility* and *prerogative* of a Divine Being. No created being (including Satan or any angel) has the ability, authority, or right to do these things.

Finally, Jesus is revealed throughout the NT as the Creator of all that exists, and that "in Him all things hold together" (Col. 1:17). He is not Someone to be second-guessed, disregarded, or dismissed as unimportant or expendable. Through the authority given to Him by God the Father, Jesus is the source of all earthly life; by this same authority, He is also the source of all spiritual life. No one lives apart from Him; no one can come to God apart from Him (John 14:6); and, in the context of salvation, we can "do nothing" apart from Him (John 15:5).

Given all this, how is it that Jesus is so doubted, discredited, and disparaged in the world? How can One who is perfectly good, all-powerful, and supremely loving—One who always and *only* serves our best interest—be set aside for anything or anyone else? Why is One who offers redemption, salvation, and an eternal home in heaven—something not a *single one of us* deserves—be treated with such suspicion, ridicule, and contempt as we see in so much of the world today?

The whole world lies in the power of Satan who operates in the realm of spiritual darkness. It is unnerving—even downright terrifying—how successful he has been in deceiving so many millions, even *billions*, of people to turn away from their benevolent Creator. Yet, all souls—those who believe in Jesus as well as those who have been blinded by Satan—will one day *leave* this earth and stand trial for the decisions they have made.

This world is not your home. Dwelling in the presence of God is *intended* to be your real home, but you do not have to consent to this. Jesus Christ, because of His love for you, allows you the freedom to choose your own future—even your own failure. You do not have to live with Him; you *can* live elsewhere if you want to. But the only "elsewhere" in the hereafter that is not *in* God's presence is to be completely separated *from* His presence. Instead of being enveloped in God's light, love, and joy forever, such people will be swallowed up in the "outer darkness" where "there will be weeping and gnashing of teeth" (Mat. 8:12).

Given these two options, the best choice seems most obvious, but it is still yours to make. And, it is a choice that must *be* made while there is still time to do so.

Chapter Twelve: What Happened at the Cross

In 2004, Mel Gibson co-produced, co-wrote, and directed a blockbuster movie called *The Passion of the Christ*. Maybe you've seen it; maybe you haven't. It took me about seventeen years to getting around to watching it myself. The basic plot involves Jesus Christ's final hours of His life, from the Garden of Gethsemane in which He was arrested to—*spoiler alert*—His death on the cross. The movie is very much from a Roman Catholic perspective, and is the highest-grossing religious movie of all time.[105]

The Passion, if nothing else, does force one to think (or, perhaps, re-think) about what Jesus actually endured in His betrayal, arrest, trials, scourging, and crucifixion. I'm not here to applaud nor denounce Gibson's portrayal of Jesus, except to say that he took a great deal of creative license with the original script (i.e., the biblical gospel accounts). He also interjected into this time period a number of elements and conversations that actually took place at different times in Jesus' life. Even so, the movie does not pretend to be completely accurate, and does draw on certain Catholic traditions as well as biblical texts.

One thing that particularly caught my attention, however, was an early scene in the movie where Jesus is agonizing in the Garden of Gethsemane. "Gethsemane," incidentally—and, given Jesus' ordeal there, appropriately—means "olive press." Jesus, the Olive Tree of Israel (Rom. 11:17), certainly felt the incomprehensible and crushing weight of carrying the condemnation of all of human sin on His shoulders. His *blood*, not olive oil, is what came from this dreadful experience. In the movie scene concerning this ordeal, Satan appears in human form in front of Jesus. Satan is depicted as a shrouded, pale-skinned, and (of course) creepy personage rather than the traditional Hollywood depiction of him as a red-skinned, horned, and overtly ghoulish figure.[106] Well done, Mr. Gibson.

As Jesus is tormented by what lies before Him, Satan asks Him, "Do you really believe that one man can bear the full burden of sin?" While an understandable question, there are two huge problems with it. First, this encounter and any conversation with Satan in the Garden is most certainly fictitious. If it happened at all, we have no record of it. Second, it assumes that Satan fully understood what was happening—namely, that Jesus' death would fulfill God's "eternal purpose" (Eph. 3:11). There is no doubt that Satan wanted Jesus to suffer and die, since he did his best to orchestrate this (to the degree that he was allowed to do so). But the idea that Satan knew *why* Jesus would die, and would die in the manner and under the circumstances that He did, is contrived.

"No man can bear this burden," Satan continues in a surly, mocking tone. "Saving their souls is too costly." This statement is loaded with theological implications, but it betrays Satan's own participation in the death of Jesus. The movie seems to imply that Satan wanted Jesus dead, to be sure, but that he also believed that His death would be catastrophic to His cause rather than victorious. After Jesus' death on the cross, the movie does show Satan screaming in rage, horror, and frustration in some empty, hellish location, but offers no explanation. I realize, of course, that this is just a movie, but I wonder how many people really believe in this convoluted portrayal of Satan. Mel Gibson is free to his own interpretation of both Jesus and Satan, but the truth is what we should pursue above all else.

God's Promise through the "Seed"

To understand the big picture of the biblical confrontation between Satan and Jesus, we need to go all the way back to the beginning. In Gen. 3:15, God promised to put "enmity" (i.e., hostility or hatred) between the "seed" of the serpent and the "seed" of the woman (Eve). "Seed" here refers to offspring or posterity, which is an unusual expression here since it is a human male that provides "seed," not a woman. But, since the serpent deceived Eve, and since Eve listened to the words of the serpent, the enmity is expressed as being between these two parties.[107]

As for the serpent, it would bruise the heel of the woman's "seed" (someone significant in her posterity). This alludes to the *limitation* of the injury, as well as its *inferiority* in comparison to what the woman's "seed" would do to the serpent. God had just cursed the serpent to crawl on its belly in the dust of the earth all the days of its life (Gen. 3:14). This not only took away the serpent's ability to lift itself to the level of a human being (literally, in height; figuratively, in speech), but also humiliated it to the ground level of animal life. While other higher animals can walk on feet, hooves, or paws, the serpent is forced to crawl in the dust, like one that grovels for its existence. Thus, God removed from the serpent the ability to reason with a human being and even deceive him. Thus, the best the serpent can do is to bite the heel of a woman's "seed." This afflicts pain, to be sure, but it will not destroy the one who is afflicted. The "seed" of the woman, however, "shall bruise [the serpent] on the head," indicating a fatal wound and a full destruction of the creature.

It is clear, as God's plan of redemption unfolds in Scripture over time, that He was not only talking about serpents and the woman. He was talking about Satan and Jesus—Satan taking on the humiliating, limited, and inferior role of the serpent, and Jesus being "born of a woman" (Gal. 4:4) but also being the infinitely superior "begotten" of God (John 3:16). Paul says explicitly that Jesus is the "seed" that fulfilled both God's prophecy to Adam and Eve *and* His promise to Abraham (Gal. 3:15–16). While Satan once enjoyed a position of preeminence and respect, he has been degraded to that of a groveling demonic creature. Satan would in due time "bruise" Jesus on the heel—i.e., through his manipulation of evil men, he would cause Jesus great suffering and affliction. But Jesus would "bruise" Satan on the head—indicating not a temporary wound, but a catastrophic injury that will bring about the very end of Satan.[108]

Much has been written on this scenario over the ages. Still, it is something often overlooked and under-appreciated by many Christians today. As the world quickly descends into madness and godlessness, it is easy to become preoccupied with all the seeming success that Satan is enjoying. Since millions—even *billions*—of people are being swayed by his lies and deceptions, it would seem that *he*—and not Christ—is in control, and that God is wringing His hands in worry over Satan's many victories. It would seem that Satan is very much alive today, and that Jesus is a 2,000-year-old memory that has long since faded or become irrelevant. It would seem that Satan has defeated Jesus—that he has bruised Jesus on the head, and that Jesus had only bruised Satan on the heel—and Jesus is worriedly striving to regain control of all that Satan has taken over.

None of these pictures are true or accurate. While Satan is still in operation and manages to oversee a kingdom of demons and wicked men, it is not true that he has been victorious over Jesus in any sense of the word. Furthermore, his kingdom is a doomed one: its downfall and full destruction have already been prophesied by a God whose word has never failed. In an illustration based on the prophecy in Gen. 3, Satan has bitten Jesus on the heel, but this is not a mortal wound since "it is impossible for [Jesus] to be held in [death's] power" (Acts 2:24).[109] Meanwhile, Jesus stomped upon Satan's head, robbing him of the power to accuse redeemed people of their sins—in effect, robbing him of *any* legitimate power.

This otherworldly picture deserves further examination. It is not enough to say that "Jesus conquered Satan at the cross" if we fail to understand what this really means. At the same time, we are unable to know *fully* what this means, since only so much has been revealed to us in God's word. Even so, what we do know is powerful information, and it should give us deeper faith and greater courage in seeking out a Savior who, quite literally, *cannot be destroyed.*

What Jesus Accomplished through His Cross

We have been led to believe—by human intuition, religious tradition, or simply our assumptions concerning Scripture—that Satan truly understood what was going on at the time of Jesus' crucifixion. After all, he is a spiritual being and therefore (we assume) must know everything going on in the spiritual realm.[110] Yet, if he did, why was he so insistent on putting Jesus to death? Why did he purposely, knowingly, and even agreeably play right into Jesus' hand to bring about his (Satan's) own demise? And, why would he do the very thing that would rob him of the only legitimate "power" that he had—namely, to rightly accuse people of being altogether unworthy of God's forgiveness or fellowship?

We are left with one of two choices: either Satan was completely stupid to do all this, or he simply did not comprehend exactly what was happening. Satan has long been proud, wicked, and filled with darkness, but stupidity—as in, lacking in intelligence or cunning ability—is not one of his characteristics. We might *call* him "stupid" for choosing to sin against God, but that decision falls into the category of moral rebellion rather than intellectual deficiency. The same can be said of ourselves when *we* choose to sin against God. This leaves us with the other scenario: Satan thought he was going to defeat Jesus by seeking His crucifixion when in fact Jesus was about to beat Satan over the head with his own stick, so to speak. In other words, Satan thought he would defeat Jesus through *death*, and yet Jesus *used* His own death to accomplish great things (Heb. 2:14–15). These things include:

- Jesus unmasked sinful men's hatred for Him (God's Son) simply because He exposed them for who they really were. And, He said, if anyone hates Him, they hate God the Father as well (John 15:18–25). This exposure was necessary because in order to save people, Jesus had to open their eyes to just how *lost* they really were. The Jews in particular painted themselves as "sons of God," yet Jesus said they acted instead like Satan's children (John 8:41–47). The vicious manner in which they plotted against Him, called for His execution, and then gloated over His crucifixion (Luke 23:35–37) only underscored what Jesus had said about them. But it was not only the Jews who were evil while claiming to be good. All of us have done the same thing. We have *all* fallen short of being good, despite our claims otherwise (Rom. 3:23).
- He fulfilled all the prophecies concerning His violent and unjust death (notably in Psalm 22 and Isa. 53). These prophecies not only predicted what would happen, but also the purpose for which it would happen. Jesus called upon these prophecies as witnesses to the truth of His words, the fact of His identity as the Son of God, and the fact that all of them directly, specifically, and necessarily pointed to Him (Mat. 26:56, 27:9, John 5:39–47, Luke 22:37, 24:44, etc.).
- He showed mastery over the darkness that overtakes those who are condemned to (spiritual) death. The darkness is powerful and mesmerizing, as we have seen, but Jesus is infinitely wise and powerful and could not be seduced by its power or charm. The Light can dispel the darkness, but the darkness cannot overtake the Light: "The Light shines in the darkness, and the darkness did not comprehend it" (John 1:5). If Satan is filled with darkness,

then he too cannot "comprehend" the Light. Satan knew who the Light *was* (Luke 4:34, etc.), but he did not know all that He was capable of doing.

- He showed mastery over the purported king *of* the darkness—Satan himself. Satan thought he could contend with Jesus in a head-to-head confrontation (as he attempted to do in the wilderness—Mat. 4:1–11), but he is no match for the Son of God. Jesus referred to Satan as "the strong man" who guards his kingdom and seeks to protect all that belongs to him. But He also claimed that He was "someone stronger" than the "strong man"—someone whose power and authority are considerably greater than Satan's (Luke 11:21–22). Through His death, Jesus robbed Satan of that by which he had imprisoned men for so long: "the power of death" and "the fear of death" (Heb. 2:14–15). The "power of death" is sin (1 Cor. 15:56); the "fear of death" is the future unleashing of God's wrath against sinners in the Judgment (Rom. 2:5–6). Jesus takes all this away when He forgives believers of their sins, thus freeing them from Satan's accusations.[111]

- He showed mastery over death itself: the grave could not hold Him in its power (Acts 2:24). This is crucially important. First, physical death is feared by all people who anticipate an accounting—and judgment—of their lives in the hereafter. Second, physical death is the worst feature of God's curse upon humankind for having sinned against Him (Gen. 3:17–19). For this reason, "the body is dead [or, destined to die—MY WORDS] because of sin" (Rom. 8:10), and this curse has haunted people ever since Adam and Eve were banished from the Garden. But Jesus' death—and, by implication, His resurrection *from* physical death—showed His supremacy over this curse. As the innocent and virtuous Son of God, not only was this curse inapplicable to Him, but *through* Him we are able to overcome it ourselves. This is not to say that we will not experience physical death, but that we can live to God forever (Eph. 2:1–5) *and* can anticipate a bodily resurrection from our own grave in the future (John 5:28–29, Rom. 8:11, 1 Cor. 15:35–44, etc.).[112]

- He provided His own body as a perfect sin offering "once for all" (Heb. 1:3, 10:10, 14). Satan must have thought that killing Jesus would destroy Him, when in fact he unwittingly helped Him to become that perfect sacrifice. Of course, it was not Satan who offered Jesus as this offering—this would be unholy to the core!—but *God the Father* "gave" His Son for this purpose (John 3:16). This is what "propitiation" refers to (Rom. 3:25, Heb. 2:17): God appeasing (or, satisfying) His own wrath through providing His own offering (His Son) in order to fulfill His own divine justice. This is something we could not do for ourselves but that God did for us. If it were not for the body and blood of Jesus—in essence, His *life*—being given as a sin offering, forgiveness *for* our sins would be impossible and all of us would be hopelessly lost. Jesus took upon Himself the enormity of what was required to free us from our self-inflicted condemnation. The full force of that requirement was made graphically and horrifically evident in the ordeal of His crucifixion (including the scourging and humiliation that preceded it). Satan, apparently, was oblivious to all of this, otherwise he would have done everything to prevent it rather than spur it on as he did.

- His resurrection *from* death irrefutably proved His power over the grave *and* the spiritual realm. While Jesus performed numerous miracles during His earthly ministry, His greatest and most convincing miracle was that of Him walking out of His own grave after being dead for three days and three nights (Mat. 12:40, 16:21, etc.). The reason why this miracle is greater than all others is because it requires mastery over the physical realm *and at the same time* the spiritual realm. Jesus could not have risen from the dead apart from this kind of power. No other miracle Jesus performed equaled this in scope; there is nothing else He could have done to improve upon this. He Himself said (John 10:17–18):

> For this reason the Father loves Me, because I lay down My life so that I may take it up again. No one has taken it away from Me, but I lay it down on My own initiative. I have authority to lay it down, and I have authority to take it up again. This commandment I received from My Father.

Satan threw everything he had at Him while He was here, and thought he had scored a victory by having Him crucified. But when Jesus rose from the dead, Satan's days were numbered and his final doom was sealed.

- He overcame the world (John 16:33). Everything that the sin-filled, unjust, and hopeless world is and stands for, He showed Himself to be superior to it. He overcame everything the world inflicted upon Him—threats, intimidations, temptations, torture, and even death itself. In every case where people have failed, He succeeded; where we all "fall short" (Rom. 3:23), He stood fast and never wavered. He "has been tempted in all things as we are, yet without sin" (Heb. 4:14). In this sense, He most appropriately serves as the Son of Man—an uncorrupted, flawless, and epitomized specimen of humanity—as well as being the Son of God.

Satan, blinded by his wicked ambition to destroy God's plan of salvation by destroying the Savior Himself, did exactly the opposite of what he intended. This is not to say that Jesus tricked him, since trickery involves deceit, and there was no deceit in Him (1 Peter 2:21). Satan had access to all the Scriptures, since he quoted them when he wanted to (Mat. 4:6). Yet, he failed to grasp the same thing that Israel failed to grasp: the concept of a *suffering Savior* (Luke 24:25–27) and His *resurrection from the dead*. Thus, while Satan saw the cross as his victory, it quickly became instead his own death-knell.

The apostle Paul, in responding to the Jews' desire for displays of God's power and the Greeks' philosophical quest for knowledge, says simply, "we preach Christ crucified" (1 Cor. 1:23). The event of Christ's death, of course, seems pathetic to unbelievers of any ethnicity, but God's plan is not about impressing people according to human expectations. It is about taking care of the problem (sin) that keeps people from eternal fellowship with their Creator. Many Christians latch on to the event itself, as though crucifixion itself was the means of God's deliverance from sin. Yet, many people were crucified in the ancient world, and two other men were crucified alongside of Jesus. It was not crucifixion itself that saved anyone; it was *who* was crucified, and *why* He was crucified, and all that was *accomplished* through His crucifixion. "'We preach Christ crucified'—

we don't preach the crucifixion of Christ. It isn't the crucifixion that gives glory to Christ but Christ gives meaning and glory to the crucifixion."[113]

Satan missed all this. The Jews who boasted in God but acted like children of Satan (John 8:44) missed all this. The Greeks, in their hopeless pursuit of human wisdom as a means of "saving" humankind, missed all this. All those *today* who are also blinded with pride, blinded with self-ambition, or blinded by human wisdom, are missing all this. Even *Christians* who are more concerned with "contemporary" religion, "casual worship," or the highly-politicized and hopelessly-flawed social justice are missing all this.

Christ did not come to the world just to die on a cross. He came to destroy Satan, Satan's world, and any belief, religion, or lifestyle inspired by Satan's deceptions. But He also came to *save* as many people as want to *be* saved. He came to save us from the darkness, from Satan, and from ourselves. While He is capable of destroying—and He *will* exercise this power in the future—His mission is to "seek and save the lost" (Luke 19:10). Retribution is coming for all who refuse (for any reason) to believe in Him, but salvation is coming for all who *do* believe in Him (Heb. 9:27–28).

God's "eternal purpose" (Eph. 3:11) is not about church services, social reform, or making everyone feel happy and comfortable. Rather, it is about giving us—*any* of us—an opportunity to walk obediently with God in this life, in anticipation of living forever with Him in the life to come. Christ is not merely a major part *of* this "eternal purpose"; He is the *summing up of all things* that God set in motion in the eternal past (Eph. 1:9–10). "And having been made perfect"—i.e., having demonstrated His perfect obedience in His human life—"[Christ] became to all those who obey Him the source of eternal salvation" (Heb. 5:9).

Who or what else can make this kind of offer—and *guarantee* its outcome?

Summary Thoughts

The truth of Scripture is more important than lushly-produced movies (such as *The Passion of the Christ*) or popular consensus concerning either Jesus or Satan. The serpent's "seed"—a lying deceiver in the likeness of the serpent's own lies to Eve—most certainly did "bruise" Jesus on the heel, so to speak. But this injury to Jesus was not catastrophic—humiliating, excruciating, and bloody, yes, but not destructive. Jesus' blow to Satan, however, was indeed catastrophic, since it meant the overthrow of his power and the ultimate destruction of Satan himself. While Satan continues to deceive the world, he is already doomed and his time is limited.

This admission does not for a moment diminish the pain and reproach that Jesus underwent in being treated like an expendable piece of trash, robbed of all human decency and dignity. His arrest, scourging, and crucifixion were acts of appalling injustice, and He suffered in ways that we will never understand, since He also took upon Himself a *spiritual* burden that defies human comprehension. But Jesus rose victoriously out of that awful situation and now sits enthroned in heaven at the right hand of His Father. Satan, meanwhile, has been forcefully removed from Jesus' presence, and has nothing but an eternity of unspeakable suffering to look forward to.

This present world is not your home. In the end, you will either be with Jesus in His glorious world or you will join Satan in his awful suffering. There is no third alternative available, and you have no authority or power to create one. No man-made religion or religious authority can create one for you, either. After all that has been said about Satan's repeated and abysmal failures as well as Jesus' triumphant and undeniable victories, the choice as to which personage to be with seems abundantly obvious. However, the freedom to choose your own future remains yours and yours alone.

Chapter Thirteen: "And There Was War in Heaven"

It seems that many people (Christians included) take one extreme or the other when dealing with Satan and his wicked realm. Some are led to believe that Satan has divine qualities—he can create something from nothing, work genuine miracles, and read your mind. He will *possess* you by taking over your mind and forcing you to sin. And, he is the only one powerful enough to give God a run for His money, so to speak.

The other extreme sees Satan as a harmless, cartoonish character that no one should take very seriously. He is the figment of the collective imagination of millennia of guilt-ridden consciences, preying upon our fears but not really being able to do us any real harm. He talks big, struts around the fiery caverns of hell, and tries to scare us whenever he can. But, in the end, he can be easily dismissed, and people can go about their lives without ever really worrying about who he is or what he is up to.

Both of these extremes are patently false. As we have already discussed, Satan's power, ability, and knowledge are *not* on par with Christ's; he and Christ are *not* equals; the two are *not* both vying for control of the universe. Satan is *not* a divine being: he is a created being that has chosen to partake of the darkness rather than remain in God's marvelous light. On the other hand, he is a real personage and a real force to be reckoned with. He is scheming, highly deceptive, and malicious. He is a formidable adversary to Christians, and he most certainly is seeking their spiritual ruin (1 Peter 5:8).

Just as Satan has been so misunderstood and wrongly identified by so many people, so has Jesus Christ. Some see Jesus as an overly-muscular, Rambo-like, comic book-variety superhero, ready to go head-to-head with Satan in a cage fight at any moment. He takes on Satan much in the same way that Batman takes on the Joker or Lex Luthor. He has super powers, including a magical sword and a mythical army of angel-warriors. His scriptures, when uttered, also have magical properties. He (and the Holy Spirit—a kind of Robin to Jesus' alleged Batman persona) can be called down from heaven to fight our battles, perform miracles, and give us stuff.

The other extreme sees Jesus as an effeminate waif of a man who is incapable of an angry thought, raising His voice, or saying anything that would make anyone feel uncomfortable. He floats around our world, our church buildings, and our minds like a storybook fairy, cheering us on and telling us to "be strong" and "keep the faith" and "you can do *all things* through Me"—whatever *that* means. He gives His blessing to whatever "good deed" we come up with, because He doesn't want to discourage us with correction or discipline. Yet, we can easily dispense with Him by setting Him on a shelf like a household idol when we have everything under control, "Thank you very much." Even so, He is always ready and waiting to be called upon when we get ourselves in a pickle. When we need Him, we simply invoke His name like a magical spell and suddenly we feel a swelling of heavenly joy, peace, and supernatural presence. He is our favorite life-coach—never critical, always "understanding" because He just loves us *so much*.

Such portrayals of Christ, on either extreme, are not based on the Scriptures, but human imagination. In some cases, false religion (often posing as Christianity) has given us these warped and skewed versions of Him. Sadly, many people simply hear what others *say* about Jesus (or, they regard their self-determined conclusions about Him to be the gospel truth) and refuse to learn about Him from God's word. The same source material that tells us about God, our souls, and the afterlife, also tells us who Jesus is and why we need Him. Ignoring the source material (the NT gospel) leads us to a warped and inaccurate view of Christ. This is not only irresponsible on our part, but (if left unchecked) leads to the ruin of our souls.

The Supremacy of Christ

There is no contest between Jesus and Satan. Jesus is a divine being with full power, full authority, and full understanding over all that has been created. Satan is a fallen angel that has limited power, limited authority, and limited understanding. Jesus does not answer to Satan for anything, but Satan must ask permissions of Jesus (Mark 5:6–13, Luke 22:31).

Jesus, in His pre-earthly existence, created the entire universe (John 1:3, 1 Cor. 8:6, Col. 1:15–16, Heb. 1:2, etc.). At some point,

Jesus Himself created *Satan*—not the monster that Satan has become, but what he was before he gave himself over to the darkness. Satan, however, has created nothing: all he does is twist, malign, and imitate whatever Jesus has done (including what Jesus made him to be). God gave all authority to His Son, Jesus Christ (Mat. 28:18), but Satan's authority—whatever he does have—can be curtailed or overruled whenever God wants to do so (Rev. 20:1–3, in principle).

In the wilderness encounter between Jesus and Satan (Mat. 4:1–11), Satan tried to get Jesus to use His power for His own benefit rather than for God's glory. Satan even quoted from Scripture, but took it out of context. He tempted, tried to deceive, and boldly even told Jesus to bow down to him, but he was not in a position to tell Jesus to *do* anything.[114] If ever there was a time for Satan to show his alleged superiority over Jesus, it would have been on that occasion, and he failed to accomplish anything. Remember, too, that Jesus was in a very weakened state, having fasted for forty days, whereas Satan was in his prime. In the end, Jesus told Satan to "Go!"—and he did. He did the same thing with Satan's demons as He exorcised them: not one demon ever refused His authority (e.g., Luke 4:31–36). Satan never told Jesus to go away, and even if he did, Jesus would have simply ignored him.

Jesus called Satan "the ruler of this world" (John 12:31); Paul referred to him as "the god of this world" (2 Cor. 4:4); John called him "the evil one" in whose power the "whole world lies" (1 John 5:19). Certainly, Satan is a force to be reckoned with. And, yes, he does have a tenacious grip on "the world"—i.e., the realm of ungodly, unconverted, and carnal-minded people. But Jesus also says that "the ruler of this world will be cast out" (John 12:31); Paul says that "The God of peace will soon crush Satan under your feet" (Rom. 16:20); and John says that "The Son of God appeared for this purpose, to destroy the works of the devil" (1 John 3:8). In other words, Satan's power is not only limited in scope; it is also limited in time. Most importantly, it is limited *by Christ*—the One to whom Satan himself will answer in the end.

In the cosmic scene of the Final Judgment (Rev. 20:7–10), Satan is not merely told to "Go!" but he is permanently, humiliatingly, and catastrophically destroyed. While Christ's depiction of this (as revealed to the apostle John) *is* in a highly symbolic vision, it nonetheless conveys very real and important truths. After Satan has been "bound" for a long time—not rendered helpless, but limited from what he was able to do when Jesus came in the flesh—he will finally be released. At that time, he will try once again to overthrow God's people (the church on earth). This ambitious plan will utterly fail, just as every plan of his has always failed, and Satan will no longer be given opportunity to devise any future plans. Instead, he will be "thrown into the lake of fire and brimstone" to be "tormented day and night forever and ever." While the "lake of fire" is no more literal than the "chain" that bound Satan (Rev. 20:1–3), it describes a horrific scene of unspeakable suffering, and something that will never end and from which he will never escape.

All said, the idea that Satan has even a sliver of a chance of victory over Jesus is just another one of the lies he has fed to people. He has no chance of defeating Christ; he has never been victorious against Christ; he cannot escape the ultimate doom that Christ will bring upon him in the end. Paul calls Satan "the prince of the power of the air" (Eph. 2:2)—an ironic description, and very telling of his (Satan's) limitations. To be the ruler of the air is to have *no real power at all*, since "the air" is empty and cannot be grasped. Furthermore, Christ is the One who *created* "the air," so Satan only is a "prince" because Christ allows him to be one (for His own purposes). Yet, as we have seen, this "prince's" doom has already been spelled out: we know that his reign will end, and there is nothing he can do about it.

The Scene Behind the Curtain

In Rev. 12, we are given a visionary glimpse into the conflict between Satan and Christ. Christ showed the apostle John a behind-the-scenes look at the spiritual realm and how this affects the brotherhood of believers. In 12:1–2, John saw a "woman" who was "with child" and about to "give birth." This "woman" was the faithful remnant of Israel—those Jews who remained faithful to God despite all the great unfaithfulness of the rest of Israel. They honored God's law, believed in the prophecies of the coming Messiah, and kept alive the promises of God regarding the redemption of Israel. The "twelve stars" alludes to the twelve tribes of Israel; "the sun" alludes to the providential care by which God has protected her until this event (Rom. 11:1–7).

Immediately after seeing this, John saw "a great red dragon" that is described as having great power and authority (symbolized by heads, horns, and crowns) (Rev. 12:3–4). This is undoubtedly Satan, who made himself the great enemy of God's Son and who sought to destroy Him. The "stars" that the dragon "swept away" likely refer to the many angels that he convinced to follow him in his rebellion against God. These had been thrown "to the earth" to afflict (at least) the nation of Israel—no doubt a reference to the many demons that Jesus encountered during His earthly ministry. This dragon "stood before the woman" as she was ready to give birth, in order to destroy the Child who was undoubtedly Jesus Christ. This attempted destruction likely refers to Herod the Great's attempt to kill Jesus, as well as possible threats by his son, Archelaus, and possibly other unrecorded threats against Jesus (Mat. 2:16–23).

From the "woman" (the faithful remnant of Israel) came the Child of promise: the Messiah. His earthly life fulfilled the promises and prophecies of God which the remnant had kept alive for centuries, and He was born to be their King (Isa. 9:6–7, Luke 1:30–33, and John 18:37). Satan's attempts to destroy the Child had failed; his attempts to destroy Jesus on the cross also failed. The Child/Redeemer, however, never failed at anything. Having succeeded in all that He had come to earth to do (John 17:4–5), Jesus was "caught up to God and to His throne"—a clear reference to His ascension from the earth to receive "all authority" given to Him by God the Father (Mat. 28:18, Acts 1:9–11, 2:33, etc.).[115]

"When [Jesus] had made purification of sins, He sat down at the right hand of the Majesty on high" (Heb. 1:3). In other words, Jesus' sacrificial offering of Himself on the cross provides for the forgiveness of all those who call upon the name of the Lord for salvation (Acts 2:21). The implication is that Satan previously had stood before God to accuse all such people of being *unworthy* of redemption and *undeserving* of God's fellowship. But when Jesus Christ took His seat at the right hand of the Father, He purified these people's souls through His own blood and therefore "made them to be a kingdom and priests" to God (Rev. 5:9). Now that Christ rules over all things, there is no longer any basis for Satan's accusations for those who belong to Christ (Rom. 8:33–34). The awful weight of guilt and the terrifying fear of judgment that Satan held over every sinner's head is removed by Christ's blood (Heb. 2:14–15). He interceded for the transgressors and delivered them from condemnation by absorbing *in Himself* the penalty for sin (Isa. 53:12, 1 Peter 2:24–25).[116]

Having set the stage for what happened between Satan ("the dragon") and Christ ("the Child"), we are then told what happened to Satan after this. "And there was war in heaven, Michael and his angels waging war with the dragon. The dragon and his angels waged war, and they were not strong enough, and there was no longer a place found for them in heaven" (Rev. 12:7–8). Christ's ascension to the right hand of God evaporated all of Satan's vicious accusations against God's people. Seeing how he had failed (over and over again), Satan chose to assert himself through a battle in heaven. The details of this battle are withheld from us, and we probably would not understand them anyway (given the spiritual context in which all this took place). The battle is not against Christ Himself—He is too powerful to be conquered or destroyed—but is between Satan's angels and the angels of heaven. Michael is one of God's powerful archangels that had battled against wicked adversaries before.[117] It appears that Michael and the heavenly angels initiate this battle when they were instructed to prevent Satan and his angels from having further access to God's throne. Satan and his angels put up a fight, but their resistance was useless and hopeless, as "they were not strong enough" to contend with the heavenly army.

"[A]nd there was no longer a place found for them in heaven" (Rev. 12:8). This does *not* mean that Satan was entirely removed from the spiritual realm, since he is a spiritual being that operates in a dimension invisible to the human eye. However, it does mean that Satan has forever lost his once-privileged place to stand before God and rail against His people and all their deficiencies. God will not hear his ranting anymore; Christ's ascension has removed any validity to his complaints. It seems—although we cannot know for certain—that this has been the core conflict between Satan and God all along: God created human beings who, because they (and *not Satan*) were created "in His image," would one day be placed *above Satan*. Satan's proud, jealous, and defiant response to this was: "Unfair! Unfair! *Unfair!*" And, if it had not been for the redemption offered to us through Christ's blood, Satan's accusations would have been *true*. But now, the fairness (or, justice for sin) has been achieved through Christ's supreme sacrifice on the cross. Now, it is unnecessary for *Satan's accusations* to be endured any longer.

The Choice That Must Be Made

I realize there is a lot of detail in the preceding explanation. Yet, the information covered is all contained in Scripture and is meant for us to know and take to heart. The idea that Jesus and Satan are equal powers vying for supremacy and control is blasphemous to what the Bible actually teaches. Jesus did not make Himself an enemy of Satan; rather, Satan made himself an enemy of God by turning aside from Him to go to his own place, so to speak—the same words that Peter said concerning Judas, Jesus' betrayer (Acts 1:25). And, having made himself an enemy *of* God, he will ultimately be destroyed *by* God. Satan literally does not have any chance to escape his future doom.

Jesus Christ is in full and absolute control. Satan is a created being, but Christ is the Son of God—a divine Personage who was never created but has always existed (John 1:1–2, 8:58). Satan chose to fill his heart with the darkness, but Christ is filled with God's Light and is Himself the Light of the world (John 8:12). Christ has been given "all authority...in heaven and on earth" (Mat. 28:18), but Satan only has limited and temporary authority to oversee a perverse kingdom that is doomed to fail. Christ is the Creator of all that exists, whether in the physical realm or the spiritual realm, "whether thrones or dominions or rulers or authorities—all things have been created through Him and for Him" (Col. 1:16). This means that Satan and his domain of darkness, while seemingly having the upper hand in the world today, actually must submit to Christ. Satan cannot do anything that Christ does not *allow* him to do.

This last point begs some difficult (and, for many Christians, *uncomfortable*) questions. For example, upon His ascension to the right hand of God, why did Christ not just destroy Satan then and there? Why instead was Satan cast out of heaven and thrown down to the earth? On the surface, it might appear that Christ got rid of *His* problem by throwing it into *our* laps. But this kind of thinking misrepresents all that we know about Christ, God's "eternal purpose" (Eph. 3:11), and the *need* for Satan (or, a satan/adversary) in the first place.

In allowing Satan to continue to exist, and to reign within a domain of darkness, Christ gives the world a decision to make. While He is the "Light of the world," this Light must be *chosen* in order to mean anything to the one who receives Him. Likewise, the darkness in which Satan operates also must be chosen—and a deliberate rejection of the Light is an active choice for the darkness. Jesus spoke of this while He was here on earth (John 3:18–21):

> He who believes in Him is not judged; he who does not believe has been judged already, because he has not believed in the name of the only begotten Son of God. This is the judgment, that the Light has come into the world, and men loved the darkness rather than the Light, for their deeds were evil. For everyone who does evil hates the Light, and does not come to the Light for fear that his deeds will be exposed. But he who practices the truth comes to the Light, so that his deeds may be manifested as having been wrought in God.

The human experience—what it means to live in this earthly context—is all about choices. People do not accidentally become Christ-followers ("Christians"); they *choose* this. Likewise, people do not accidentally follow Satan; they *choose* this when they give themselves over to the same power of darkness to which he gave *himself*. No one inexplicably finds himself in heaven any more than one accidentally ends up in hell. Christ provides the opportunity for each person to choose his own future, but He does not make the choice Himself.[118]

Satan, as powerful as he seems to be—and as powerful as he thinks he is in his own inflated ego—cannot make you do anything. He cannot force you to be evil, and he cannot keep you from pursuing good. He cannot make you sin, and he cannot keep you from following the Light. If your soul is lost, it will do no good to blame

Satan for your demise, since it was *you* who made the decision to follow him rather than to give your allegiance to Christ.

Of course, no one likes to hear this kind of talk today. People want to hear that they will *all* be "saved" simply because God loves them. Or, it is not their *fault* that their lives are filled with debilitating or self-destructive habits. Or, they just cannot *resist* the temptation to do evil, because, well, "The devil made me do it." The truth is—and this is *God's* truth, not mine—the devil cannot *make* you do anything. If you "do" evil, it is because you *chose* to do it. Granted, there may have been a great deal of persuasive factors in your life that pressured you to make that particular decision (bad influences, peer pressure, godless environment, misleading information, etc.), but ultimately it is you who made the final decision.

The same is true concerning the Light. "If anyone wishes to come after Me," Jesus said, "he must deny himself, and take up his cross and follow Me" (Mat. 16:24). No one will deny himself for Christ, sacrifice his life for Christ, or follow Christ who does not first *desire* to "come after" Him and thus *choose* to do these things. Just as no one can force you to sin, so no one can force you to "come after" Christ and seek righteousness. Never mind the millions of people who have been pressured by friends and family to go to church, be baptized, and comply with a Christian code of conduct. Coercion, intimidation, and peer pressuring are not acceptable ways to "come after" Christ. Such people have been converted to churchgoing, not to Christ. No one is saved through churchgoing, but only through *Christ-following*. Jesus is clear: "if *anyone*" makes this an individual and personal decision, not a family one, a group one, or a forced one.

Thus, while Christ is unquestionably the most powerful Being that exists (outside of God the Father), He does not force you to love Him, obey Him, or follow Him.[119] In fact, He gives you, me, and every person on the planet an opportunity to seek Him, pursue Him, and discover Him. While the world is indeed filled with darkness and "lies in the power of the evil one" (1 John 5:19), it is still not hard to find the great and irrepressible Light of the world in the midst of all this darkness. He remains "the true Light which, coming into the world, enlightens every man" that is searching *for* the Light (John 1:9). In other words, if someone really wants to discover the truth—not *their* "truth," nor someone else's, but *God's*—then Christ will make sure that they find it. How they respond to that truth once they learn it is up to them, but God will not hide the truth from anyone who seeks it.

What all this means is: while there was war in heaven—Michael and his fellow heavenly angels versus Satan and his demonic angels—there is also a war going on within every person. This war is not over whether to go to church, or whether to indulge in alcohol or pornography. It is much deeper—much more *involved*—than these things. Rather, it is a war over who will receive your love, your allegiance, and your dominant attention from this point forward. Just because God "has made [Jesus] both Lord and Christ" (Acts 2:33) does not mean you will choose Him to be *your* Lord or *your* Christ. If you listen to your heart—something the world is always telling you to do—and follow the impulse of your own human desires, this will lead you to follow Satan, not Christ (James 1:13–16). Christ never tells you to listen to your heart; He tells you to listen to *Him*.

This ongoing struggle—to listen to your heart or listen to Christ—continues throughout the life of every person who has not fully given himself over to the darkness. The Bible does talk about those who have so completely surrendered to the darkness that they are no longer interested in "the truth," God's grace, or even God's love. Such people have so adamantly—and so consistently—rejected "the truth" that now they believe Satan's lies to be true, and God's truth sounds like lies to them (2 Thess. 2:10–12). I don't know who these people are by name, and I could not pick them out of a crowd, but the word of God clearly says that such people do exist.

But for the rest of us, the battle continues aggressively, bloodily, *relentlessly*. Peter warns us to avoid the "fleshly lusts which wage war against the soul" (1 Peter 2:11). When we pursue these lusts, we give life—and strength—to them, and this creates a conflict within our soul. When Michael and the angels of heaven went to war against Satan and his wicked angels, you can be sure that no one in the Lord's army gave any sympathetic attention to the demons. Instead, they sought to cast them out of their sight. This is similar to what Jesus said about anything that tempts you: cut it out of your life and *cast it away from you* (Mat. 5:29–30). Whatever is a "stumbling block" to you is poison to your soul: you do not *need* it and must not *desire* it.

The problem is: even when we give our allegiance to the Light, there remains within us the residual darkness from when we were still enemies of God. This darkness does not just evaporate upon our conversion to Christ. Our baptism signified a change of allegiance—Christ is now our Lord, not sin—but whatever opposes Christ *within us* still needs to be dealt with (Rom. 6:3–11). This is why, soon after talking about how Christians are "dead to sin, but alive to God in Christ Jesus," Paul says we need to be "putting to death the deeds of the body" (Rom. 8:12–13).

In an analogy to what has just been said, just because you are made a king over a certain domain does not mean everyone in that domain suddenly or automatically submits to you. There will always be those who refuse to recognize your kingship, who become your enemies (see Luke 19:11–14, for example). Similarly, even though Christ has been exalted to the right hand of God, there remains within the realm of His authority many demons and unbelievers that remain defiant to that authority. Just as God is in the process of putting an end to all those who resist His Son, so you must put an end to the deeds of darkness (Gal. 5:19–21) that wage war against your allegiance to Christ. You are not only fighting to purify your own soul, but also to defend your loyalty to your new King.

The war in heaven has long since been over, but the war in our souls continues on throughout the course of our earthly existence. I'm speaking specifically to Christians, not to unbelievers. Those who have not yet named Christ as their Lord may wrestle with moral dilemmas from time to time, but they still remain under the control of the darkness. Even Christians have not yet "overcome" (Rev. 2:7, 11, 17, etc.) because the possibility of falling from grace still remains (Gal. 5:4). If it did not, there would not be numerous warnings in the NT to be strong in the Lord, stand firm in the strength of His might, put on the full armor of God, do not be overcome by evil, and many others. The fact that this possibility still exists is unnerving, and ought to compel us to be very serious about remaining loyal to our Lord. We are "saved" in promise, but we are not yet in heaven, and we have not yet literally and absolutely escaped hell.

Summary Thoughts

Many people—including some Christians—either give Satan way too much or way too little credit. We should never respect what Satan *is*—a liar, a schemer, and a monster unlike anything we have seen on earth. On the other hand, we should respect what he can *do*—his lies, deceptions, and manipulations can be extremely persuasive and effective to those who are not paying full attention.

Similarly, many people—including some Christians—have a warped and very unbiblical view of Jesus Christ. He is not a muscle-bound superhero who operates in a Hollywood-style world of amazing cinematography and dramatic effects. He is also not an effeminate, pale-skinned, and nearly helpless waif who speaks softly and tries not to upset anyone. He is *powerful* and *commanding*—the depiction of Him as a warrior-king riding on a white hose and carrying a sword in Rev. 19:11–16 is both impressive and a bit terrifying. Yet, He is also gentle and compassionate toward those who need gentleness and mercy, as He is to those who seek "help in time of need" at His throne (Heb. 4:14–16). However, it is easy to mischaracterize Him if we allow our human imagination (or Hollywood, popular culture, or tradition) to describe Him rather than appealing to the word of God.

All myths and fanciful depictions aside, Satan and Christ are not in a constant cosmic battle for control. In reality, the battle *in heaven* has already been fought, and Satan was decisively overwhelmed, defeated, and humiliated. The battle *on earth*—and the battle that wages in the heart of every person who has pledged loyalty to the Light and denounced the darkness—does continue, but it is not Satan versus Christ. Instead, it is every believer *in* Christ putting on the "full armor of God" (Eph. 6:11–18) and engaging the enemy every day in the world, in the church, and even within himself. The world is filled with satanic enemies, impostor Christians, and hypocrites of every kind. Yet, Christ is more powerful than them all, if we trust in *Him* and the strength of *His* might rather than our own.

Part Four: Preparing for the Afterlife
Chapter Fourteen: The Problem of Your Evil

For my 16-year-old son's first car, I wanted something old and classy—on a budget, of course. I found him a 1972 Chevy Nova two-door sedan, in which someone had taken out the straight-six engine and dropped in a 316-cubic inch V8, to which we added a few other improvements. The engine was built for racing, so it sounded like it had attitude (a good thing!), and it could get up and *go!*

When it ran, that is. Besides numerous smaller issues, the engine would inexplicably—and always inconveniently—die. In most cases, we could not get it started again. I would get phone calls from my son on his way to school: "Hey Dad, I'm stuck on [insert: busy road], and the car died again." Together with a friend, my son and I went over all kinds of possible scenarios as to what would cause this to happen. We replaced key parts; we did all kinds of diagnostic tests; we spent a great deal of time and money. One day when the engine had died not far from my house, my friend and I stood there with the hood up (again), peering bewilderedly at the engine. Suddenly, my friend said, "I think I found the problem." The cold-start wire from the ignition coil that went to the starter solenoid had somehow come undone and was hanging loose. This meant that, when it brushed against the engine block (on any random turn of the car), it would short the ignition—effectively stalling the engine on the spot. I don't know how we had missed that before, but we hooked it back up and…problem solved.

In a similar way, sometimes we know there is a debilitating problem with our lives, but we may spend a lot of time and energy fixing all the wrong things. Maybe we don't know what to look for. Maybe we are distracted with other, lesser problems that do need to be addressed but are not nearly as serious. The biggest problem may go undetected—for months, years, even decades—until someone comes along who knows what to look for and how to fix it. And, while non-Christians are often unwilling to admit this, the biggest problem is not marital, familial, economical, or political. Instead, it is *spiritual*. And, while the world certainly creates a number of problems for us all, the most important spiritual problem you should be concerned about is *your own*. That is, your spiritual problem is your number one, most important, and most debilitating problem of all. Furthermore, this spiritual problem is not merely related to the darkness that we have been examining. Rather, it *is* the darkness.

What Is Your Problem?

If people were to write down, say, the top three or four problems in their lives, it is unlikely that spiritual problems would even be on their list. They would likely cite financial difficulties, marital problems, health and/or weight issues, or simply "I'm unhappy." Of course, these are all legitimate problems for many people. But these are not the biggest problems in anyone's life.

Many people talk about "the problem of evil" in the world, but not everyone sees their personal connection to this problem. Evil—or simply, *sin*—is not just a problem in "the world," but it is the biggest problem in every *person* in the world. The world is unquestionably a sinful place to live, but one's *own* sin is a much bigger problem than that, simply because of how it affects him personally. The troubles we face on an everyday basis—or even life's big tragedies—will all disappear when we leave this world. But if we have not taken care of the sins we have committed in this life, they will be the cause of our ruin in the life to come.

But most people do not think this way. Many think that spiritual problems are lesser, not greater, than their earthly circumstances. Because of this, spiritual problems can be dealt with at a later time (so they reason). In all honesty, trying to get someone to think about his eternal soul when that person is deeply in debt or facing a health crisis can be a hard sell. After all, dealing with sins does not put money in one's bank account, put gas in his car, or remove his need for surgery. So, that's a fair point. It also misses the most *important* point completely.

To illustrate, imagine someone going deep into the woods for a nice long hike. It's a gorgeous day, he is surrounded by natural beauty, and he is in prime health. Now imagine that during the course of his hike, he accidently scrapes alongside some poison ivy, causing a terrible rash on his legs. Then, a stray arrow of an out-of-view hunter glances his femoral artery, but the arrow is so sharp that he barely feels anything. Then, on top of this, he runs into a mosquito swarm and is bitten all over. And, if this were not enough, suddenly the weather changes and he finds himself in the midst of an awful storm.

Now suppose you had opportunity to enter this scene and ask the hiker what his greatest problem is. And suppose he said, "Are you kidding? This poison ivy thing is *painful!*" And then he goes on to complain about the mosquitos and driving rain. Meanwhile, you are paying attention to the all the blood spurting out of the wound in his thigh. Clearly, this is his most serious and immediate problem, but he seems oblivious to it. Or, he thinks that it is something to address at a later time. Yet, if he does not do something urgently, he will bleed out and soon be dead. The other problems that he chose to focus on instead will not kill him, even though he gave *them* his full attention.

So it is with most people. They focus on the wrong problem(s) even though they are, for all intents and purposes, bleeding out (spiritually). They feel the pain of their seeming "pressing" problems of the moment (or year), but miss the most debilitating problem of all: the condition of their soul. They focus on relationship troubles, bad behaviors, house payments, job stress, or maybe the latest health scare, but they neglect the one thing that, in the end, will have the greatest and most catastrophic effect on their existence. These people are dead even while they live (Eph. 2:1–3), but they don't *feel* dead, so they ignore the true state of their situation.

What is *your* problem? For your own soul's sake, be honest and realistic. Just because your spiritual condition "feels" well does not necessarily mean it *is* well. God deals with facts, not your (or my) feelings. Just because you may have learned to cope with sinful behavior does not make it no longer sinful. Just because you may have justified being irresponsible with your time, your marriage, your health, or your life does not mean that everything will somehow work out fine in the end. Just because people have done you wrong or life has been unkind to you does not mean your moral responsibility to God simply evaporates into thin air—God does not buy into victimization claims. Just because you may have learned to manage an addiction on your own terms does not mean you are conforming to the image of Christ or surrendering to His will. Just because you "don't have a problem in the world" does not mean God has no problem with you.

Where are you at with all of this? Are you dwelling on the relatively insignificant pain of poison ivy when in fact your soul is bleeding out? Or, have you taken care of your most serious problem *first*? Even if you want to address this latter problem, the nature of it is so difficult, so great in scope, and so beyond your ability to resolve it that neither I nor any human on earth can help you. What you need—what *all* of us need—is none other than the Great Physician (Jesus Christ) to take care of it.

Sin Is a Choice, Not Something that Just "Happens" to You
Sin is a direct violation of either God's law or one's own conscience. Anyone can violate God's law, and such violation incurs divine wrath; if there was no law, then there would be no charge of sin (Rom. 4:15). Only *you* can violate your own conscience, however; no one else can do this for you. Your conscience serves as a "law" unto yourself, to the degree that it declares your intuitive sense of right and wrong (Rom. 2:12–16). Whatever is not in agreement with one's conscience (or, "is not from faith"—Rom. 14:23) is a sin *against* his conscience—in effect, a sin against the righteous standard that God instilled within us. Just as we can *know* that there is a God through the evidences He has provided in "what has been made" (Rom. 1:18–20), so we can know what is right and wrong through the moral compass that God has given to all people. Just as we are "without excuse" to deny God's existence, so we are without excuse to assume there is no absolute standard of righteousness or to deny that any violation of it is *wrong* (sin).

Many people have been taught that sin is not a choice but is something into which we are born. Such thinking is popular but not biblical.[120] Sin is a choice, not our default "nature," not an accident, not a birth defect, and not a genetic disposition. Paul told the Ephesian Christians, "And *you* were dead in *your* trespasses and sins, in which *you* formerly walked according to the course of this world, according to the prince of the power of the air, of the spirit that is now working in the sons of disobedience" (Eph. 2:1–2, emphases added). Notice the personal responsibility: *you* did this; these are *your* trespasses (not Adam's or anyone else's); *you* walked according to the world; etc. As it was for them, so it is for you and me. Whenever we sin against God, we are legally, personally, and morally responsible for what *we* have done.

Just as we can choose to be obedient and faithful to God, so we can choose to be lawless and wicked. God does not *make* us one way or the other (any more than He *made* Satan a fallen angel), but we choose our own path. When we choose to give life to the wicked lusts of our own heart, then sin is "born." Whatever God creates is good and perfect; whatever we create through our rebellion to God is demonic, evil, and unholy (James 1:13–16). Once sin is committed, death follows, "For the wages of sin is death…" (Rom. 6:23). "Death" in this context is *spiritual* in nature, not physical. Initially, it is a death *sentence*—a pronouncement of condemnation like what is made to a convicted murderer by a court of law. While Satan wants you to believe that *he* has the power to destroy you, it is in fact *God* who does the destroying. Remember that even Satan himself will be destroyed by God because of his own sin against Him.

Sin is not a minor indiscretion, momentary lapse of judgment, harmless mistake, or figment of your imagination. It is an objective reality, which means that once it has been committed (or, brought into existence through a decisive act), it *will not go away* unless it is removed through the justice that God requires for it. Since sin is a spiritual problem, it can only be remedied by a spiritual solution. Since it is a human problem, animal sacrifices (or anything less than, in essence, a *human* sacrifice) cannot fix it (Heb. 10:4).

Sin is not a mere religious concept; we cannot deal with it conceptually.[121] It is not an emotional state of being; we cannot deal with it subjectively. It does not matter what you feel about your sin, or whether you feel anything at all. If you have committed sin, then it *does exist*, and it will lead to your spiritual ruin unless you avail yourself of God's solution. "If we say that we have no sin, we are deceiving ourselves and the truth is not in us" (1 John 1:8). Once we have sinned, we are no longer law-*keepers* but law-*breakers*. It does not matter whether we have broken one law or a million—the consequence (spiritual death) is the same.[122] Once we have broken *a* law, we have broken *the* law. This is not a semantics game, but an undeniable teaching of Scripture (James 2:10–11).

Many people seem to think that sin is a problem only if we believe in God, want to be religious (or pious), are plagued with guilt, or want to ease our conscience. Otherwise, it is assumed, sin is not real and/or does not matter. We can just live our life without worrying about sin or guilt, and just learn to be happy and content on our own terms. When such people die, however, they will be immediately and frighteningly confronted with the fact that God is real, their soul is real, the afterlife is real, and their *sin* is real. Sadly, that is an awful time to come to terms with reality since there is nothing one can do to address his spiritual problem once he has left his earthly life. Self-delusion is an irresponsible and pathetic way to leave this world.

Your sin is your number one, most important, and biggest problem. Your sin—not the world's or someone else's, but *yours*—is what will separate you from fellowship with God. Your sin—not the world's or someone else's—is what will cause your soul to be lost forever in the "outer darkness" if you ignore it or deal with it inadequately. There is no other problem in this world—no matter how big you think it to be—that can have this effect on you and your spiritual future.

God's condemnation is what you incur when you sin, not merely His displeasure. God's forgiveness is what you need, not therapy, sermons, or religion. Those who leave this life unforgiven will face God's dreadful, horrifying, soul-destroying *wrath*, not a stern lecture and then a full pardon (John 3:36, Rom. 1:18, 2:5–8, 4:15, 5:9, Eph. 5:6, etc.). A seemingly harmless fling with the darkness will cost you your entire future existence, if not for the forgiveness that Christ offers through His gospel. Your sin—*every* sin, not just the one(s) you might be thinking about right now—is an enormous, insurmountable, unfixable problem, left to yourself. Your sin is not just "a" problem; it is not just "problematic"; it is the *only* problem that can lead to the destruction of your soul. Car problems, house problems, job problems, relationship struggles, health issues, and even earthly tragedies are not your biggest concern. Your biggest concern, as God sees it, is the evil in your heart.

Positive thinking and religion cannot take away sins; feeling "spiritual" is not the same as being forgiven. It took a blood sacrifice of the highest order—an innocent heart, a perfect human specimen, and (at the same time) a *divine Personage*—to remove the evil with which you corrupted your soul. In other words, it does not take a church service, a heartfelt prayer, or tears of remorse to remove sin, but a literal *act of God*. And, it continues to take an act of God to remove any sin you might have right now or that you will commit in the future. The darkness in your soul is too powerful for you to remove by any human effort.

Christians Who Live in Delusion

You might be thinking, "I took care of this 'sin' problem when I became a Christian." If Christians should no longer have any problem with sin, then why are there so many warnings in the NT *to* Christians about staying faithful, persevering, enduring, and "[abstaining] from every form of evil" (1 Thess. 5:22)? Why are we instructed to be constantly "[putting] to death the deeds of the body" (Rom. 8:13) if indeed we already did this upon our conversion? If there is no battle, why does Paul urge you to "take up the full armor of God" and stand firm "against the world forces of this darkness" (Eph. 6:11–12)?

Far from being finished with dealing with the darkness, I propose a far different scenario: we who are Christians will spend the rest of our lives confronting, combating, and striving to overcome the darkness that tenaciously seeks a place in our own heart. I will go a step further: when you were not a Christian, there was little confrontation between you and the darkness because you were already immersed in it. Now that you have become a Christian—if indeed that is even the case—you have changed your allegiance from sin's mastery over you to Christ's mastery. In essence, you did not just choose to leave the darkness behind, you openly condemned it. And the darkness is now coming after you with an awful vengeance because you dared to leave it and it wants you back.

Christians often fail to see things this way. We think our biggest problems are marital spats, an occasional friction between fellow church members, uninspiring sermons, or maybe a few bad habits we are trying (not always very hard) to overcome. We are often unaware that the real problem—the real *battle* for our souls—is taking place in our hearts, not in our home or a church building. We think that the darkness is not something that can affect us or harm us, since, after all, we *are* Christians. We are often oblivious of the fact that *all* friction between spouses, church members, and everyone else is *not* merely a difference of opinions, seeing things differently, or a harmless disagreement. Rather, it is the darkness attempting to compromise our faith, inflate our pride, or poison our heart. A bad heart is one in which the darkness has gained control and established a base camp, so to speak. A good and faithful heart is one in which Christ reigns as Lord and Savior, and thus *everything* that person does is dictated by His will, His love, and His gospel. "Do not be deceived," we are warned over and over in Scripture. Do not think your problem is one thing when in fact it is really something else.

The world is filled with sin—we have already established this—and "the whole world lies in the power of the evil one" (1 John 5:19). But just because you may have become a Christian does not mean the "whole world" no longer has any effect on you, no longer has an attraction *for* you, or that you no longer have any affinity for *it*. Just because you dealt with sin once, or twice, or a couple of thousand times, does not mean that the power of the darkness finally gives up, walks away, and leaves you alone forever. Whenever we talk about "sin," we are talking about the power of the darkness. And whenever we (or you) talk about *your* sin, we are talking about *you* having dabbled in that darkness, looking for something that (you think) God cannot provide for you. Or, maybe you were looking for something *more* than what God offers you, and the darkness smilingly beckons, "Come, find it here."

It is true that the world is filled with darkness, and it is also true that you must live in a constant state of *resisting* that darkness because "sin is crouching at the door; and its desire is for you, but you must master it" (Gen. 4:7). You will not escape the influence of sin—it is everywhere. You will not be free from temptation *to* sin—it is ever-present. You will not escape the followers of sin, the harm that sin causes among people, or the consequences of sin in the world—you will have to *leave* the world to do this. Sin is the darkness, and the darkness is powerful, pervasive, insidious, and *relentless*. If you stamp it out in one area of your life, it will raise its ugly head in another. It is always seeking "an opportune time" to trip you up and then devour you (Luke 4:13).

Christians tend to overgeneralize this subject. We say things like, "sin is a problem," but we do not always say, "sin is *my* problem." We talk about "the problem of evil," but we seldom discuss the problem of *our* evil—as though "evil" was something that happened only to non-Christians or, at least, *other* Christians. We scoff at how ignorant or naïve or oblivious the world is toward the activity of Satan, but we may not admit when Satan is having a field day with us. We need to stop this diversion of attention *away* from ourselves and start focusing *on* ourselves. We need to stop talking about "the world" and first of all deal with *our* world—the only one *we* have control over, the one we sometimes invite the darkness into, the one we corrupt through our decision to give life to the carnal desires of our heart.

Summary Thoughts

What, exactly, is your problem? It is not me (although you may not be too happy *with* me right now): it is *your sin*. Sin, if it is present, is always "the problem." All other problems of life are temporary in nature, outside of your control, or just plain insignificant in comparison. Sin, however, will erode your integrity, compromise your conscience, and rot away your soul. You can leave this world having not resolved all other problems, but if you leave this world without having taken care of your sins, you "have no hope" in the world to come (1 Thess. 4:13). That is a blunt statement, I realize, but it is better that you hear it now than in the hereafter. And, the only time you have to *deal* with this problem is in the here-and-now, not in the hereafter.

Remember the illustration with my son's 1972 Nova? We tried to fix a number of problems that either were *not* real problems or not the *biggest* problem. The big problem did not go away just because we took care of a bunch of little ones (or phantom ones). People do this all the time: they focus on all the distractions on the periphery while ignoring or being oblivious to the soul-threatening issue in the center of everything. We tend to focus on mosquito bites and stubbed toes rather than the fact that we are bleeding out from a ferocious predator's lethal attack. If your soul is not right with God, then ignoring this will only make things worse, not better.

On the other hand, if your soul *is* right with God, then no number of earthly troubles, trials, or tragedies can overcome you, as long as you remain faithful to Him. God cannot force you to *be* faithful, but He can transform your heart (if you let Him) to increase your faithfulness. Even trials of faith, when responded to properly, will give you endurance and spiritual maturity, "so that you may be perfect and complete, lacking in nothing" (James 1:4). "With God all things are possible" (Mat. 19:26)—this does not mean all things are easy, are easy to understand, or that all your troubles just melt away when you turn to Him. It means, in essence, that no matter what you face in this life, your soul rests in God's hands. And in God's hands is an excellent place to be.

Chapter Fifteen: Christ Can Overcome Your World (If You Let Him)

Coming to terms with the seriousness of our "problem"—our own sinful condition—is not easy. In fact, it is one of the more difficult things we will ever do. It is not so hard to admit that we *have* this problem. However, it is very hard to do what is necessary to *resolve* it. And what is necessary to resolve it requires a commitment on your part that continues to grow over time rather than fade and diminish.

Dealing with sin is a lifelong process, not a one-time conversion event. This does not mean that we are to intentionally drag out our "dealing with sin" *for* the rest of our lives. It means that no matter how well you deal with it now, you will have to deal with it again—and again, and again, and again, *ad infinitum*. People tend to focus on the event of their conversion, baptism, and initial celebration rather than digging in for the long haul. Yet, our human lusts do not simply disappear upon our conversion; in some respect, they are intensified because we are now, for the first time, denying them. These lusts (and the human pride that drives them) do not take kindly to being denied. In other cases, it is not carnal lusts that are the problem, but indifference, apathy, and laziness. The lack of motivation to follow Christ is just as debilitating as serving one's base human appetite.

In many cases—I speak from decades of observation as well as my own personal experience—we tend to leave Christ out of the picture. We deal with sin, but we do so on our own terms, and often professionally or clinically rather than "in spirit and truth" (John 4:24). Or, we sideline Christ to a subordinate role, like that of a cheerleader, life coach, or motivational guru. We may work on the business of religion, the mechanics of church services, or tackling our own bad habits—all good things, in themselves—but without allowing Christ to fill our hearts and draw us closer to the Father.

Christ is not calling us—you, me, or anyone—to a lifetime of church services, sermons, and potlucks. He is also not only calling us *out* of the darkness but also *into* the Light: we are not only saved *from* our sins, but we are also saved *for* fellowship with God through Him. In coming into Christ—i.e., establishing a covenant relationship with the Father through the mediation of His Son—we are *born of*

God rather than born of this world (John 1:12–13). In doing so, God "has qualified us to share in the inheritance of the saints in Light. For He rescued us from the domain of darkness, and transferred us to the kingdom of His beloved Son, in whom we have redemption, the forgiveness of sins" (Col. 1:12–14). Your deliverance out of the world and into fellowship with God is, as far as you are concerned, the most important rescue mission in all of history. This is how God *wants* you to see it.

Remarkable as this is, the work is not over. You must never give up, "For you have need of endurance, so that when you have done the will of God, you may receive what was promised" (Heb. 10:36). There will still be sin to deal with, and some sins are far more difficult—more insidious, ingrained, and tenacious—than others. Such sins need to be identified, confronted, and then removed. While you are responsible for getting these actions accomplished, you are *not* able to carry them out on your own. If you were, then you would not need Christ, His grace, or any divine help. Instead of taking on the enemy on your own—something every Christian (myself included) has done at one time or another—you must seek the constant help of One who is more powerful than what ails you: Jesus Christ. He is not only the Savior of the world, He must be made the Savior of *your* world—not only of your earthly life, but your spiritual existence.

But we have gotten ahead of ourselves. The best way to know what has been just been covered is to take a bird's-eye approach to the subject. From there, you will know what is required of you, as well as all that Christ will do for you. Both parties—you and Christ—have great responsibility, but be sure that His is immensely greater than anything He asks of you.

Victory in Jesus

The apostle Paul wrote, "The sting of death is sin, and the power of sin is the law" (1 Cor. 15:56). This "sting" is not a mere hiccup in your schedule or an inconvenience to your normal routine; it precipitates your spiritual ruin. When you sin against God, you are condemned *by* Him. This is just as true for Christians as it is for unbelievers. In a real sense, your defiance of your Creator renders you damaged goods. The "power of sin" is in the violation of God's law. His law (or word) defines what sin is and condemns those who commit it. Once you sin, you are no longer a law-keeper but a law-breaker. You are no longer innocent but guilty before the highest authority in the universe. Thankfully, God not only exposes the problem, He also provides the solution (1 Cor. 15:57). Your "victory" is not in what you do for God, but what Christ the Savior does for you.

"With people [salvation] is impossible, but with God all things are possible" (Mat. 19:26). When you give "all things" over to God, then salvation is not only "possible" (as a potential solution) but will be yours (for real). If you wish to solve your own problems in your own way, then salvation will be impossible for you. Or, if you wish to solve your own problems in your own way and are convinced (wrongly) that God approves of this, the darkness has a firm grip on your heart and is deceiving you. I know it sounds like I am only speaking to those who are not Christians, but in fact this applies to *all* people—Christians or not. Having become a Christian does not make you immune to being deceived by the darkness.

If "all things are possible" *with* God, this means that *without* Him no amount of human effort, ingenuity, or even procrastination will save us from our sins. Jesus' statement also means that something has to be done, something needs to change, and (thus) something needs to be given up. What needs to be given up is not merely your time, your old habits, or your addiction(s), but your *proud resistance of God's grace*, if indeed you stand outside of that grace. Human pride allies itself with the darkness, never with God, and finds in the darkness a favorable environment and plenty of like-minded company.

The key to God's salvation is the mediatory work of His Son, Jesus Christ. Jesus gave up *His* world in order to come to *our* world. He did this in order to provide a ransom (or, payment) for our sins—mine, yours, and everyone's. This ransom was not in the form of money, but was His actual life, as manifested through His blood sacrifice. In providing such a priceless ransom (1 Peter 1:18–19), He has no interest in preserving the life that *you* have created apart from Him. Through Him, you are capable of far *greater* than what you have come to know. While your pride (in whatever form) can sabotage everything, the offer still remains. Perhaps you have already surrendered to His will and are enjoying the fellowship of His grace—an excellent choice! Or, perhaps you have tried to marry your world with the one He has planned for you—a choice that is guaranteed to fail.

If you really wish to be with God in the afterlife, you must listen to His Son *now*. He knows what He is talking about, and He is more than capable of guiding you to His Father.

Do you believe this?

"I Have Overcome the World"

On the final night of His life on earth, Jesus gave many encouraging words to His disciples. Near the end of this discourse, He said, "These things I have spoken to you, so that in Me you may have peace. In the world you have tribulation, but take courage; I have overcome the world" (John 16:33). This is a strange thing to say for someone who is about to be arrested, brutally whipped, and then humiliatingly executed in front of the entire world. Given this, how can—or, why should—anyone put stock in such a statement? It would seem that, if anything, the world is about to overcome *Him*.

One of the great paradoxes of the gospel is this: *things are not always as they seem*. Jesus would allow Himself to be *portrayed* as a sinner deserving to be executed. He would allow wicked men to *appear* to be victorious over Him. It *seemed* at first that He had failed, the manipulative Jewish leaders had indeed won, and Satan had gained the upper hand. Yet, nothing could be further from the truth.

When He said these words to His disciples, Jesus was about to take on Satan, death, and the darkness head on. He could not have overcome the world unless He first allowed Himself to be *confronted* with all of its menacing power and ungodly horror. He had to "taste death for everyone" (Heb. 2:9) as a sublime representative of all humankind. This means much more than Him simply *dying*, since all people eventually die. It means that He died in order to demonstrate that *His* power was infinitely greater than the *world's* power. The only way to do this was to undergo the most awful death that men could inflict upon Him and then to *overcome* this death by coming back to life despite it all.

Since He knew beforehand all this was going to happen, Jesus spoke confidently, boldly, and reassuringly to His disciples on the night He was betrayed. He knew they would watch Him be arrested, beaten, and nailed to a cross; He knew their hearts would sink within them, thinking they had wasted the last three years of their lives, Jesus wasn't who they thought He was, and all was lost. He knew they would be filled with tears, disappointment, and disillusionment soon after He spoke to them. But He also knew He would face whatever the world threw at Him—and the world threw *everything it had* at Him—and still be victorious.

Jesus' confidence—"I have overcome the world"—was not that of a man who taunted death foolishly or arrogantly. These were not the words of a smug, cocky, alpha-male trying to sound tough in the company of those who looked up to him. He did not merely predict what He *thought* might happen (if nothing went wrong); He predicted exactly *what had already happened*, in essence, because of who He was and the power He possessed. Being the Son of God, nothing *could* go wrong for Him: He could *not* fail, and *no one* could stop what His Father had put into motion since before the world was created (Eph. 3:8–12, 2 Tim. 1:8–9, etc.). This is why Jesus said, "I *have* overcome the world"—*past tense*—before He had *literally* overcome the world's best effort to destroy Him and the grave's best effort to contain Him.

In fact, this idea of Jesus being victorious over the world (and death itself) was embedded in Scripture long before Jesus "became flesh" and dwelt among men (John 1:14). God has been forgiving people of their sins since the days of Adam, and yet the only possible way for Him to do this was for a once-for-all offering *for* sin to be made on behalf of all humankind. In other words, God the Father forgave sins in the ancient past because He knew absolutely that His Son would, "in the fullness of the time" (Gal. 4:4), provide such a sin offering. The Father's own unfailing reputation, and the forgiveness of every single faithful soul that had ever lived, rested upon this confidence.[123]

Even so, Jesus (the Son of God) had to experience what it means to be human (the Son of Man). He had to "be tempted in all things, as we are" (Heb. 4:15). He had to "[learn] obedience from the things which He suffered" (Heb. 5:8). This does not mean He had to learn obedience in the same way you and I learn it—through trial and error—but that He had to demonstrate His obedience to God even in the face of awful suffering. And, again, He had to face death and the grave just like everyone else (Heb. 2:9).

Still, in experiencing all these things, He *overcame* each one. He was "tempted in all things," yet "without sin." He suffered more than we will ever suffer, yet without a single failure in His obedience to God. And, He died like all men die, but He rose from His grave without any human intercession and will never die again—something *no other man* could ever do. In doing so, He "[put] an end to the agony of death, since it was impossible for Him to be held in its power" (Acts 2:24). And, He "[rendered] powerless him who had the power of death, that is, the devil" (Heb. 2:14). And, He "abolished death and brought life and immortality to light through the gospel" (2 Tim. 1:10). In other words, He overcame *the darkness* with the irrepressible, unstoppable, and indestructible Light of His divine power.

Faith and Forgiveness

Because of all that Jesus has done—and He has never and *can* never fail at anything—we also are able to "have peace" and "take courage" in Him (John 16:33). He has overcome "*the* world," but He also has the power to overcome *your* world. He has overcome Satan, but you also can overcome all of Satan's schemes *through* Him. And, He has overcome the power of darkness, but the darkness is robbed of all power in Jesus' presence. No one who belongs to Jesus and follows Him has to be afraid of the hereafter (John 10:27–28).

"God is love, and the one who abides in love abides in God, and God abides in him. By this, love is perfected with us, so that we may have confidence in the day of judgment; because as He is, so also are we in this world" (1 John 4:16–17). The "day of judgment" is coming for all people, whether they believe in God or not. Yet, those in whom God abides—which are the same as those who belong to Christ—do not have to *fear* this "day" because they "have an Advocate with the Father, Jesus Christ the righteous" (1 John 2:1), and He will provide them with safe passage into eternity.

Left to yourself, however, you have good reason to be afraid. You cannot "overcome the world" on your own, because the world is too big, Satan is too clever, and the darkness is too powerful for you. You cannot overcome the world simply by saying prayers, reading Scripture, or going to church. Even calling yourself a "Christian" identifies what you *ought* to be—a Christ-follower—but not necessarily who you really *are*. As we covered earlier, your biggest problem was never that you had a "church deficiency," but that you stand condemned because of your sins—and no one less than a divine being can help you.

"[T]here is now no condemnation for those who are in Christ Jesus" (Rom. 8:1). Christ is, in fact, the only solution to your problem. It is necessary that you are *in* Christ in order to expect help *from* Him, and I will talk more about this later. Anyone who dies outside of Christ dies outside of the mercy and grace that are found only *in* Christ. It is impossible—and unrealistic—to think that He will deliver you just because you are in trouble. Everyone who has sinned is in trouble, but most people still listen to the god of this world (Satan) rather than the One whom the God of heaven has declared "both Lord and Christ" (Acts 2:36). No one should expect Christ to help the one who refuses to commit his or her soul to His care. He is the Great Physician, not a paramedic.

Upon giving your allegiance to Him, Christ is made *your* Lord and *your* Savior. You can overcome whatever is outside of Christ because you are *in* Him. This overcoming, however, is not an unconditional offer. It is not one that you control to your liking. That Christ *can* and *will* help you is a fact, but *how* and *when* He does so must be His call, not yours. It is always amazing to me to hear people taking ten or twenty years to mess things up very badly but wanting Christ to fix everything overnight. Do not confuse Christ's ability to *forgive* you with His plan to *transform* your heart. His forgiveness is instantaneous; transformation will take the rest of your life, regardless of your situation.

But forgiveness is also dependent upon your willingness to be transformed—which requires submission to Him and not resistance every step of the way. Christ does not need people to tell Him how to respond to all the damage that we have caused. He does not need you to "fix" yourself first before coming to Him. He does not need you to approach His throne of grace covered with bandages, duct tape, and splints—repairs of your own making. He needs you to come to Him *broken* and *with all your messiness*, but with faith that He can and will heal you.

Faith is a critical element in this process, because "without faith, it is impossible to please Him, for he who comes to God must believe that He is and that He is a rewarder of those who seek Him" (Heb. 11:6). Christ is not asking for your input on how to overcome your world; He only asks for your faith in Him that *He* will overcome it. Just as you would not tell a brain surgeon how to operate on your head, so you should not tell Christ how to "do surgery" on your spiritual heart. While we are all quick to tell Christ how to do His job—how to heal us, save us, and handle our problems—this assumes our control over Him rather than allowing Him to have control over us. For you to put your faith in Christ means that you give Him full control over your heart from this point forward. Anything less than this is not faith, but resistance. And all resistance is unbelief, which is a sin.

"For whatever is born of God overcomes the world; and this is the victory that has overcome the world—our faith. Who is the one who overcomes the world, but he who believes that Jesus is the Son of God?" (1 John 5:4–5). Well, there it is, plain and simple. Christ has overcome the world—the entire gospel of salvation is founded upon this monumental fact. In the context of the entire NT, to "believe" that Jesus is the Son of God is to *obey* Him. To disbelieve Him is to *disobey* Him; compare John 3:16 and 3:36, for example. In the exchange for your belief in Him, Christ overcomes your world and prepares you for the eternity to come. This makes your belief in Him the greatest investment that exists, period.

Overcoming Your World
So then, what is in your world? Sin, to be sure. I can say this with confidence because *every one of us* is imperfect, and *all of us* fall short of God's holiness (Rom. 3:23).[124] But, what kinds of sin? Some sinful behaviors are more difficult to put an end to than others. Remember, Christ's forgiveness is immediate, but the transformation is not. This

is not to be understood as permission to sin in the meantime. Sin is *never* permissible; we are *never* to tolerate it under any circumstance. On the other hand, some sinful behaviors will take far greater effort to overcome than others. Christ promises to be there on the entire journey, from beginning to end. He will provide the moral strength, moral courage, and whatever else is necessary for you to overcome these things. Your job is to trust in His provision and to do your part in complying with what He tells you to do. "Faith" is not a mere religious feeling, mental exercise, or church experience, but an active obedience to the One whom you have made your Master.

"To him who overcomes," Jesus promises a tremendous reward (Rev. 2:7, etc.). But He never said *what*, exactly, must be overcome. While sin is your and my biggest problem to overcome, you may have other struggles in your life that will challenge your faith in Him. Marital problems, health problems, financial problems, job problems, etc. are pretty common, but not necessarily sinful in nature. Sexual frustration, mental illness, and depression are (sadly) also fairly common, but are not sinful in themselves. Chemical addictions, sexual addictions, and *all* behaviors that exercise satanic control over us *are* sinful. These are also more difficult to overcome because they are often deeply entrenched in our bodies and/or minds. Your financial worries can change overnight with a sudden increase in income; your chemical addiction may take a long time to master.

Christ does not describe every possible thing that must be overcome. He simply says, in essence, "You *can* and *must* overcome whatever is in this world that keeps you from Me." He also says, in essence, "This problem is too big, too powerful, and too much for you to handle on your own, so trust Me to see you through it." Through Christ, you *can* overcome anything in this world—including "the world" itself. He is more powerful than whatever now imprisons you; "greater is He who is in you than he who is in the world" (1 John 4:4). There is nothing in the world—not even the *entire* world—that can prevent you from being saved and serving Christ.

Again, if Christ can overcome the world, death, and Satan himself, He is most certainly able to overcome whatever problem stands in the way of your fellowship with God. He will not do this *instead* of you, but *through* you. Being saved by grace *through* faith (Eph. 2:8) implies a working relationship between what you do (in faith) and what Christ does (as an exercise of divine grace). This means you need to put forward your own effort as well as depend upon His ability to perform. Whatever makes you stumble, *you* are told to "cut it off and throw it from you" (Mat. 5:30)—Christ will not do this for you. You cannot cling to your sin, make provision for it, keep a fondness for it in your heart, or keep practicing it in hopes that Jesus will magically end it one day. You do your part in faith, and Christ will do His part in divine grace. This is how the gospel works.

But just because Christ can remove *all* of your problems does not mean that He will do so entirely. The only problem He promises to remove entirely is your sin—this is what His forgiveness is all about. Sin must be removed in order for you to have fellowship with God. Lesser things—earthly struggles in general—do not necessarily *have* to be removed in order for you to have fellowship with Him. However, Christ does provide you with the means to deal with these other things so that they will not overcome *you*. How, when, and to what extent He does so is up to Him, not you.

This may sound like I'm saying, "Christ *can* help you, but maybe He won't." This is not true. Christ *can* help you, and with reference to whatever is trying to destroy your soul, He *will* help you. But He does maintain the right to exercise His help in whatever manner *He* sees is best, not according to what you want Him to do. For example, left to my own self-serving human understanding, I would want Christ to take away *all* of my problems so that I could be deliriously happy in this world. But Christ, in His wisdom and full control of my situation, allows me to endure certain problems so that I can learn how to be happy *in Him*, not in the removal of every earthly struggle. This world is not the source of my spiritual happiness; He is. This world is not my home; Christ is my "home," so to speak (Col. 3:1–4). I need to learn how to be happy (as in, content) with Him, not with a trouble-free life. And so it is for every believer in Him.

Summary Thoughts

Christ has overcome the world, and He is ready and willing to overcome *your* world, too. He has proven ability; He cannot lie and has never failed at *anything*; and He promises to help you. He is not only trustworthy, but He is the only One in whom you *can* trust. He deserves your trust—your faith, your confidence, and your dependence—more than does anyone else, including yourself. Putting faith in Him does not mean sitting around waiting for Him to act, since there are things each of us must do in faith. It does mean, however, that you believe in Him and are actively demonstrating that belief by submitting to whatever He requires of you. So then, you do your job, so to speak, and let Him do His. He will not do what He has told you to do, and you are completely unable to do what He alone is capable of doing.

Think deeply on what is being said here. You literally do not have all the time in the world to make wise decisions or act in faith. I don't want to be too *forward* here, but it is *your eternal soul* we are talking about. Even having taken on the name "Christian" does not guarantee you will be saved no matter what. God does not save people according to names, seniority, or church status. He only saves people who live by faith in His Son. The problem of unbelief—ironically, one of the most insidious sins among Christians—can be dealt with through a humble appeal to God through the blood of Christ (1 John 1:9).

Christ loves you more than you will ever know. Because He loves you, He wants to help you—not just now, not just in the day of trial, but from this point forward and *always*. He has proven to you, me, and the entire world that He is fully *capable* of helping us. But He will not help you to overcome this world without your full and committed consent. If you have already become a Christian, you still need His help every day, no matter what. But if you are not yet a Christian—a Christ-follower as defined in Scripture—then a major, life-changing decision stands before you. And, again, you do not have all the time in the world to make it. This world is not your home, and you may be leaving here far sooner than you had once thought.

Chapter Sixteen: A Message to Christians

Most of this book has been talking to *all* people, regardless of their religious beliefs. I have attempted to speak to the pressing need at hand—being prepared to leave this world successfully—rather than deal only with those who have already become Christians.
To become a Christian means: to believe in Christ as one's Savior (Rom. 10:9–10), to repent of one's sinful practices (Luke 24:45–46), to "clothe" oneself with Christ in baptism (Gal. 3:26–27), and to walk with Him in obedient faith (Eph. 4:1–6). This is what the Bible teaches, regardless of what one chooses to believe otherwise.

Given all that has been said, becoming something *other* than a Christian will not help anyone. It may bring a measure of spiritual gratification for now, but it will prove to be useless in the life to come. Also, becoming a specific *designation* of "Christian"—identifying with a denominational brand rather than simply identifying with Christ—also will not help anyone. Christ is saving only one church: the body of those who believe in Him *apart from* any human interference with His authority.

I have written on all this at length in other books.[128] As to the subject at hand, let me speak now directly to Christians for a moment. Having been a Christian for over forty years (and over twenty-five years as a gospel minister), I know how we "tick." I also know how we can be mistaken about what it means to *walk* like a Christian, or how we can misrepresent Christ to others. I know this well because I have gone down these roads myself, all the while thinking that I was on the right track. "The gospel truth" is a heavy and sobering responsibility, and yet some of us have let it go to our heads rather than allow it to transform our hearts.

Despite all my personal and our collective errors, I have a special kinship to these people, since we are, after all, brothers and sisters in the Lord. Because of this, it disturbs me greatly to see what has happened to so many of them—how they have become soft and undisciplined, how they have gone astray, or how some have simply given up and resigned themselves to mere religion *about* Jesus Christ rather than a joyful and fulfilling relationship *with* Him.

Our Citizenship Is in Heaven, Not Here

"Set your mind on the things above," Paul instructed Christians, "not on the things that are on earth. For you have died and your life is hidden with Christ in God" (Col. 3:2–3). Christians are those who have "died" *to* this world and *for* Christ. The symbolic but necessary ritual of that death was carried out in our baptism, in which we shared in "the likeness of His death" (Rom. 6:3–7). In other words, our baptism in water imitated what Jesus underwent in His literal death, burial, and resurrection. One cannot be "born again" (1 Peter 1:3) until he has first died to the world, to sin, and even to himself. One cannot *live* to the Son of God until he has *died* to the condemnation that his law-breaking brought about (Rom. 7:4–6).

"Set your mind on the things above"—because "above" (where God dwells) is where you want your soul to be in the hereafter. The journey to that pristine existence begins now, both in your heart and through your conduct. It is something that must be believed as well as lived out visibly, literally, and measurably. No Christian is setting his "mind on the things above" if he continues to practice sin, including the sin of unbelief. Faith is not a Sunday service experience; it is a real-life, full-time, and here-and-now demonstration of your trust in the only One who loves you more than anyone else. Your faith in His ability to perform is what He requires of me, you, and every person who wishes to be with God in the world to come.

One of the paradoxes of Christians is this: we want to be with God in *His* world, but we have serious reservations about leaving behind the familiarity of *this* world. There is an old African saying: "Everybody wants to go to heaven, but nobody wants to die." It's not just the dying experience itself that bothers us, but also that to *which* we must die. It is not uncommon for Christians to say (or sing), "I'm ready to die for the Lord!" But many of these same people cling tenaciously to the life they have carved out for themselves, and they refuse to let go of *that* in order to pursue Christ. They claim a willingness to *die* for Him, but are in fact unwilling to *live* for Him.

Jesus won't have any of this duplicity of heart. Being a disciple of Christ, He says, will take everything you have (Mat. 16:24–25), cost you everyone you know (Mat. 10:34–39), and require your highest loyalty (Luke 9:57–62). There is no place for half-hearted disciples in Christ's church. This is not to say that such people do not exist in His earthly churches; it means that they will not be ushered into glory with His eternal church. What Jesus asks of us—of *me* and *you*—is difficult, to say the least. And, paradoxically, it is also the most rewarding: He promises nothing less than an eternal, heavenly, and *problem-free* existence in return. Far more than this, He promises that *we* will be with *Him* in this perfect and sinless home.

This thought deserves a deep pause for reflection. Heaven is not all about crystal mansions and streets of gold—or whatever Christians look forward to seeing there.[129] The greatest aspiration of human existence ought to be to live with the One who gave us life—our Creator. To be with the Creator in *His* world—not a temporary world that He made *for* us—is what He has intended for us all along ("I will be their God, and they shall be My people"—2 Cor. 6:16). Instead of living in the shadow of the Creator—a world filled with types, foreshadows, and anticipations of things to come—we are invited to live with the Creator Himself. Instead of simply being made "in His own image" (Gen. 1:27) but never actually seeing the One whose image we reflect, we are invited to see Him face to face (1 Cor. 13:12).

The emphasis here is not just on the scenery of heaven (although this will be fantastic, to be sure). Rather, it is on the *company* we will keep in heaven. John's glimpse of Christ's church in glory reads: "I saw no temple in it, for the Lord God the Almighty and the Lamb are its temple. And the city has no need of the sun or of the moon to shine on it, for the glory of God has illumined it, and its lamp is the Lamb" (Rev. 21:22–23). No temples, no church buildings, no church parking lots, no pews, no pulpits, no need for the sun or artificial sources of light. Instead, the One who *is* Light will illuminate the entire world of heaven. Or, as Paul says (with regard to the promise of heaven), "For God, who said, 'Light shall shine out of darkness,' is the One who has shone in our hearts to give the Light of the knowledge of the glory of God in the face of Christ" (2 Cor. 4:6). Imagine basking forever in a Light that can be *felt* and *embraced* as well as *seen* and *enjoyed*.

"God is Light, and in Him there is no darkness at all" (1 John 1:5). The darkness will be forever removed from God's people. Since we will be in the presence of Him in whom there is no darkness (James 1:17), no darkness will be in *our* presence. For now, we must coexist with an evil, satanic, and godless world, but this will not carry over into the world to come. In the future world, the division between the kingdom of Light and the domain of darkness will be made permanent. Those who refused to follow Christ in this earthly life will be cast into the "outer darkness" (Mat. 8:12), while those who genuinely *did* follow Him will be ushered into the eternal Light.

In heaven, God promises comfort, aesthetic beauty, and the cessation of physical labor. However, these pale in comparison to the real reward. For example, whenever Paul spoke of life in the hereafter, he never mentioned the *environment* of heaven but always the *One* with whom he wished to be forever: Jesus Christ (2 Cor. 5:8, Phil. 1:23, etc.). By implication, wherever Christ is will be the most *excellent* environment! Yet, the emphasis is not on the surroundings, but the glorified One who made it all possible for us. Apart from all that He did (and does) for us, none of us could be there.

The New Circle That Will Never Be Broken

Unfortunately, many Christians tend to think of heaven as a mere glorified extension of this life—particularly, a continuation of the relationships that began here on earth. Many people equate heaven with seeing all the loved ones, relatives, friends, and good people that have already died.[130] Thus, instead of envisioning an eternal *union* with God's Son, they long instead for a grand *re*-union with family and friends. While there is nothing wrong with desiring to be with loved ones who have died in the Lord, it is God and His Son who will bring us all together.

If you are in heaven, *everyone there* will be a "loved one": everyone will love you and be loved by you! No one will be left out, lonely, or forgotten. Since everyone in heaven chose to love God on earth, so they chose to love all who belong to Him—and to be loved by all who also chose to love Him. This ethereal, beautiful, and absolutely fulfilling fellowship will never be marred by sin, will never grow old or too familiar, and will never end. The love we will experience, share, and be forever immersed in will be far more excellent than any love we have known among fellow humans in this present life. In heaven, there will be no need for husbands, wives, children, siblings, cousins, aunts, uncles, or friends. *Everyone* in heaven will be related by blood—not biologically, genetically, or racially as now, but by the blood of the Redeemer. We will be one new family, "one new man" (Eph. 2:15), and one glorious Bride (Rev. 21:1–2).

People look forward to a recreation of "the circle"—i.e., the circle of family and loved ones they enjoyed on earth—but they do not always think about a *new* circle that infinitely exceeds the former one in every way. Will the circle be unbroken?—no and yes. The original circle will be forever broken, because sin corrupted it and made it impossible for it to carry over into eternity. But the *new* circle will be that of God's people of all time, from every nation, and from every walk of life. These will come together in one great company to worship the One who saved them from the darkness and filled their souls with light instead. "Behold," God promises, "I am making all things new" (Rev. 21:5). This *new* circle will be forever intact: it will never be broken. It will remain forever complete, and we will forever be complete *in* it.

When you chose to follow Christ, you voluntarily left everyone and everything else behind. You *died*, in essence, to everyone who is outside of Christ. This was a necessary and purposeful separation. While being eternally separated from loved ones sounds unbearable in the world to come (and, yes, I struggle with this, too), believers have already made this decision. Some of our loved ones turn away from us to follow this world, and *we* turn away from them to follow the Lord. This reminds me of a story of a father who was lying on his death bed, saying goodbye to his family. He was a Christian, as were his wife and two of his three adult children. One adult son, however, chose to live for the world and dwell in the darkness. The father was smiling and cheerful toward his wife and two children, but hugged and cried over the wayward son. "See," the son proudly said to his mother afterward, "he obviously loved me the most." "No," the mother replied sadly, "he knows that he will see the rest of us in heaven, but he will never see *you* again, and this is breaking his heart."

"It is so unbearably sad," Christians will say, "knowing that [insert: name of loved one] will not be there." But it will not be sadness we will feel, not then. It will be *full understanding* of the situation. That person, whoever he or she is, had just as much opportunity to follow Christ as you did, but refused it. You chose, and that person chose: you chose the Lord, and the other chose Satan; you chose the Light, and the other chose the darkness. This is heartbreaking for now, because we do not have the full knowledge and perspective that being with God will provide us. Even so, we will then understand that every person—including the one whom we love to pieces right now—makes his own decision as to which path he will take: the wide path or the narrow one (Mat. 7:13–14).[131] In the end, God's love, and our love for God, "will wipe away every tear" from our eyes, and we will not spend eternity mourning over those who were lost. Instead, we will spend eternity gratefully worshiping the One who *saved us* from being lost. "From God's standpoint, it is better to have loved the whole world (John 3:16) and have lost some than not to have loved them at all."[132] He does not save us because we are worthy; He saves us because He *loves* us and we loved Him in return.

We Still Have Much Work to Do

But, as much as Christians long for heaven—and we *should* long for it, and *deeply*—we are not yet there. Having "heaven in our hearts" ought to dictate how we live, but it is not equal to actually *being* there. Unnervingly, we must admit that, until we find ourselves in the Savior's loving embrace, the possibility of falling still remains. We will "never stumble" *if* we remain faithful to Him, but this requires an ongoing and ever-deepening commitment to Him (2 Peter 1:10–11). "[T]here remains a Sabbath rest for the people of God" (Heb. 4:9), but this "rest" will only be given after our work here is carried out, and—because we still remain on earth—our work is not yet done.

It is not time for Christians to rest, relax, and retire from the Lord's work. Instead, it is time to throw our heart into this work, for there is much to do and every one of us has a responsibility to do it. We are to make the most of our time and "understand what the will of the Lord is" (Eph. 5:15–17). We cannot afford to make excuses, for "the night is almost gone, and the day is near. Therefore, let us lay aside the deeds of darkness and put on the armor of light" (Rom. 13:12). We cannot afford to take the path of least resistance, because this path leads to ruin and we may not have opportunity to get off of it before we leave this present world.

It is time for Christians to endure the scoffing, ridicule, and contempt of those who hate God, reject His authority, and despise Christianity. Instead of cowering in the shadows (or in our church buildings), we need to stand boldly before our accusers and not be intimidated by them. Instead of curling up in a fetal position and surrendering to the darkness, we have been called to "stand firm" and to "be strong in the Lord and in the strength of His might" (Eph. 6:10–14). Instead of discovering how close we can get to sin without "technically" sinning, we must learn to *hate* sin while at the same time *love* sinners, since this is what God does.

It is time for Christians to stop reminiscing about how things "used to be" when we just went to church and sang songs and listened to sermons without really *becoming* anything more than what we were. "Do not say, 'Why is it that the former days were better than these?' For it is not from wisdom that you ask about this" (Eccles. 7:10). While seemingly safe and comfortable, the former days were not as good as we thought they were if indeed we did not appreciate what we had or make the most of the opportunity handed to us. Instead, "you have need of endurance, so that when you have done the will of God, you may receive what was promised" (Heb. 10:36). To "endure" does not mean merely to tolerate through gritted teeth, but to *finish what we started*. And, because we are still here, we have not yet finished what we started.

It is time for Christians to suffer for what is right, not avoid suffering and running from our moral responsibilities (because they are hard, uncomfortable, and disruptive). Many Christians are trying to make their own heaven in the here-and-now rather than working toward the heaven to come. In other words, they are padding their lives with creature comforts, filling their schedules with sports, social media, or entertainment, and then telling church leaders that they are "too busy" to be engaged in church work. Such people are wasting valuable time and energy; they are burying their talents in the ground. Instead, they would do well to make the sacrifices of discipleship to Christ and learn to be industrious for the Lord.

It is time for Christians to choose life, which means choosing Christ above all else. Heaven will be filled with such people; hell will be filled with everyone else—all those who chose lesser things. Here, there are many persuasions, distractions, and false hopes, and we are warned in Scripture against following any of them. "Do not be deceived" is a pervasive teaching of the NT, and we must make strenuous effort *not* to be deceived. The world is filled with spiritual fool's gold—things that look real, that glitter and sparkle, and seem worth pursuing. Yet, fool's gold has zero value, and everyone will find this out in the world to come.

It is time for Christians to show the world what godly love really looks like. It is not the flowery, plastic, and hollow "love" of mere well-wishers, hand-shakers, and "God bless you"-sayers. Real love—*godly* love—is a love that does not cave under criticism, does not compromise, will not buckle under the slightest pressure, and refuses to be soft and lazy (1 Cor. 13:4–7). Real love speaks the truth to all who need to hear it, regardless of how uncomfortable it might be to say it. "Tough love" is still *love*, as long as it seeks what God says is the best interest of the one being loved. Godly love honors God above all and champions what is right, not merely what is popular, tolerated, or "unoffensive."

Summary Thoughts

Dear Christian, are you being honest with God—and yourself? Are you allowing your heart to be exposed by the Light rather than hiding behind the shelter of your baptism status, family pedigree, or church membership? Where will you be when this life is over? This is a strange question to ask *Christians*, to be sure, but not everyone who wears the name of "Christ-follower" has kept his original promise to Him. Have you?

Christ promises a "crown of life" for all those who have "fought the good fight," "finished the course," and "kept the faith" (2 Tim. 4:7–8). Paul wrote these expressions in past tense, since they speak of what *had* been done, not what still *needed* to be done. In order for Christ to put a crown of life on your head—the most amazing experience imaginable!—you must be faithful till death, persevere through every trial, stay the course, and live for Him above all else.

This is a difficult, narrow, and often lonely path to walk, but it is doable. Even if all others abandon you, Christ will never do this (Heb. 13:5–6).

The theme of the entire Bible is: "I will be their God and they shall be My people." In order for you to be one of *His* people, you must consciously, actively, and even sacrificially make Him *your* God. You must carry out His work here on earth *and* be prepared to leave this earth in anticipation of an altogether new life with Him. You must not simply be waiting to "die in the Lord," but you must first prove to *live* in faithful obedience to Him.

Once we are in heaven, "faith" will be no longer, since we will see the object of our love in fact. Also, "hope" will not be necessary, since we will forever be with the One in whom we now long for. But *love* will last forever—and our love for God in the hereafter will never wane or grow old, but will be immediately and forever full, rewarding, and perfect. "For now we see in a mirror dimly, but then face to face; now I know in part," Paul says, "but then I will know fully just as I also have been fully known. But now faith, hope, love, abide these three; but the greatest of these is love" (1 Cor. 13:12–13).

Appendix I: The Problem of Evil

Moral evil is a problem. "Evil," according to God's world, is whatever opposes His authority or contradicts His revealed truth. Evil, wickedness, and unrighteousness are all synonymous: it is impossible to practice one without being guilty of the others (Rom. 1:18–20).

The "problem" is not only that evil exists—a point which no one seems to dispute—but *why* it exists, or exactly where it *came* from. Seldom does anyone ask where "good" comes from, because goodness is not a problem for anyone. We all want to believe that moral goodness (or virtue) does exist, and we all want to be the recipients of it. But here is where the moral struggle begins: If God is completely and perfectly good, then how can good and evil coexist in the spiritual realm as well as the world that He created? Simply put: how can a *good God* allow anything *but* good to exist?

Some say that evil is *our* problem to which God offers His solution. Some make Satan fully responsible for all evil; others focus only on *human* evil—the unkind, unjust, and unholy way in which we treat one another. Still others want to lay the full responsibility for evil at God's feet. If everything that has a beginning was created by God, then evil itself must be of His creation (otherwise wickedness, like godliness, is eternal). Or, at the very least, He is responsible for evil simply by the fact that He did not (and does not) prevent it or abolish it altogether. A famous quote from the Scottish philosopher David Hume: "Is [God] willing to prevent evil, but not able? Then he is impotent. Is he able, but not willing? Then he is malevolent. Is he both able and willing? Whence then is evil?"[133]

You can see how this subject can get rather deep very quickly. Theologians have labeled this discussion "theodicy," which means "God's justice (despite the existence of evil)." It is a subject—a *problem*—that has vexed and disturbed many people for many centuries. "From a purely apologetic perspective, more skepticism, agnosticism, and atheism have sprung from an inability to answer various aspects of evil than from any other single issue. What is more, when doubt begins in this area, it moves quickly to other areas."[134] In other words, wrestling with the problem of evil can serve as a gateway to other spiritual difficulties, which can lead people to throw up their hands and give up altogether.

This begs the question: should we be discussing this subject *at all*? If grappling with this "problem" may cause us to lose our faith in God—to even deny His very existence—then should we simply set this thing down right here and walk away from it? My strong opinion is: *absolutely not*. Many men and women have chosen to become atheists because they could not (or, more accurately, *would* not) reconcile a good God allowing evil to exist, but upon further inspection every one of these have other "issues" with God and His word that have contributed to that decision. The "problem of evil" is, for some, the grand unicorn argument that people who are mad at God, disappointed with Christians, and/or fed up with "organized religion," like to cite in order to justify their own moral irresponsibility. Throwing a seemingly unanswerable theological argument in Christians' faces is like throwing down the unbeatable trump card in the middle of a card game.[135] Since no one can come up with a conclusion about God's justice that satisfies everyone else, it seems safe to deny His existence altogether.

I give you the benefit of doubt that you are not one of those people whom I just described. If you are reading this, it is most likely that you are searching *for* the truth, not looking for some way—a justifiable loophole—to avoid or even deny the truth. This does not mean that my conclusions *are* "the truth," but that you and I are doing the same thing: we respect God's existence, His word, and His holiness. We know that just because *we* may not have all the answers does not mean that answers do not exist, or that God is incapable of providing them. God has revealed what He wants us to know for certain; He has also chosen *not* to reveal what He wants us to wrestle with. He wants us to have faith in His goodness despite what happens otherwise. Given this, there is no good, logical, or anticipated reason why we should lose our faith over discussing His holy nature or the moral evil that opposes it. Instead, we ought to find our faith in God made even stronger through the experience.

Moral Authority Is Required in Order for Good and Evil to Exist
God exists. Any honest, objective, and truly open-minded person who examines the design, engineering, complexity, and diversity of the natural world will admit this. This same person will reach the same conclusion upon examining the spiritual (i.e., non-physical; metaphysical; invisible) dimension of every human being. One's internal dialogue, conscience, moral intuition, emotions, capacity for love (as well as hatred), consciousness of justice (as well as guilt), and a number of other considerations can never be chalked up to "pure chance." Instead, we have been designed, engineered, wired, and programmed (to some extent) by an all-knowing and all-powerful Being that transcends us in every way.

The Bible itself provides another testimony to the fact of God's existence. It is illogical to cite *only* the Bible for this conclusion, because this is circular reasoning ("Why does God exist? Because the Bible says so. Why does the Bible say this? Because God exists"—and so on, *ad infinitum*.) On the other hand, the Bible confirms conclusively, even unapologetically, that the Being who created the world and is the source of all human life does indeed exist. Even more, it reveals His name, His divine nature, His personality, His intentions, and even His master plan. The biblical record does not so much defend God's *existence* as much as it explains—especially through Christ (John 1:18)—who God *is* and why we should listen to Him.

Evil also exists. As "good" is real, so is evil; as "good" visibly manifests itself in manifold ways, so does evil. The *kind* of evil we are talking about is *moral* evil, not the so-called "evil" of animals killing and eating each other, or the so-called "natural evil" of the physical world (i.e., destruction caused by famine, plague, severe weather, tornadoes, etc.). What animals do to each other in order to survive is an inappropriate means by which to determine God's moral justice. Likewise, the material world does not make decisions to either hurt or benefit people; it has no capacity for reasoning, malevolence, compassion, or decision-making. It follows physical laws absolutely; it cannot choose to do otherwise. Earthquakes, for example, are not cruel any more than a pristine mountain setting is kind.[136]

Moral evil has to do with one's moral decision—always a human choice, never an accident or automatic reflex—to oppose God rather than to live in harmony with His divine nature. This divine nature serves as a moral *law* for us, and this law will either be honored and obeyed, or it will be defied and violated.[137] Animals live by instinct, not moral law; the earth operates by natural laws (gravity, thermodynamics, electromagnetism, hydraulics, meteorology, etc.), not moral law. Humans are the only living beings on the planet that can make *moral decisions* concerning the *moral law* under which God has placed them.

Atheists believe that evil is real, but that God is not. This, however, is an illogical position and impossible to defend. "It's difficult to argue the problem of evil when your worldview provides no basis for believing in evil."[138] People only seem to have a "problem" with evil but not with good. Yet, apart from God, neither one makes sense or can be validated. "Good" can only exist if there is an absolute standard of good; evil can only exist as a departure from this absolute standard. Ultimately, trying to define either "good" or "evil" necessarily requires the existence of a Higher Authority—an absolute authority that defines absolute morality, rather than relying on human authority. "If there is a moral law demanding that we ought always to be just, this leads us right back to a Moral Lawgiver."[139] It is logically (and, of course, biblically) impossible otherwise.

But, again, if God is good, then where did "evil" come from?[140] If God is Light, then where did the (spiritual) darkness come from? We know that darkness is only the absence of light; darkness does not "come from" anywhere. There is nothing that actually *creates* darkness, whereas light requires a source (Gen. 1:1–5). In any context in which God's *Light* is ignored, denied, or defied, *moral* darkness envelops the one doing the ignoring, denying, or defying (Eph. 4:17–19).

Asking where evil came from is like saying, "Where does cold come from?" when in fact "coldness" is merely the absence of heat. There is no way to understand, explain, or measure "cold" without some reference to heat. Nowhere in the physical universe is there a source of "cold"; there are only places where *heat* is created or where heat is not present. Likewise, there is no source of *darkness*—something that actively produces darkness on its own, with no reference to God's Light—but only a realm of the *absence* of

God's Light. Take away God's Light, and what we know to be "the darkness" would disappear altogether: it would have no distinction whatsoever. One who is blind from birth, for example, does not "see" darkness, because he has never seen *light*. All he "sees" is, from his perspective, the *only* thing to exist.

Evil is not a creation of God, but is the corruption of (or, turning away from) whatever He *has* created. It is a meaningless concept without recognizing this original point of reference. Just as one cannot turn left if there is no right, or go south if there is no north, so there cannot be evil unless it is the *opposite direction* of something else. Calling something "evil" without also admitting an absolute "good" from which it has departed is like talking about a hole in the ground without acknowledging the *missing ground* as well as the *surrounding ground* that marks the perimeter of the hole in the first place. Evil cannot exist unless good exists because it is always a departure from or corruption of what is good rather than something that stands by itself. Again, describing "evil" apart from the good from which it departed or which it corrupted simply does not make sense.

In choosing to be good, we choose to conform to God's own standard *of* good. A choice to be evil necessitates that we have turned away *from* this divine standard to pursue a lesser standard—comprehensively known as "the darkness." Paul talks about this in 2 Tim. 4:3–4: people who want a religious doctrine that satisfies their carnal appetite (instead of seeking "sound doctrine") turn away *from* the God's truth and turn aside *to* myths instead. Both "the truth" *and* "myths [or simply, false teaching]" must exist, be real, and be objectively defined in order for either one to exist. No one can turn aside to false teaching unless he first turned away from the truth. Likewise, no one can be evil unless he turns away from a perfect standard of "good."

God has given us freedom—a free will—to choose between good and evil. We can choose good *over* evil, which is the same as choosing to stand *with* God over choosing to stand *opposed* to Him.[141] If we did not have this moral freedom, then we could not be responsible for our own actions. Yet, because we do have this choice, what we choose to do becomes our responsibility. Our freedom is an extremely powerful and dangerous gift. It is powerful because with it, we can make decisions that extend into eternity. It is dangerous because we can choose to defy both our own Creator and the very reason for our existence.[142]

God is the Ultimate Cause or Prime Mover of all things—what one author calls the "Unlimited Limiter."[143] This makes Him responsible to *oversee* all that has been created, but it does not make Him responsible for every decision *within* the Creation. Every created entity that has been given free will, whether angelic or human, may be compared to a dog on a long leash: it can move around in a number of directions, and even cause a great deal of trouble, but it is only able to move so far. The leash is not responsible for what the dog does, but only for how far it can go. Likewise, God limits the extent of our travel, but He does not control what we do *in* our travels.

The Goodness of God

But the bigger question still remains: Is God *Himself* "good"? It stands to reason that, if He does indeed exist, He must be either "good" or "evil," because He cannot be both. If He is evil, then this begs the question: Why would an evil God allow *good* in the world? Why would He do anything good at all? And why are people so upset that a *good* God might allow evil to exist (for now) but no one seems upset about the possibility of God being *evil*? And if He is evil, then there can be no transcendent "good" by which to measure anything, no standard of justice, and nothing good to look forward to in the afterlife. It would be *good*, and not evil, that we should be wary of in this life. And it will be evil, and not good, that will indeed triumph in the end.

But if God is good, then He must be *wholly* good, since otherwise He would be no better than we are. Basically "good" people prone to error, capable of sin, and able to be corrupted. If God, being good, can do evil things, then He is really not "God" at all, since He will have submitted to an influence outside of Himself and done the bidding of power greater than Himself. Thus, He is not a Sovereign God, but simply "a god" that has all the faults and weaknesses of human beings. This describes, in essence, the entire pantheon of Greek and Roman gods. Mythology is filled with "gods" who are merely glorified men—with all of men's flaws, weaknesses, and carnal desires.

If God *is* good, He is good because He told us so, not because we told *Him* so. In other words, it is not our place to define "good" apart from God, and then measure Him against our self-determined standard. Much of what drives the idea that God is *not* good is a subjective definition and application of what is "good" in the first place. Yet, our understanding of "good" must be measured against God Himself, since He is the universal and transcendent standard. This is why, when Jesus was called a "good Teacher," He replied, "Why do you call Me good? No one is good except God alone" (Mark 10:17). This does not mean that no one can *be* or *do* good, but that no one's "good" means anything by itself. God is the measuring stick by which all "good" is defined. Jesus even measured Himself against this standard rather than assuming His own.

If this is true about what is good, then anything *short* of this defines what is evil. Jesus hinted at this with regard to our answers to people: either say "yes" or "no," because "anything beyond these is of evil" (Mat. 5:37). In other words, if we are not going to imitate God's honesty, integrity, and straightforwardness, then we fall *short* of all this—in reality, we fall short of God Himself. To fall short of God's standard of righteousness (or, goodness; holiness) is to fall short of God Himself (Rom. 3:23). To fall short of God is to sin—to reject the Light and choose the darkness instead.

A Good God and an Evil World

Rubbing God out of existence because we are unhappy with the fact that a good God would allow evil to exist is illogical and extremely shortsighted. This approach fails to acknowledge all the positive evidence of God's existence, but dismisses Him based upon highly opinionated views of what we think God should do if *we* were Him. "If *I* were God," the contemporary narrative says, in essence, "*I* would not allow evil and suffering in the world. *I* would eradicate all misery, disease, abuse, and injustice in the world. *I* would do this, *I* would do that, etc. etc." This view is very popular, to be sure, but it accomplishes nothing. It is pure fantasy and, even worse, assumes that we have a clue about how to oversee the entire world and all of humankind.

We all speak from an extremely limited, finite, and self-serving point-of-view. God, on the other hand, speaks from perfect knowledge, infinite wisdom, and a completely objective foresight. Not only are we unable to be on par with His perspective, we cannot even comprehend it beyond what He has revealed to us. Not only are we unable to prove the non-existence of God, we are unable to *dis*prove all the positive evidence that defends Him. There is sufficient evidence for God's existence; there is also sufficient evidence that He is altogether good without any "variation or shifting shadow" (James 1:17). He cannot deny who He is and still remain "God" (2 Tim. 2:13); He cannot be any better or worse than He is at any given moment. Anyone can deny all this if he wants to, but he will not be able to offer a valid argument that nullifies any of it.

Even when one accepts God's existence, he may cringe at all the evil going on in the world. The path of least resistance here is to make God responsible for all of it. Such people will reason, "If God is in charge of the world, then He is also responsible for what happens in it—both good and bad." In a sense, they want God to be held accountable to *them*—to answer for His crimes, so to speak—rather than *them* being held accountable to God.[144] All the pain, sadness, human suffering, and injustice that is going on in the world is ultimately, according to some, God's fault. He may not be the initial cause of it, but He created the environment in which it is happening, and He has not prevented it *from* happening.

There are a number of subjective and unwarranted assumptions with this kind of thinking. It ignores the fact that God has complete and infallible knowledge about what is going on, while we speak from an extremely inferior and finite position. It ignores the perfect world that God once created for people, which was corrupted not by His failure to keep it pristine but *our* (human) failure to honor our Creator and His gifts to us. It specifically ignores the gift of free will that God has given to people to exercise independent of His intention for them. If we were unable to choose to be unkind, dishonest, and wicked, then it would make our kindness, honesty, and virtue meaningless. We would have no more righteousness than a rabbit or a tree. What separates us from the animal kingdom is (among other things) our ability to *choose* to defy our Creator rather than to be completely governed by instinct or physical laws that we cannot violate. "[I]f it is good to be free, then evil is possible. Freedom means the power to choose otherwise. ... If one is free to love, he is also free to hate. ... The very nature of our divinely-given freedom makes evil possible."[145]

It *is* true that God has not prevented evil from occurring. In the scope of moral freedom, there must be the freedom to choose evil *over* good—a choice that God does not sanction, but allows nonetheless. However, our ability to choose to be evil does not make God guilty of the evil crimes that we commit. This is like holding you guilty for murders committed by your 16-year-old son because he is *your* son and the product of *your* household environment. While you might have negatively influenced your son to murder people, he still (in our hypothetical situation) is the murderer, not you. In sharp contrast, God has never influenced people to be wicked, but to be just, show love, demonstrate kindness, and be humble (Micah 6:8). We never learned wickedness from God, but from Satan and all those whose hearts were given over to the darkness.

Our sins are our decisions, not God's; likewise, our *faith* in Him is our decision, not His. The choice to be faithful to our Creator is as much a part of our free will as it is to choose to be evil. Jesus said as much in Mat. 12:33–37: each person (a "tree" in His analogy) has the free will *and* ability either to be good or bad, and his "fruit" (outward actions) will expose the true nature of his heart. He also says that there will be an accounting for our moral choices: rather than God standing trial before us, we will most certainly stand trial before Him.[146]

But there remains the question of human pain and suffering: how can a good God allow this to happen, especially to innocent people, including children? I recently watched a MADD-produced documentary ("Impact: After the Crash" [2013]) that covered the horrific 1998 crash in Kentucky between a pickup truck and a school bus being used for a church-sponsored outing. A drunk driver, going the wrong way on an interstate freeway, plowed into the bus at night; the bus's gas tank immediately exploded, sending a fireball through the bus which quickly incinerated the entire vehicle. While several people managed to escape, twenty-seven others (mostly children) died.

The truck's driver survived, however, with only minor injuries. Where was God when all this happened? How could a *good God* allow *innocent children* to be burned alive in a situation over which they had no control?

This is just one story out of perhaps *millions* of stories worldwide where human irresponsibility led to a tragic conclusion. In assessing such tragedies, people seem to gravitate toward blaming *God* for them rather than the *person/people* directly responsible. God did not kill those twenty-seven people on the bus crash that I just cited. Instead, a very drunk driver did *and* the bus manufacturer's poor design indirectly contributed to it.[147] God allowed each party—the drunk driver *and* the bus designers—to exercise free will, and they did. Free will does not always end well.

Could God have *prevented* this bus crash? Of course. Why *didn't* He? Now we are treading on difficult ground. To expect that God *should* have prevented it not only robs the free will of those responsible for what happened, but it also critiques God and His decisions without having His knowledge, authority, or ability to perform. In other words, it condemns God for something that we are incapable of even understanding at His level. Now we have the creation judging the Creator. While we are free to ask God the question of "why," we have no business answering it *for* Him— especially, to hold Him in contempt because we do not understand the full scope of the situation.[148]

Responsibility for Pain and Suffering

Aside from natural evil (i.e., the harmful dynamics of our own planet or random disease), *all* human suffering is the result of human beings violating God's laws regarding Him, one's fellow man, one's own body, and stewardship of the earth itself. Those who do not believe in God will, of course, reject this answer, but it is evident from observation, our own personal experience, and the biblical record. Every "suffering"—a subjective term that is often difficult to measure or define—can be traced back to human sin. Greed, abuse of power, rejection of God's laws, conflicts of interest, etc. lead to oppression, thievery, sexual abuse, murder, and crimes against humanity. People injure themselves through reckless living, personal irresponsibility, substance abuse, and immoral behavior. As we discussed in chapter 7, God is not responsible for these things, people are. God allows them to happen because of the free will He has given us, but He condemns every decision that violates His own holy nature, which serves as a moral law for all people.

The modern mindset seems to categorize *all* "suffering" as bad, as though nothing good could possibly come from any of it. In this view, all suffering must be eliminated through whatever means—money, medicine, medical practices, and social legislation. Even the "suffering" of disagreement (of certain lifestyles, sexual preferences, and beliefs) must be removed, which requires the elimination of all those who are voicing the disagreement. This implies the eradication of Christianity. The reasoning is: Christians are the source of all social "hatred," since they are "intolerant" of certain lifestyles and beliefs. The utopian idea behind this is that we all should be able to live in a trouble-free, disease-free, and injustice-free world in which everyone can do anything they want without criticism from anyone else. Yet, this is sheer fantasy: it is impossible to achieve, impossible to sustain, and impossible to even envision without a higher—and, apparently, morally-neutral—authority being in charge of it all.

No one wants to suffer, of course, and no one—myself included—is trying to diminish or even trivialize one's suffering simply because some good may ultimately come from it. Such hollow platitudes are common at funerals of those who have just died a tragic death ("I know your loved one just died a horrible death, but *God has a plan!*"). Overlooking one's suffering, or ignoring that person's tremendous emotional grief, by pointing out a "silver lining" is, quite simply, rude and uncompassionate.

On the other hand, suffering can and has often snapped the attention of those involved back to where it should be. God does not want us to suffer *needlessly*, but He does not prevent us from feeling the painful effects of living in a sinful world. There are some basic lessons to be learned from the presence of suffering:

- There are consequences to sin—not just consequences to *you* for *your* sin, but consequences for *all* of us for *everyone's* sins. God's authority and power provide law and order for the world;

His oversight maintains the balance and control of the realm of humankind. Sin disrupts the sacred balance of the natural order of Creation. God is the only One capable of enforcing these laws and re-establishing this balance. Meanwhile, "the whole creation groans and suffers" under the weight of His condemnation of human sin (Rom. 8:22). Yet, in Christ, "there is now no condemnation," but spiritual freedom (Rom. 8:1–2).

- We really have no control over this world's maladies. Sickness and disease bring debilitation, suffering, and death to people every day. Despite our best efforts, we cannot stop this from happening. Such things cause us to yearn for a world in which these things do not exist, protected by One who can permanently heal us of all diseases (see Exod. 15:26, in principle).
- We really have no control over the dynamics of this world. The natural forces of this planet (earthquakes, tornadoes, tsunamis, famine, etc.) bring their own form of pain and suffering to people. Suffering the effects of a planet that is in a constant state of change symbolizes the instability and unreliability of this world in general. We are made to think of a far better world that *never* changes because it is already perfect in every way—i.e., *God's* world.
- This world is not your home. If God is good and His ultimate intention is for you to be with Him in a world without suffering (Rev. 7:16–17, 21:3–5), then a world *with* suffering is not your final destination. This is only true if you choose to be faithful to Him; otherwise, *all you will know* is suffering in the world to come, absent of anything good.
- Satan *wants* you to suffer in order to ruin you. He wants you, like Job's wife, to "curse God and die" when you are faced with the trials and traumas of this life (Job 2:9). He wants you to believe that a good God would not allow you to suffer, so either God is *not* good or *you* are expendable. If you are a Christian, Satan wants you to abandon your faith, renege on your promises to God, and be miserable and hopeless.
- Faith does not make suffering go away, but gives us the proper manner in which to deal with it. No one should assume that by becoming a Christian, life will be easier. In fact, life is likely to become more difficult. Similarly, faith is no guarantee against

being harmed by evil, but trusts in God's providence—His "provide-ability"—to safeguard us from being destroyed by it. "Faith tells us we can hope for the end of whatever evils plague us. Not now, perhaps. ... Still, we can hope confidently, knowing that God's way is going to win out in the end, and *perhaps* right now for others if not for us."[149]

- God *needs* you to suffer, but not to destroy you. He wants you to know for certain that this world is not your home, to look to Him in anticipation of a far better home in which there is no suffering. He wants your trials and ordeals to seek a higher explanation, a better healing, and a greater purpose than whatever you will find on earth without Him. If you are a Christian, He *calls* you to suffer in order for you to identify with the price His Son had to pay for your sin (1 Peter 2:21–25). He *invites* you to suffer for your faith and His name's sake—in ways that unbelievers will never *have* to suffer—in order to refine, strengthen, and complete you. "Satan and God intend the same suffering for entirely different purposes, but God's purpose triumphs."[150]

The *experience* of suffering is bad, but the *purpose* for (and *result* of) suffering does not have to be bad. If you are outside of Christ (i.e., not a faithful Christian), then for you to overcome your trials is really no great accomplishment, since it has not drawn you closer to God. Not only this, but if you remain outside of Christ, your afterlife is filled *only* with suffering without any change, reprieve, or ending. If you *are* a faithful Christian, then whatever you experience here on earth can contribute to your faith and draw you closer to God. In your afterlife, if you "remain faithful until death" (Rev. 2:10), you will be ushered into a world in which there is no more pain, loss, suffering, separation, or death.

Summary Thoughts

God does exist, and He is good to all people, both the righteous and the wicked (Mat. 5:43–45). This does not mean He will spare either group from trials, adversity, pain, loss, or even death. It means He is a benevolent God who seeks the best interest of *every* person. How each person responds to His kindness does determine whether or not he will benefit from this. People tend to limit God's kindness to comfort, safety, material prosperity, and a seemingly advantageous station in life. Yet, God seeks a much better objective, namely, the salvation of each person's soul and a growing relationship with Him. In this respect, His goodness is magnified far beyond creature comforts and being spared from life's pains and inadequacies.

Evil also exists, but it is not able to exceed the limits which God has imposed upon it. Evil *is* a problem, in that it causes all kinds of trouble, heartache, loss, and suffering for all of us. But evil is not a problem that is too big for God to handle or contain. God keeps evil (and evil people) on a leash: it (they) can do a lot of damage wherever it goes, but it can only go so far. God allows evil to be present in the human realm to allow us an opportunity to exercise our free will: we can choose to put our faith in God, despite what happens to us, or we can pursue evil and suffer the consequences of that decision. In choosing evil, not only does one forfeit the *good life*—a life of fellowship with Christ, sealed for the day of his redemption (Eph. 1:13–14)—but he also guarantees himself a future life of awful pain, suffering, and torment.

"For God so loved the world, that He gave His only begotten Son, that whoever believes in Him shall not perish, but have eternal life" (John 3:16). An evil or corrupted God would never make this sacrifice for us; He would never offer us such an undeserved gift; and He would not care that we are "perishing" in our sins. A good God, however, provides the priceless gift of His Son, then offers each person the priceless opportunity to choose *between* His Son and the temporary sparkle of this present world. People in both groups will suffer in this life—and those who choose Christ will suffer in ways that unbelievers will never know—but one group's suffering will be limited to this life, while the other group's suffering will never end. God is *good* in providing *each one of us* the opportunity to choose our own future rather than choosing it for us.

God allows everything to run its course for the time being, but He has a master plan which has yet to be fully realized. For now, He is being patient about bringing an end to this physical world, but His patience is meant to be taken as opportunity to turn to Him, not a sign of His weakness, forgetfulness, or inability to deliver. Sometime in your future, whether in this life or the next, you will see with your own eyes exactly what He has been waiting for all along.

Appendix II: Near-death Experiences

Some people allegedly have traveled to the afterlife and returned to tell us about it. Are we supposed to believe in what they claim to have seen and heard? (Do *you*?) How are such claims to be regarded in light of biblical teaching? Is such teaching to be re-evaluated or even modified by such claims? Should an alleged journey *to* the afterlife become an authority *about* the afterlife? And if so, whose "journey" are we to believe—and why?

We are talking here, of course, about so-called "near-death experiences," or NDEs. Some people claim to have had some otherworldly experience—not a dream or vision, but a *visit*—to the spiritual realm. This happened invariably while they were faced with some extremely stressful or traumatic event in which they thought they were going to die or had *indeed* died and then were resuscitated. Somehow, apart from normal human experience, these relatively few people retained some conscious recollection of this "near-death" incident.

Such people want us to believe that they visited heaven (or, in some cases, *hell*) and then returned to tell us about their experience. These have a great story to tell, it would seem, and there are many who will listen to it. But in order to be taken seriously, they are going to have to provide greater authority, greater proofs, and greater testimony about the afterlife than what God has already provided us in His revealed word. Simply put, it is a foolish thing to set aside the veritable record of the NT to accept *instead* the fanciful account of someone's journey into the afterlife—one that was admittedly experienced under extreme duress.

Even so, we cannot deal responsibly with the subject of the afterlife without confronting the NDE phenomenon.

Laying Some Ground Rules

Before we go any further in this discussion, it is important for us to establish an objective basis for it. We are supposed to be rational, competent, and critical-thinking people. We are supposed to be objective in our thinking, not subjective; we should be looking for facts, evidences, and proofs, not led astray by fiction, fantasy, and emotions. Any discussion about the afterlife necessarily involves a discussion about God, the human soul, and the ultimate destination of that soul. In other words, it is serious business. It is not a subject to be explained by "I think," "I feel," or "I believe." You and I are allowed our opinions on things unknown to us. But these opinions cannot *replace* the unknown, and they certainly cannot supersede what *is* known—namely, what God has already said on the matter.

Having said that, consider the following ground rules for this kind of discussion:

- Just because we do not have information on or an explanation of something does not mean such information or explanation *does not exist*. It simply means we do not know these things. God, for whatever reason, has not provided us with such details (and He does not have to explain why); or, we are not privileged to know them.[151] We would do well to accept this: not only do we not know everything we want to know, but we do not *need* to know it, either. For example, what we *do not* know about the afterlife is considerably greater than what we *do* know. Yet, this does not mean this unknown information does not exist, only that we are not (for whatever reason) privy to it.
- The examination of whatever subject we wish to consider (and especially one of a spiritual nature) can be divided into three general categories: what we know for certain; what we *think* we know; and what we do not or cannot know. What we know for certain is what has been proved to be true (or, *the truth*). It is supported by relevant evidence, credible witnesses, sound reasoning, and (in the case of divine revelation) miraculous authentication. What we *think* we know also may be supported by evidence, witnesses, etc., but is limited in nature. We do not have enough evidence to come to a final, absolute, and universally-applied conclusion. It remains only our opinion on the matter. We may have a very well-supported, well-reasoned, and plausible opinion, but it is an opinion all the same. What we *do not* know or *cannot* know refers to things that are simply outside of human knowledge, experience, or access. Either we do not know these things *yet* because they remain undiscovered, or they are

undiscoverable. Only God Himself knows them, and, for His own reasons, He has not disclosed them to us.

What we know for certain:	What we *think* we know, but cannot be proved:	What we *cannot* know, but are free to speculate:
Whatever truths God has revealed in His word; or, whatever is proved to be true by incontrovertible and impartial evidence	Educated opinions based on principles and patterns of God's revealed word; or based upon intuition, personal experiences, or deductive reasoning	Anything that God has not specifically revealed, or for which He has said nothing
These cannot be changed, but are facts and constants	These *can* be changed, as our understanding of God's word increases or develops, or as we receive new or better information	These *can* be changed, but such changes are irrelevant since they are based only on human imagination

- If we are going to be logical, objective, and critical thinkers, we are not allowed to make unwarranted, unjustified, and fanciful leaps from negligible or questionable evidence to a factual conclusion. You might recall infamous cases of scientists finding some miniscule bone evidence of what they called prehistoric man and then creating an entire skeleton, lifestyle, culture, and sometimes even a wardrobe from this scant evidence. Thus, Java Man (1891), Piltdown Man (1912), Peking Man (1928), and Neanderthal Man (1950s) have all been proven to be misdiagnoses, blunders, or outright frauds.[152] This approach is not science, and it is not scientific; it is not made any *more* scientific just because "scientists" are involved. Wishful thinking must never be mistaken for critical thinking. Keep this in mind when considering "authorities" or "experts" who, in essence, claim to

be smarter than God on subjects about which they know little or nothing (1 Tim. 1:6–7).
- We cannot determine a universal certainty—i.e., something that happens to *all* people, regardless of time in history, ethnicity, culture, gender, or personal circumstances—by the testimony of an extremely small percentage of people. Such testimonies are even further unusable or altogether discredited when they have nothing but these people's own very private experiences to support them. Claims about "what happens to us when we die" ought to be regarded with a great deal of skepticism. "When *we* die" is a broad, universal statement; it can only represent what *all* people experience if the one telling us this has the credentials to speak for all of humanity—or is *transcendent* of humanity (as God is). An exception to this would be a person who has been given authority *by* God to speak for Him *and* (not "or") provides miraculous proof of this authority. Even Jesus told us *not to believe Him* unless He provided miraculous proof that what He said was indeed from God (John 10:37–38). The apostle Paul spoke with great authority, but backed it up with demonstrations of great power (Rom. 15:18–19, 1 Cor. 2:3–5, 2 Cor. 12:12, etc.). Remarkable claims require remarkable proofs (Heb. 2:3b–4). Words alone are not enough, and earthly claims of the spiritual realm are not enough, "For the kingdom of God does not consist in words but in power" (1 Cor. 4:20).
- Just because a person *thinks* he saw, felt, heard, detected, or experienced something that contradicts natural expectations does not mean he *did*. The human mind, especially when under great duress or facing highly traumatic circumstances, can produce all sorts of false information. Anyone who has dealt with the manic episodes of someone who is bipolar knows that something can seem *very real* to the one having the episode but *complete fiction* to the one observing him. This is not to suggest for a moment any ill-intent or purposeful deception on the part of the one who "saw" something. In his mind, he *did* see it—but he "saw" it *in his mind*. That doesn't make it real, even though it seems incredibly real to *him*. It is not my responsibility to explain what a person claims to have seen; it *is* my responsibility to withhold accepting

his claim as *the gospel truth* in the absence of factual, objective, and corroborating evidence.

- Finally, whatever a person thinks he saw, felt, heard, etc., is *most certainly false* or simply *his imagination* if it contradicts whatever God has already revealed. The Holy Spirit does not give conflicting revelations to us; He does not speak out of both sides of His mouth. God is not going to give a person undergoing a traumatic experience a *different* truth (or gospel) than what He has revealed to everyone else. To claim otherwise is to incur His divine judgment (Gal. 1:8). And yes, what God has said about the afterlife is part of His gospel, since it has to do with the disposition of human souls in the spiritual realm—a subject on which He is the highest and best authority.

Again, none of this is meant to call a person's *intentions* into question, only the reality of what they believe to have seen while in an allegedly "dead" state of being. Our beliefs about the afterlife must not rest upon the claims of a relatively few extraordinary testimonies. "As Christians, intellectual honesty compels us to candidly acknowledge that...our hope of conscious life after death is rooted and grounded in the Biblical revelation."[153]

Subjective Experiences

God "has spoken to us in His Son, whom He appointed heir of all things, through whom also He made the world" (Heb. 1:2)—a most profound claim. Yet, Christ has validated this "speaking" with eyewitness accounts, fulfillment of hundreds of ancient prophecies, and numerous miracles. He has told us whatever He wants us to know about the afterlife; He has withheld from us far more than He has revealed. He has told us everything we need to know "pertaining to life and godliness" (2 Peter 1:3); He has purposely *not* told us what it is like to die, what we will see upon our own death, and *nothing* about encounters or conversations with angels along the way.[154]

Then some random person comes along and gives us his truly *incredible* story about what he "saw" beyond this world. He claims to have detailed knowledge about things that (it is thought) he could not have known otherwise. He provides a graphic and fantastic depiction of what no one else has seen, often including angelic encounters, conversations, and even prophetic utterances. He returns to the world of the living and tells everyone what he "saw," and many people, predisposed and maybe even desperate to believe that what he said is true, listen to him as though listening to an angel—or even God Himself.

This is amazing. Jesus came *from* the spiritual realm, provided credible proofs *of* this fact, then returned *to* the spiritual realm after walking out of His own tomb (without any human assistance), and most people shrug, yawn, and turn away in disinterest. But some woman (like Betty Eadie, author of *Embraced by the Light*), some doctor (like Eben Alexander, author of *Proof of Heaven*), or even a very young boy (like Colton Burpo, whose story is told in *Heaven Is for Real*) unleashes a fantastic tale, each person having no divinely-supported credentials, and we need to write a book about it, make a movie about it, and believe it as though it were the *gospel truth*. Suddenly, everyone is all ears! Suddenly, we have "proof" that there really *is* an afterlife! Jesus' testimony was apparently not enough: we need this *new* testimony to convince us. What just happened? What are we to do with this?

Some will argue that it is not just one or two random people who have these experiences, but thousands of people over a period of time. The online Near Death Experience Research Foundation (NDERF) makes the statistical claim that there are 774 NDEs in America every year.[155] The math is fuzzy, however, and the "research" involves information-gathering techniques that are extremely subjective in nature. Furthermore, "It is of no small interest that when certain psychic phenomena is in vogue, suddenly it becomes epidemic. Many begin to share the same experience."[156] This is as true about NDEs as it is about UFO sightings, alien abductions, and paranormal experiences. NDEs are among the spiritual trends of the late 20th century, now spilling into the 21st century. Prior to this, hardly anyone ever heard of such a thing. The term "near-death experience" was not even coined until the 1975 publication of Raymond Moody's book, *Life after Life*. Proponents of NDEs counter such skepticism, however, by saying that "as public acceptance has grown, more people are willing to tell their own stories."[157] This is a convenient, yet not convincing, response.

I am not here to argue whether a person can be clinically "dead" and then resuscitated from that state. That is a subject for medical doctors; I accept their scientific conclusions. I also accept the idea that a human being's perception of what is happening to him may be influenced by subconscious input rather than conscious.[158] There is a great deal about the subconscious human mind that remains little understood or altogether unknown to us. Thus, a person may "see" the details of the life-saving efforts of doctors and nurses while being unconscious. He may claim to have watched from above as people attempt to save his life. However, as a listener to such an account, I have no reason to set aside all biblical evidence about God, the soul, death, and the afterlife simply because of what that person claims to have experienced. There is a huge, impassible gulf between these two things.

Claims about God, the soul, and the afterlife involve the spiritual realm, not the human psychological realm. We cannot enter voluntarily into the spiritual realm unless we are *invited* to do so and then *taken* there by an authority that far exceeds our own. Thus, the apostle Paul was "caught up" to God's world where he saw and heard things that the subconscious mind cannot see or hear on its own power (2 Cor. 12:2–4). If it *could*, then why does it need some "near-death experience" to do so? Why aren't people doing this *at will* whenever they choose, regardless of their circumstances?

Likewise, the apostle John was invited and then ushered into God's heavenly throne scene (Rev. 4:1–2). We ourselves can stand before God's throne *in faith*—that is, we can "go" there according to our spiritual belief system—but we cannot literally *be* there unless we are invited and taken there. A traumatic experience does not qualify as such an invitation; a near-death experience does not have the power, so to speak, to escort us to where God is.

Given this, it matters little what patients or medical doctors say about what people experience when a soul is directly confronted with death. This is an area where God alone has the right to speak. And what does He say on the matter? NDEs are foreign to the revealed word of God. There is no account in the Bible of someone who *almost* died but was revived and resuscitated. "The Scriptures report a number of resurrections. It is significant that none of the resurrectees [*sic*] is reported as discussing anything that was 'experienced' in the interim twixt death and the resurrection."[159] Lazarus' resurrection from the dead would be a case in point (John 11:17–44); nothing has been recorded about what he "saw" or did not see while he was dead for four days. Jesus' own resurrection would be another: He did not say what *He* saw or experienced, even though as the Son of God we can safely assume that He *did* have conscious knowledge of what was happening to Him—or, more accurately, what He was *making happen*.

In other words, people are claiming to have experiences about the spiritual realm that the Holy Spirit *never* revealed (or, at least, was never recorded *as* divine revelation). This should make any objective thinker highly skeptical of such claims. The burden of proof is not on me, the listener to such stories; it is upon the one who tells them. Even if they believe with all their heart that they are honest, sincere, and really did experience what they claim, they still have to *prove* it in order for it to be believed as fact.

The Typical Near-Death Experience

There is an established pattern to the typical NDE, as collected over time.[160] This includes but is not limited to:

- An event brought on by a specific life-threatening trauma. In other words, it is not something dreamed at night, a conscious hallucination, or self-induced situation (except in cases of failed suicide attempts).
- Some form of out-of-body experience: floating over one's own body; cognizance of one's surroundings; and able to see and/or hear specific details or conversations (even though unconscious).
- The sensation of going through a long tunnel at great speed; the awareness of lights and colors; and a bright and comforting light at the end of this tunnel.
- The tunnel opens up to a brilliant light that is not only seen, but also felt: it conveys warmth, peace, and joy. There is no sense of

weight, only a floating sensation, like swimming in light (as if in warm water).
- An overwhelming sense of love, clarity, knowledge, beauty, and completeness; the ability to "see" striking details. Often, this is accompanied by music or songs one has never heard, and/or smelling aromas that one has never known.
- Seeing one's entire life as though re-living it (as if in a timeless state). During this, one is aware not only of what *happened*, but also what he was thinking, what he felt, and how what he did affected other people.
- Being met by and engaging in conversations with some angelic being(s). Often, this being would be like a narrator or tour guide, explaining what the person was seeing or who he was meeting. In some cases, the person meets and talks with people whom he once knew but have since died.
- In some cases, an encounter with Jesus (or, someone who calls himself or refers to himself as "Jesus"), and/or God Himself (or, someone who claims to be "God"). In this encounter, one receives special information or instructions. In some cases, this "Jesus" or "God" will tell the person that it is time for him to return to his earthly life.
- Some are given the choice to return to life; others are told that they *will* return; still others are *forced* to return (against their own will).
- A return to earthly life with a strong sense of "mission" or a resolution to live without fear and to love more deeply than ever before. This person claims that his life from that point forward is far more fulfilling and rewarding than before his NDE.

The fact that numerous people have had a similar experience is not convincing, if indeed this is simply how the human mind responds to tragic situations. What such people may well be experiencing is, for all intents and purposes, a psychotic episode rather than a genuine visit to the afterlife. Such episodes can manifest similar characteristics even though spread across a broad variety of people. A *mental projection* is hardly interchangeable with a *spiritual teleportation*.

The details of a common NDE testimony (above) does represent a large percentage of the cases documented, but not all are so positive or comforting. Some recall the same out-of-body sensation, and the same floating at high speed through a tunnel. But at the end of this tunnel is not a warm and comforting light, but an overwhelming feeling of fear, gripping terror, and abject hopelessness. Such people report being surrounded by demonic beings that inflict horror and pain upon them. Some enter what has been dubbed "the void"—a completely dark, timeless, apathetic, and *empty* state of being. In this "void," one is intimately confronted with his sins, his lack of love for others, and the darkness of his soul. Leo MacDonald, a self-proclaimed expert on the subject, writes:

> For some souls, the void is a beautiful and heavenly experience because, in the absence of all else, they are able to perfectly see the love and light they have cultivated within themselves. For other souls, the void is a terrifying and horrible hell because, in the absence of everything, they are able to perfectly see…the lack of love and light they have cultivated within themselves. For this reason, the void is more than a place for the reflection of the soul. For some souls, it is a place for purification. In the latter case, the void acts as a kind of time-out where troubled souls remain until they choose a different course of action.
>
> The void is not punishment. It is the perfect place for all souls to see themselves and to purge themselves from all illusions. For those souls who are too self-absorbed in their own misery to see the light, there are a multitude of Beings of Light nearby to help them when they freely choose to seek them. The nature of love and light is such that it cannot be forced upon people who don't want it. Choosing love/light over darkness is the key to being freed from the void. The moment the choice is made, the light and tunnel appears and the soul is drawn into the light.[161]

What is the objective reader to make of such accounts? Where does someone come up with such information about this "void," and what makes that person qualified to know it? How (and why) are we to believe this explanation? What makes this person so special (if that's the right word) so as to have received this information? Why was he selected for this above billions of other people?

I have read through many books, articles, and published accounts of NDEs. In doing so, I felt like I was reading through someone else's fantastic dream—or drug-induced hallucination. The accounts lack authority, believability, and *purpose*. I am *not* saying all those involved did not "see" or "feel" something. I *am* saying that they cannot provide convincing proof of such experiences that do not have some *other* explanation than being projected into the afterlife. For example, recreational *and* some prescription drugs, anesthetics, delirium tremens (a.k.a. DTs, experienced during alcohol detoxification), UTIs (in elderly people), extreme sleep deprivation, and trauma itself can create false mental images that seem very real. I have dealt with a number of people who "saw" things that simply did not exist, yet swore what they saw was real. If this is possible during a conscious experience, it stands to reason that it can be just as possible during an unconscious one.

If NDEs of the afterlife are prompted and orchestrated by someone (or something?) in the spiritual realm, as many NDE-ers believe, this begs the question: what purpose do these accounts serve? Why *these* people and not *everyone* (or at least far more than what is claimed)? Why only under extreme duress and not at other times? What message is being communicated? What message could these people be given that is better or more important or even more believable than the gospel message of salvation that God has revealed to *everyone* for *all time* (Jude 1:3)? What proof do these people present as credible and irrefutable, aside from their own intensely private testimony that was admittedly induced by extraordinary circumstances?

Conspicuously, in some cases, those who claim to have had a NDE have profited handsomely from telling or selling their stories in the form of interviews, books, TV appearances, or movie rights. Where some *have* profited, you can be sure that others will say whatever they have to in *hopes* of cashing in on the trend. Yet, even in the cases of those who swear to be honest and sincere ("I am *not* making this up!"), their stories lack proof or substantiation. In other words, some people are seeking fame and (hopefully) fortune by making fantastic claims that appear uncontestable.

Second Chances and False Prophets

Many NDE accounts reveal a "second chance" opportunity. A person may not have thought too much about God, his soul, or where his soul was headed, but suddenly an NDE changes his mind. Allegedly, the message from the great beyond was, "Now that you've had this brush with death, go back to your earthly life and do better!"[162] Interestingly, *not once* in any account that I read did someone become a Christian (in the way the Bible instructs) because of their experience. Many became more "spiritual," "spiritually-aware," or "religious-minded," but that is not the same thing as becoming a disciple to Christ. My questions are: Why are these few (select?) people given this alleged second chance, but not everyone? Why are they never told to go back, read the Bible, obey the gospel of Christ, and lead a Christian life thereafter—like what you and I are expected to do? Why is what they "see" in their preferential vision so much more important than what you and I are expected to "see" by faith in God and His word? And, *who decides* all these things without providing excellent and believable reasons for them?

We are not to believe everything a person says—especially things about God and His doctrine (1 John 4:1). In Jeremiah's day, people were claiming to have had heavenly visions that contradicted what God revealed to His prophet. "Then the LORD said to [Jeremiah], 'The prophets are prophesying falsehood in My name. I have neither sent them nor commanded them nor spoken to them; they are prophesying to you a false vision, divination, futility and the deception of their own minds" (Jer. 14:14). This still happens today. An NDE testimony, whenever and however it contradicts what God has already revealed in His gospel, is a *false vision* and a "deception of [one's] own mind."

A person does not have to have demon horns and carry a pitchfork to be a false prophet. He simply offers a teaching that poses to be *from God* that he knows is wrong *or* contradicts what God has already declared is right. An NDE-er may claim, directly or by implication, "God gave me this message—it is a truth that *supersedes* what was written earlier in the Bible!" Just think about how this sounds.

Divinely-revealed truth was given by Jesus Christ and His hand-picked apostles, verified by numerous miracles and eyewitness accounts, and has survived intact for some 2,000 years. Now, suddenly—without explanation, and without even *greater* proofs than before—a few people come along and claim their message "supersedes" what was written. This sounds like propaganda from Satan, not inspired teaching of God.

In *most* cases of NDEs, people claim to be loved, accepted, and approved by God (or Jesus, and/or His angels). God loves everyone, so there is no surprise here. But God does not accept or approve of *anyone* who does not belong to Him "in Christ." Those who reject God, reject His Son, or reject His word will not be warmly welcomed into Christ's presence. Such people are "hostile" to God and therefore remain "dead" in their sins (Rom. 8:6–8, Eph. 2:1–3). Those who reject Christ also reject God (Luke 10:16), and no NDE can resolve this. We have no reason to think that an alleged NDE duplicates what the blood of Christ does in atoning for sin—or worse: renders His blood *irrelevant* or *unnecessary* for salvation.

This presents a serious and irreconcilable dilemma: either what God told us (through Christ, His Spirit, and His apostles) *was not true* or *does not matter*, or such NDE accounts are *not real*. By "not real," I do not mean that such people necessarily made up their NDE. Rather, their claimed experience, vision, or encounter with God was not really with God at all, but is something else. If a person told me that he had an NDE in which he saw, heard, or experienced things that compromised or contradicted the gospel record, I would answer: "I don't know *what* you saw, felt, heard, or experienced, but—with all due respect—I cannot accept this as a message *from God*. Whatever you believe God told you in your NDE, it cannot be anything different than what He has already told *everyone* in His gospel. I strongly caution against assuming your personal conviction or an unexplainable experience to be a 'heavenly message.'"

Many researchers and psychologists claim that NDEs about hell, torture, and encounters with demons are simply a projection of a person's tormented soul. That person's guilt, intense shame, rejection, and despair are visually formed in a terrifying experience that projects his fear of the loss of his soul. But why not apply this same explanation for people's NDE accounts of heaven, ethereal peace, angels, and God Himself? What if people who (real or imagined) are at peace with themselves, relatively content, well-adjusted, etc. are simply visually forming their own anticipation of a happy future? Why is an NDE merely a "mental projection" when it is negative, but must be accepted as real and believable when it is positive? This logically-inconsistent approach reveals some of the bias toward this subject, and does irreparable damage to its credibility.

An Authentic View of the Spiritual Realm

The book of Revelation opens as follows: "The Revelation of Jesus Christ, which God gave Him to show to His bond-servants, the things which must soon take place; and He sent and communicated it by His angel to His bond-servant John, who testified to the word of God and to the testimony of Jesus Christ, even to all that he saw" (1:1–2). I realize this is not an NDE, but it is God's prophetic communication to the seven churches of the Roman province of Asia Minor (1:4) and remains a primary and authoritative record of the spiritual world. John's otherworldly, behind-the-scenes, heavenly vision begins in Rev. 4:1 and ends in 22:9. While he saw many amazing scenes, wonders, and creatures, and heard many remarkable words, there are some essential truths that we would do well to recognize:

- John himself was a credible eyewitness of these things. He was one of Christ's hand-picked apostles; as such, he was the highest authority on earth for all things heavenly and doctrinal (for Christ's church). He was endowed with authority to communicate divine truth to God's people, and proved this through the performance of miracles (Heb. 2:3–4).
- What God revealed to John in this revelation is consistent with what had already been revealed, although in a different format (i.e., in a highly symbolic vision vs. literal instruction). John did not see *or* record "a different gospel" (see Gal. 1:6–8), but the *same* gospel in a different mode of communication. The gospel Paul preached and the gospel John underscored in Revelation are not two separate (or competing) messages of salvation, but one and the same.

- Thus, whatever John "saw" in his vision did not contradict, modify, or even cause us to question whatever the Holy Spirit had already revealed to men who wrote the rest of the NT. That message is essentially this:
- There are only two groups of people in God's sight: those who stand with Christ, and everyone else.
- Despite the fantastic scenes John saw, it is still necessary to become a Christian to be saved. He is not given and does not offer a separate or alternative method of salvation.
- This earthly life is the *only* opportunity to choose your allegiance, whether to Christ or something else. There are no second chances; there is no purgatory (of any kind); there are no special cases; and there are no exceptions or exemptions—NDEs notwithstanding.
- Christ personally admonishes all Christians to "be faithful until death" (Rev. 2:10)—not just "faithful" to whatever seems real, true, or important to each person, but to what *God has revealed* is real, true, and important. Being faithful to one's own heart is not necessarily the same thing as being faithful to Christ.
- There most certainly *is* a spiritual realm, a human soul, an afterlife, a Judgment Day, and a final and irrevocable separation between those faithful to Christ and everyone else.
- There most certainly *is* a heaven *and* a hell. Heaven is where God is and where His church will be in glory. Hell is where Satan is and where all who follow him will be in the "outer darkness" (Rev. 20:11–15, 22:14–15).
- The only group of people entering into glory with God will be Christ's church (His "bride"—Rev. 19:7–9, 21:1–5). There will be no other church, no other religious group, and no other body of people.

John's vision of the spiritual realm—for all intents and purposes, the *afterlife*—is not a personal, trauma-induced, hallucinogenic experience that cannot be corroborated by anyone or anything else. Instead, it is a genuine and believable prophecy designed to inform, inspire, encourage, and warn God's people not to give up their faith but to *uphold the gospel of Christ*, even in daunting circumstances. This should be our message as well: *not*, "Do whatever your heart tells you"; *not*, "Believe whatever some angelic being in an NDE told you"; and *not*, "Do whatever God told you in your alleged conversation with Him." Rather: Do what Christ has declared to be true—not just for you or a handful of NDE-ers, but for *all* people, regardless of what they face in this life.

Summary Thoughts

The NDE discussion actually is a fascinating one, but this is because of the power of the human mind and imagination rather than learning about the afterlife. Even so, we can choose to approach this subject subjectively (allowing our emotions and personal biases dictate our judgment) or objectively (by considering the facts, and comparing "what happened" with what we know to be true). Those who claim to have had an NDE usually believe what they saw or experienced while near death was real. But something can seem very real to an individual person and still not be objectively true. Likewise, just because someone chooses *not* to believe in something does not, by itself, make it untrue.

Remember the "ground rules" stated in the opening of this section. These use a critical-thinking approach to the subject rather than merely a religious one. We cannot approach something so important as the afterlife just by guessing, being creative, making unwarranted leaps of logic, or imposing a universal teaching based on a few very subjective experiences. Furthermore, *whatever* a person thinks he saw, felt, heard, or encountered in an NDE *most certainly is* false (or, is a projection of his own imagination) *whenever* it contradicts what God has already revealed to be true. You and I have no good reason to accept as true the fantastic claims of people who ultimately have no proof other than their own personal conviction. Authority is a huge factor here, as it always is in biblical teaching, because without it we are deceived into trusting in things that are not true or have been plucked out of thin air.

Are people really having NDEs? According to those who swear by them, *yes*. Their NDEs, however, were *not* necessarily trips to the "great beyond," but likely were creations of their human imagination when confronted with an extreme situation. How much stock should the rest of us put in these accounts? My strong advice is: *not very much*. This is not a personal dismissal of those people's integrity; rather, we would be wise to choose the facts of the biblical record over their testimonies.

What you choose to believe about the afterlife, however, does not change what you will really encounter there. Once you die and leave this earthly context that you have enjoyed until now, you will be fully engulfed in God's world. When that happens, you will no longer be able to make personal choices and believe whatever you want, as you do now. Then, all your choices will have already been made, and God will simply finalize them forever. And, the only thing that you will believe is *the truth*, since this is the only belief system in the heavenly realm. There will be no more alleged NDEs, no delusions, no false conclusions, no false religions, and no false claims of any kind.

Given this, the big question has nothing to do with NDEs. The real question is: Are you ready for what you will be confronted with after your *own* death experience? This is what should be of the greatest importance to you.

Sources Used for This Study

Alcorn, Randy. *If God Is Good*. Colorado Springs, CO: Multnomah Books, 2009.

Allen, Jimmy. *What Is Hell Like? (and Other Sermons)*. Dallas, TX: Christian Publishing Co., 1965.

Barker, Dan. *Godless*. Berkeley, CA: Ulysses Press, 2008.

Barnes, Albert. *Barnes' Notes on the Old Testament*, electronic edition. Database © 2010 by WORDsearch Corp.

Bell, Rob. *Love Wins*. New York: HarperOne, 2011.

Boatman, Russell. *What the Bible Says about the End Time*. Joplin, MO: College Press, 1980.

Brogaard, Betty. *The Homemade Atheist*. Berkeley, CA: Ulysses Press, 2010.

Clark, Robert T., and James D. Bales. *Why Scientists Accept Evolution*. Grand Rapids: Baker Book House, 1966.

Dawkins, Richard. *The God Delusion*. New York: Houghton Mifflin Co., 2006.

DeSpelder, Lynne Ann, and Albert Lee Strickland. *The Last Dance: Encountering Death and Dying*, 4th ed. Mountain View, CA: Mayfield Publishing Co., 1996.

D'Souza, Dinesh. *God Forsaken*. Carol Stream, IL: Tyndale House Publishers, 2012.

Geisler, Norman L. *Christian Apologetics*. Grand Rapids: Baker Book House, 1976.

_____ *If God, Why Evil?* Bloomington, MN: Bethany House Publishers, 2011.

Geisler, Norman L., and Frank Turek. *I Don't Have Enough Faith to Be an Atheist*. Wheaton, IL: Crossway, 2004.

Hitchens, Christopher. *God Is Not Great: How Religion Poisons Everything*. New York: Twelve/Hachette Book Group USA, 2007.

Holman Bible Dictionary, electronic edition. Trent C. Butler, gen. ed. © 1991 by Holman Bible Publishers; database © 2008 by WORDsearch Corp.

The International Standard Bible Encyclopedia, electronic edition. © 1979 by Wm. B. Eerdmans Publishing Co.; database © 2013 by WORDsearch Corp.

Jamieson, Robert, A. R. Fausset, and David Brown. *Commentary Critical and Explanatory on the Whole Bible (1871)*, electronic edition. Database © 2012 by WORDsearch Corp.

Kelly, Henry Ansgar. *Satan: A Biography*. New York: Cambridge University Press, 2006.

Kushner, Harold. *When Bad Things Happen to Good People*. New York: Schocken Books, 1989.

C. S. Lewis, *The Problem of Pain*. New York: Simon & Schuster, 1996.

McGuiggan, Jim. *The Dragon Slayer: Reflections on the Saving of the World*. McGuiggan Publishing, 2004.

Mills, David. *Atheist Universe: The Thinking Person's Answer to Christian Fundamentalism*. Berkeley, CA: Ulysses Press, 2006.

Oldridge, Darren. *The Devil: A Very Short Introduction*. New York: Oxford University Press, 2012).

Onfray, Michael. *Atheist Manifesto*, trans. by Jeremy Leggatt. New York: Arcade Publishing, 2007.

Robertson, A. T. *Word Pictures in the New Testament*, electronic edition. © 1932, 1960 by the Sunday School Board of the Baptist Convention; database © 2007 by WORDsearch Corp.

Sellers, James E. *When Trouble Comes*. New York: Abingdon Press, 1960.

Streissguth, Thomas. *The Devil*. Farmington Hills: MI: Lucent Books, 2005.

Strobel, Lee. *The Case for a Creator*. Grand Rapids: Zondervan, 2004.

Strong, James. *Strong's Talking Greek Hebrew Dictionary*, electronic edition. Database © WORDsearch Corp.

Sychtysz, Chad. *The Gospel of Forgiveness*. Waynesville, OH: Spiritbuilding Publishers, 2011.

_____. *The Gospel of Saving Grace.* Waynesville, OH: Spiritbuilding Publishers, 2020.

_____. *The Holy Spirit of God: A Biblical Perspective.* Waynesville, OH: Spiritbuilding Publishers, 2010.

_____. *Seeking the Sacred.* Waynesville, OH: Spiritbuilding Publishers, 2009.

Thayer, Joseph. *Thayer's Greek-English Lexicon,* electronic edition. Database © 2014 by WORDsearch Corp.

Vincent, Martin R. *Vincent's Word Studies,* electronic edition. Database © 2014 by WORDsearch Corp.

Welch, Edward. *Addictions: A Banquet in the Grave.* Phillipsburg, NJ: P & R Publishing, 2001.

The Zondervan Pictorial Bible Encyclopedia, vol. 2. Merrill C. Tenney, gen. ed. Grand Rapids: Zondervan Corporation, 1976.

Endnotes

1 By "spiritual" here, I only mean something other than "physical." The word "metaphysical" would work, as long as it is used in a practical context with no reference to mysticism or alleged paranormal activity.

2 The evolutionist has many impossible scenarios to attempt to explain, such as how: something came from nothing; energy organized itself into material form (apart from an even *greater* energy to accomplish this); life came from non-life; simplicity leads to complexity; independence leads to interdependence; information (such as DNA) organizes itself into existence in order to determine *future* form; non-intelligence becomes intelligence; and all of the physical universe, despite winding down and cooling off (according to laws of thermodynamics) somehow achieved a far *greater* state than before without any outside intervention. This is the short list; the actual list could fill a book. Christianity, in sharp contrast, has only one scenario to prove in order for everything else to make sense: the existence of an all-powerful and all-knowing Creator. Once this is established (to the degree that is necessary, not for answering every question concerning this), everything else has a logical explanation.

3 Quoted by David Mills, *Atheist Universe: The Thinking Person's Answer to Christian Fundamentalism* (Berkeley, CA: Ulysses Press, 2006), 65.

4 Atheists are quick to say that creationism (their word, not mine), because it cannot be explained scientifically, is mere religious dogma (Mills, *Atheist Universe*, 76). In other words, if God and His actions do not conform to what we know about the physical universe, then He does not exist. This view does not disprove God; it only allows Him to *be* "God" according to present human knowledge and human expectations. This defies the very concept of God—a Being that is transcendent of the material world and the Creator of all branches of science. Atheists assume that "science" is the standard by which all things must be measured, but they have never explained, even remotely, where science itself came from.

5 Robert T. Clark and James D. Bales, *Why Scientists Accept Evolution* (Grand Rapids: Baker Book House, 1966), 38.

6 It is not that all the evidence supports Evolution (or, Darwinism), but "that the Darwinists have defined science in such a way that the only possible answer is Darwinism. ... False science is bad science, and it's the Darwinists who are practicing it. ... *Science* doesn't really say anything—*scientists* do" (Norman L. Geisler and Frank Turek, *I Don't Have Enough Faith to Be an Atheist* [Wheaton, IL: Crossway, 2004], 123–124, 128). In other words, instead of pure, unbiased, objective science "proving" Evolution, what *passes*

for "science" is nothing more than propaganda put forward by those who have a vested interest (careers, academic credentials, peer approval, grants, etc.) in protecting it. Richard Dawkins, in a 1989 New York Times book review, said: "It is absolutely safe to say that if you meet somebody who claims not to believe in evolution, that person is ignorant, stupid, or insane (or wicked, but I'd rather not consider that)" (quoted in *ibid.*, 162). Atheists/Evolutionists all claim that they want "truth" to reign supreme, as long as it is *their version* of it and that they are the only ones qualified to *know* it.

7   "Evolution is taken for granted today and it is uncritically accepted by scientists as well as laymen. It is accepted by them today because it was already accepted by others who went on before them and under whose direction they obtained their education" (Clark and Bales, *Why Scientists Accept Evolution*, 106).

8   I strongly recommend Dinesh D'Souza's book, *God Forsaken* (Carol Stream, IL: Tyndale House Publishers, 2012). He argues that the so-called "New Atheists" are obsessed with God, yet in so many cases, "[their] atheism seems to have more to do with disappointment of God" rather than any grand proofs against His existence (18–19). "With [Richard] Dawkins, as with others, we are not dealing with ordinary atheism; we are dealing with wounded theism. The wounded theist is distinguished from the atheist in that the atheist doesn't believe in God; the wounded theist is angry with God. In some cases the wounded theist hates God; his atheism is a form of revenge" against Him for whatever He has done to disappoint him (20).

9   Richard Dawkins, noted atheist, is especially malicious in his characterization of "the God of the Old Testament": He is "arguably the most unpleasant character in all of fiction: jealous and proud of it; a petty, unjust, unforgiving control freak; a vindictive, bloodthirsty ethnic cleanser; a misogynistic [i.e., woman-hating], homophobic, racist, infanticidal, genocidal, filicidal [i.e., a parent's deliberate killing of their own child(ren)], pestilential, megalomaniacal, sadomasochistic, capriciously malevolent bully" (*The God Delusion* [New York: Houghton Mifflin Co., 2006], 31; bracketed words are mine). Dawkins' complete misrepresentation of God overlooks the full context in which God and His dealings with humankind operate, but it is not his intent to be fair, objective, or even honest in his assessment. Dan Barker, another noted atheist, says of Jesus that He is selfish, callous, elite, violent, irrational, mentally unstable, ruthless, morally bankrupt, tyrannical, a thug, a lunatic, and doesn't "have the faintest concept of morality" (*Godless* [Berkeley, CA: Ulysses Press, 2008], 178–183). Apparently, vicious name-calling is all part of the atheist's "proof" that God does not exist and that Jesus failed to meet that person's expectations. This is not new: even the Pharisees called Jesus many names and accused Him of being mentally unstable and demon-possessed, yet their opinions ignored the facts and, in the end, failed to accomplish anything.

10   "[M]any of the atheists are very arrogant. I encounter them all the time. ... Reason itself becomes a casualty when people have so high an opinion of their own cleverness" (D'Souza, *God Forsaken*, 59).

11   Barker sums this up: "If God knows in advance that there will be evil as a direct or indirect result of his actions, then he is not all good. He is at least partly responsible for the harm. Since God has the desire to eliminate all evil, why doesn't he? If God truly is all-knowing and all-powerful, then he is not omni-benevolent [i.e., all-good] when he does not stop unnecessary harm" (*Godless*, 126; bracketed words are mine). Instead of admitting that he does not understand all that is going on or all that God is doing (or not doing), Barker assumes a position of moral superiority. He feels comfortable questioning God's motives and judging God by his own assessment of how an all-powerful and all-knowing Being ought to act. Since God disappointed him, therefore not only is He wrong, but He is not even allowed to exist. Sadly, this elitist approach is very common among atheists.

12   God leaves sufficient room for skepticism, doubt, atheism, and ridicule, just as He has also provided sufficient evidence for truth, understanding, belief, and marvel at His Creation. In this sense, God leaves Himself very vulnerable to human criticism. He does so only because He knows absolutely what is real, true, and meaningful; human criticism is often blinded by pride and emotions, limited in knowledge and scope, and often compromised by conflicts of interest. Just as God leaves Himself open to such criticism, so Christians accept the criticism and mockery of their faith in God simply because they believe in the reality, truth, and evidence that He has revealed in His word.

13   Betty Brogaard, *The Homemade Atheist* (Berkeley, CA: Ulysses Press, 2010), 131.

14   William Provine of Cornell University stated that if Darwinism (i.e., Evolutionism) is true: there is no evidence for God; there is no life after death; there is no absolute foundation for right and wrong; there is no ultimate meaning for life; and people do not really have a free will (cited by Lee Strobel, *The Case for a Creator* [Grand Rapids: Zondervan, 2004], 16).

15   Even so, the Evolutionist claims that the material world gave *life* to non-living, inanimate, and non-spiritual things, which defies all logic, reason, and observation—all components of genuine science. A non-living, material world cannot give to itself what it did not possess in the first place. We could say the same thing about sight, hearing, taste, emotions, love, hate, guilt, joy, and the perception of time. Just as a rock cannot give birth to a fish—no matter *how many eons of time* we throw at it—so a material world cannot give birth to a human soul.

16 "Inspired" can be a misleading English translation in the cited text. The original Greek word here [*theopneustos*] literally means "God-breathed," which tells us that whatever *is* Scripture (i.e., the sacred writings of God's spokesmen) came *from* God. In effect, the emphasis is not what God breathed *into* men as much as it is what God breathed *out* as divine truth. "God's breath is the irresistible outflow of His power. When Paul declares, then, that 'every scripture' or 'all scripture' is the product of the divine breath, 'is God-breathed,' he asserts that Scripture is the product of a specifically divine operation" (G. W. Bromiley, "Inspiration," *International Standard Bible Encyclopedia*, revised and electronic edition [© 1979 by Wm. B. Eerdmans Publishing Co.; database © 2013 by WORDsearch Corp.]. This does not mean that God determined every literal word that His apostles wrote, but that their teaching was consistent with what He communicated to them by way of divine revelation (Gal. 1:11–12). God allowed these men to maintain their personality, writing style, and (to some degree) word choices in their writings; yet, the theological statements that they made were overseen and conditioned by the influence of His Holy Spirit (see, for example, 1 Cor. 2:12, 14:37–38, 1 Tim. 4:1, and 2 Peter 1:20–21).

17 Recommended readings on this include: Dinesh D'Souza, *What's So Great about Christianity*; Norman L. Geisler and Frank Turek, *I Don't Have Enough Faith to Be an Atheist*; Josh McDowell, *Evidence That Demands a Verdict*, vols. 1 & 2; Lee Strobel, *The Case for a Creator*; Bert Thompson, *The Case for the Existence of God*; Thomas B. Warren, *Have Atheists Proved There Is No God?*; etc.

18 Norman L. Geisler, *Christian Apologetics* (Grand Rapids: Baker Book House, 1976), 135.

19 Logically-speaking, how can someone *absolutely know* that something is *unknowable*, unless he had confirmation of this from a source greater than the limits of his own finite understanding? This is like saying, "I *know for certain* that the existence of God is 'unknowable.'" Such certainty must be based upon a god-like source of information, since it involves knowledge that is beyond this person to know from his own experiences. This creates a self-refuting position: he cites god-like knowledge to "know" that God does not exist (!). Yet, not having *full* knowledge of God is not the same thing as proof positive that He does not exist.

20 Michael Onfray, a bitter critic of God and Christianity, says that with human intelligence, "We need no posthumous paradise, no salvation or redemption of the soul, no all-knowing, all-seeing God. Properly and rationally directed, intelligence wards off all magical thinking (*Atheist Manifesto*, trans. by Jeremy Leggatt [New York: Arcade Publishing, 2007], 67). And, apparently, Onfray feels qualified to inform the rest of us exactly how human intelligence is to be "properly and rationally directed." Yet, his prejudice against God and the Bible corrupts any attempt at objectivity or sincerity. After 200+ pages of scathing ridicule, misrepresentation, contortion

of facts, and ripping Scripture out of context, he offers NOTHING on the benefits of atheism except that it doesn't have religion.

21   Lynne Ann DeSpelder and Albert Lee Strickland, *The Last Dance: Encountering Death and Dying*, 4th ed. (Mountain View, CA: Mayfield Publishing Co., 1996), 552.

22   *Ibid.*, 554.

23   James Orr, "Sheol," *ISBE* (electronic).

24   Gary A. Lee, "Hades," *ISBE* (electronic). The Septuagint (the Greek translation of the Hebrew text of the Bible, ca. 200 BC) uses "Hades" synonymously with "Sheol."

25   Ralph L. Smith, "Hell," *Holman Bible Dictionary*, electronic edition (Trent C. Butler, gen. ed.; © 1991 by Holman Bible Publishers; database © 2008 by WORDsearch Corp).

26   K. A. Kitchen, "Egypt, Land of," *The Zondervan Pictorial Bible Encyclopedia*, vol. 2 (Grand Rapids: Zondervan Corporation, 1976), 254, 256.

27   DeSpelder and Strickland, *The Last Dance*, 563.

28   For an explanation and critique of Calvinism, I recommend reading chapter 17 in my book, *The Gospel of Saving Grace* (Spiritbuilding Publishers, 2020); go to www.spiritbuilding.com/chad.

29   Adam (when he was just "dust"), Jesus (in His tomb), and every sinner-turned-Christian all have one thing in common: they were all *dead* until God breathed *life* into them. Adam was given life that he never had; Christ was given life that He once had; and the sinner is given a far better life than he ever had. In each case, it is the power of God that raised each person from his dead state.

30   DeSpelder and Strickland, *The Last Dance*, 551.

31   Adapted from Russell Boatman, *What the Bible Says about the End Time* (Joplin, MO: College Press, 1980), 266.

32   Robert Jamieson, A. R. Fausset, and David Brown, *Commentary Critical and Explanatory on the Whole Bible (1871)*, electronic edition (database © 2012 by WORDsearch Corp.). on 2 Peter 3:4.

33   Boatman, *What the Bible Says*, 272.

34   Modern Premillennialism teaches that the righteous will actually live on this physical planet forever. This man-made doctrine teaches that Christ's entire church will be "raptured" from the earth at some future time. After

this, the rest of the world will endure a seven-year "tribulation" period, in which people will have yet another opportunity to obey the gospel; those that do will be severely persecuted by some global entity known as "the beast." At the end of this seven-year period, Christ will descend from heaven with an army of angels to destroy "the beast" and *his* huge army; Satan—the power behind "the beast"—will be literally "bound" for a literal millennium. While Satan is bound, Christ will identify 144,000 selected saints (allegedly, ethnic Jews) who will reign with Him in a newly-built temple in literal Jerusalem; peace will envelop the earth. At the end of the millennium, however, Satan will be released from his prison, gather all of Christ's enemies from the earth, and wage one final battle against Christ and His saints. Satan will finally be destroyed once and for all, the 144,000 will be ushered into heaven, and all the other saints will live in a newly-cleansed, refurbished earth. Such is the basic overview of Premillennialism. The theological and logistical problems are numerous, and there are many fanciful versions of this doctrine. The point is: many believe that they will simply live on a glorified earth in some future time, yet the Bible never teaches this. The Bible says we will be with God in *His* world, not away from Him in our *own* world. Premillennialists claim that those on the glorified earth will be able to "transport" to heaven to "visit" God, who will live in a 1,500-mile-square "New Jerusalem" that will apparently be floating high above the earth, but this just adds to the absurdity of their doctrine.

35   Even those who may be unhappy with the God of the Bible still want to have their personal worth—their existence—validated by an "extraterrestrial" being far superior to themselves. The irony is: God is the greatest "extraterrestrial being" that exists, and yet many people dismiss Him in hopes of finding someone else.

36   Ironically, Paul virtually states this very point in 1 Cor. 15:13–19. If there is no resurrection, then Christ is not who He said He was, His gospel cannot help us, and we have no reason to hope in Christ or His gospel.

37   In my strong opinion, if a person cannot answer three basic questions concerning his existence in the afterlife, he ought not to think that he will have any decision-making authority *in* that realm. These three questions are: 1) What authority will you have?; 2) what language or form of communication will you use?; and 3) what will you *look* like? If a person cannot answer these three basic questions, he admits that he is heading toward a realm of which he has no knowledge but blindly hopes to assert his individual control. This is a most dangerous assumption. Meanwhile, the Christian's response to these questions ought to be: 1) God is our authority, and we will be submissive to and content with this; 2) God will take care of the communication issue, so we need not worry about it; and 3) God will give us a glorified body (2 Cor. 5:1–4), so we need not worry about this, either.

38   This reminds us of Festus' outburst in Acts 26:24: "While Paul was saying this in his defense, Festus said in a loud voice, 'Paul, you are out

of your mind! Your great learning is driving you mad.'" Festus reasoned, in essence, that since he could not make sense of Paul, therefore Paul was *senseless* and could not be understood by *anyone* with intelligence. This is where many people are at today: because God, Jesus, the afterlife, heaven, hell, immortality, and eternity do not make sense to *them*, therefore the ideas themselves are *senseless* and should be regarded as foolish to *everyone* with intelligence. Given the evidence God has provided, however, this itself is a most foolish position to maintain—the very thing that Paul gently points out to Festus in his response to the ruler's outburst.

39   Joseph Thayer, *Thayer's Greek-English Lexicon*, electronic edition (© 2014 by WORDsearch Corp.), G5591.

40   It should be interesting to us that these same statements—God being the "Alpha and Omega" and the summing up of all things—are also attributed to Christ; see Eph. 1:9–10 and Rev. 22:13.

41   Think of the statements in Scripture that speak of this, such as, "God is in heaven and you are on the earth" (Eccles. 5:4) and "Our Father, who is in Heaven" (Mat. 6:9).

42   The only exceptions to this are when God has purposely *revealed* His world to certain people, such as Paul (2 Cor. 12:1–4) and John (Rev. 4:1ff).

43   This point—that "the LORD is one"—does not invalidate the triune nature of "God." The Bible teaches that "God" in the fullest sense is the sacred and humanly-incomprehensible union of God the Father, God the Son, and God the Spirit. Each of these Personages has an individual identity and function, but all three work together in seamless cooperation toward a common goal. Thus, when Jesus said, "I and the Father are one" (John 10:30), He did not mean, "I *am* the Father"—which would have been a blasphemous statement—but rather, "I am completely *united* with My Father in nature, intent, and purpose, so that there will never be any contradiction between what *I* do or say and what *He* does or says" (see John 5:18–20, 17:20–23, Col. 2:9, and Heb. 1:1–3).

44   This is a point, ironically, implied by Satan himself when he told Jesus to turn stones into loaves of bread (Mat. 4:3–4). Given the superiority and mastery God has over our world, miraculous events recorded in the Bible—everything from the parting of the Red Sea (Exod. 14) to the sun standing still in the sky (Josh. 10:12–13) to resurrections of the dead (John 11)—are completely explainable and understandable. God, the Creator and Master of our world, can supersede the natural laws of our world whenever and however He chooses in order to serve a heavenly purpose. "Whatever the LORD pleases, He does, in heaven and in the earth, in the seas and in all the deeps" (Psalm 135:6).

45 C. S. Lewis, *The Problem of Pain* (New York: Simon & Schuster, 1996), 107.

46 *Ibid.*, 103.

47 "Perish" is from the Greek word *apollumi*, which means "to destroy fully" (literally or figuratively), "die," "lose," or "mar" (James Strong, *Strong's Talking Greek Hebrew Dictionary*, electronic edition [database © WORDsearch Corp.], G622). See other similar contextual usage of this word in 1 Cor. 1:18, 2 Cor. 4:3, 2 Thess. 2:10, and 2 Peter 3:9. In Rev. 9:11, Satan is given the name "Apollyon" ("destroyer"), which is from this same Greek root.

48 Rob Bell, *Love Wins* (New York: HarperOne, 2011), 106–107. Not surprisingly, Bell does not explain any of what he talks about here. In fact, his book is filled with ideas and claims that are based on nothing more than his own speculative imagination and creative exposition of selected verses of the Bible.

49 "As one might expect, the doctrine of universal salvation without regard for what any one may have done (or may be) in this life offers little incentive for evangelism. If God will save everyone anyhow, somehow, why concern ourselves with the lost? Likewise, the position taken offers little incentive for indoctrination and edification. Christian growth and church growth suffer sorely when it is taught that those who give themselves to the pursuits of this life will be saved without exception in the end" (Boatman, *What the Bible Says*, 319).

50 "Grace" is, in effect, anything and everything God does for us that we cannot do for ourselves for the purpose of our salvation. For a fuller study on this extremely important topic, I recommend my book, *The Gospel of Saving Grace* (Spiritbuilding Publishers, 2020); go to www.spiritbuilding.com/chad.

51 This passage reveals that the "lake of fire" (from Rev. 20:14–15) was not made for human sinners, but for Satan and all other fallen angels. However, Jesus also reveals that when human beings choose to follow demons rather than listen to their Creator, they will share in the demons' destruction.

52 The Greek word for "hell" here is *gehenna* (G1067). "*Gehenna* is a transliteration from the Aramaic form of the Hebrew *gē-hinnōm*, 'valley of Hinnom.' This latter form, however, is rare in the Old Testament, the prevailing name being 'the valley of the son of Hinnom.'…In the New Testament (King James Version, margin notes) *Gehenna* occurs in Matthew 5:22, 29–30; Matthew 10:28; Matthew 18:9; Matthew 23:15, 33; Mark 9:43, 45, 47; Luke 12:5; [and] James 3:6. In all of these it designates the place of eternal punishment of the wicked, generally in connection with the final judgment. It is associated with fire as the source of torment. Both body and soul are cast into it. This is not to be explained on the principle that the

New Testament speaks metaphorically of the state after death in terms of the body; it presupposes [or, takes for granted] the resurrection" (Geerhardus Vos, "Gehenna," *ISBE* [electronic]; bracketed words are mine).

53   Boatman, *What the Bible Says*, 305–306; bracketed words are mine.

54   I am not going to take the time to address Calvinism here, a.k.a. the Doctrine of Predestination. This doctrine claims that God determines each soul's destiny before we are even born. This is an untenable, man-made teaching, not a biblical one. Again, I have covered this in detail in chapter 17 of my book, *The Gospel of Saving Grace* (Spiritbuilding Publishers, 2020); go to www.spiritbuilding.com/chad.

55   "If there is no hell, then the cross is a sham. If there is no hell, only a final nothingness, then Christ literally died to save us from nothing. In this case, Christ's death is robbed of its eternal significance. Unless there is an eternal separation from which people need to be delivered, the cross is emptied of its real meaning" (Norman L. Geisler, *If God, Why Evil?* [Bloomington, MN: Bethany House Publishers, 2011], 101).

56   Much of this discussion has to do with the damage that sin causes, and God's severity toward our sin. Many people are surprised (or disappointed) that God does not just forgive all of us and let our "mistakes" or "indiscretions" be considered the proverbial water under the bridge. But God makes it abundantly clear in the Bible that He is intolerant of sin and will not allow anyone into fellowship with Him who refuses to deal with his sin responsibly. The fact that *redemption* for sin required His Son to come to earth and die an awful and undeserved death on a cross is proof of how difficult it is for sin to be removed, even by God. Sadly, people's ignorance of God *and* the Bible have contributed to a blithe, shoulder-shrugging, "What's God's problem?"-kind of attitude toward sin. To such people, God's offer of salvation seems trite or unnecessary.

57   This gives us insight into God's response to the awful nature of sin: whatever is corrupted by sin must be destroyed. Those who sin cannot be rehabilitated or reformed; this is not a legal or moral solution to the problem. They can only be *redeemed* through the blood of Christ, because through this blood God's divine justice is satisfied: a life is given for a life that is destroyed (by sin).

58   William Evans, "Wrath (Anger)," *ISBE* (electronic).

59   Lewis, *The Problem of Pain*, 112.

60   God never says that souls will just cease to exist or disappear. He consistently speaks of a "punishment" in the afterlife for the unbelieving and disobedient. One cannot be punished if he is unable to experience it. A corpse cannot feel physical pain because it is dead to the physical world, but a soul *can* and *will* feel pain in the spiritual world. This is God's promise, which

is as powerful and guaranteed to be fulfilled as are His promises of reward to the faithful. "...[T]here's not a single solitary argument a man can make against the Bible doctrine of Hell which cannot be applied with equal force against the Bible doctrine of Heaven" (Jimmy Allen, *What Is Hell Like? (and Other Sermons* [Dallas, TX: Christian Publishing Co., 1965], 229).

61   We are speaking of "rich men" here as a typical class of people, not in an absolute sense. Abraham was a very rich man, but God credited him with righteousness (Rom. 4:3); Job was very wealthy, but God counted him as faithful; Joseph of Arimathea—the man who took care of Jesus' dead body—was "a rich man" (Mat. 27:57), but is honored for his kindness and demonstration of faith. While it is generally true that rich men (and rich *women*) are tethered to this world rather than being genuine servants of God, exceptions most certainly do exist.

62   The Greek text here (for "was laid") indicates a *casting*, implying a roughness or unconcern (A. T. Robertson, *Word Pictures in the New Testament*, electronic edition [© 1932, 1960 by the Sunday School Board of the Baptist Convention; database © 2007 by WORDsearch Corp.], on Luke 16:20). In this sense, people laid him at the rich man's gate like they were taking out the garbage. At best, the reason for his being laid at the rich man's gate was to solicit the sympathy and compassion of someone who could actually afford to feed and take care of him. "Was laid" also indicates Lazarus' utter helplessness: he was unable to walk, being so weakened by his poor health.

63   The word "Hades" (*Strong's* [electronic], G86)—not "hell" like the KJV renders it—refers to the realm of all departed spirits, as traditionally understood in times of antiquity. "Hades was originally the name of the god who presided over the realm of the dead... Hence the phrase, house of Hades. It...signifies, therefore, the invisible land, the realm of shadow. It is the place to which all who depart this life descend, without reference to their moral character. By this word the Septuagint [the Greek translation of the Old Testament, ca. 200 BC] translated the Hebrew *Sheol*, which has a similar general meaning. The classical Hades embraced both good and bad men, though divided into *Elysium*, the abode of the virtuous, and *Tartarus*, the abode of the wicked. In these particulars it corresponds substantially with *Sheol*; both the godly and the wicked being represented as gathered into the latter" (Martin R. Vincent, *Vincent's Word Studies*, electronic edition [database © 2014 by WORDsearch Corp.], on Mat. 16:18; bracketed words are mine).

64   The Law of Moses was preceded by numerous miracles in Israel's exodus from Egypt. The ten plagues against the Egyptians, the separation of the Israelites *from* the Egyptians during those plagues, the crossing of the Red Sea, the manna from heaven, the pillar of cloud by day and fire by night, etc. all provided more than enough *reason to believe and obey God*. Abraham's point in his exchange with the rich man is, in essence: one more miracle will

not change anything. If the rich man's brothers will not repent because of the record of miracles in the Pentateuch, they will not repent for any *lesser* reason, such as a customized miracle sent to prick their conscience. The same is true today: if one will not believe and obey because of the numerous miracles of Christ and His apostles, then a far *lesser* proof—a single, special miracle meant only for that person—will not matter. If one ignores the greater proofs, then he will most certainly ignore the lesser.

65 The account in Luke 16:19–31 does *not* teach, however, that all rich people will inevitably be lost or that all poor (or suffering) people will automatically be saved. We are judged by our faith in God, not our economic status or earthly circumstances.

66 Someone might respond, "But the same thing can be said about the Light: we do not understand it; we *cannot* fully understand it; and we cannot control it." But "the Light" has been very open, forthcoming, and transparent in its intentions. The Light is always beneficial and will never harm us; thus, we do not need to know anything about it (Him) beyond what it has revealed to us and the fact that it will always serve our best interest. None of this is true about the darkness: it purposely withholds critical information; it lies, deceives, and manipulates; and it seeks our ruin, never our best interest.

67 For what it is worth, Henry Kelly (*Satan: A Biography* [New York: Cambridge University Press, 2006]) says: "When all is said and done, Mark [in Mark 3:23–27] does not give the impression that Satan is a particularly important figure in the scheme of things. At most, he seems to be an obstructionist" (84). Instead of having any meaningful inherent power, it does appear that much of Satan's "power" *is* that of obstructing the means for human souls to have fellowship with their God. On the other hand, such obstructionist power is not to be taken lightly.

68 This alludes to the process of justification, in which the believer is brought back *up* to the righteousness of God from which he had *fallen*. To fall is to sin; to be justified is to be made righteous through the blood of Christ (Rom. 3:24). Falling is a serious and soul-threatening problem; justification is the process of overcoming that problem through the blood of Christ (Rom. 3:24). Falling is what *we* do; justifying fallen souls is something only *God* can do.

69 One of the best—and most disturbing—books I have ever read on this point is Edward Welch's *Addictions: A Banquet in the Grave* (Phillipsburg, NJ: P & R Publishing, 2001). I highly recommend it for anyone dealing with addiction—either their own or that of a loved one.

70 For the record, I am speaking with a measure of firsthand observation: my two younger brothers were alcoholics since their teen years. One died from suicide, the other from liver cancer—both directly related to their

alcoholism. While I am very much aware that they were initially victims of their culture, peer pressure, and their own poor judgment, the fact remains that they both continued this way of life by their own choosing and despite all the love, appeals, and professional therapies paid for by family members. I am not saying this to condemn them personally, but to underscore the point that alcoholism is ultimately a choice, not an irresistible or unsolicited "disease."

71   I am referring here to specific behaviors or practices that are the direct result of personal *choices* (such as drug use, unhealthy lifestyle, irresponsibility, etc.) rather than congenital circumstances (such as personal temperament) or emotional damage (such as from genuine childhood trauma, physical abuse, or sexual assault). In other words, I do not want anyone thinking that I am lumping those who have been afflicted by something beyond their control with those who have invited troubles and alleged disabilities into their own lives.

72   I am not saying that I celebrate these holidays, or even believe that they are biblically or historically accurate. I am simply pointing out the fact that they remind all Americans of Jesus' birth, death, and resurrection every year.

73   I want to be careful here *not* to say, "our *sinful* nature," because the Bible does not teach that we are programmed by God to sin. On the other hand, we *do* tend to be lazy, take shortcuts, and choose something pleasurable over discipline and hard work, if given the choice (and I speak from experience).

74   "It is more often the failure to act than the desire to cause harm that allows innocents to suffer. If the prince of darkness existed, he would surely rejoice that this truth is so easily forgotten. He might even…choose to encourage our ignorance by pretending he does not exist at all" (Darren Oldridge, *The Devil: A Very Short Introduction* [New York: Oxford University Press, 2012], 104.

75   *Strong's* (electronic), H7854.

76   Ibid., G1228. *Diabolos* means "slanderer"; whenever referring to Satan, it is always accompanied with the definite article ("the").

77   Oldridge, *The Devil: A Very Short Introduction*, 3. Oldridge also says: "[For many], the Devil is essentially a metaphor. He represents a conflux of influences—social, political, biological, and philosophical—that promote pain and destruction. … As the personification of all that is believed to be wicked, he can serve as a container for everything that an individual or community rejects. He is a kind of black mirror" (*ibid.*, 2–3). These are summaries of how people *see* the Devil, not accurate teachings about him from Scripture. Even so, they do provide an interesting perspective.

78   Quoted in Kelly, *Satan: A Biography*, 310. Schleiermacher also believed: there is no new doctrine in the NT concerning the Devil; the Devil plays no role in the plan of salvation; belief in God and Christ does not require belief in the Devil; and the Devil cannot be said to affect Christians (*ibid.*, 311). While he is certainly entitled to his opinions, much of what Schleiermacher concluded is at odds with clear NT teaching.

79   Thomas Streissguth, *The Devil* (Farmington Hills: MI: Lucent Books, 2005), 9, 76–77; bracketed words are mine. Interestingly, Evolution itself does not pass the test of modern "logic, deduction, and reasoning"; it also cannot be touched, smelled, seen, heard, or understood by any scientific means. It is a fairy tale that has been invented in order to explain the material world without any supernatural intervention.

80   The book of Job was likely written before the time of Moses, and probably concurrent with the time of Abraham. The ancients at that time did not have a universal or codified view of "Satan" as we have today, given our advantage from what has been revealed in the NT (Albert Barnes, *Barnes' Notes on the Old Testament*, electronic edition [database © 2010 by WORDsearch Corp.], on Job 1:6). In reading Job 1 – 2, we assume that "the satan" was an entity that everyone already knew—just like today's "Satan" is so well known—but this is inconclusive from the biblical text.

81   John sees a vision, not a literal historical diorama. We are not to literalize the "stars" here, which likely symbolize fallen angels. Power is what is being addressed here: Satan, as the ruler of the demons (see Rev. 9:11), *does* have considerable power and influence so as to convince "a third" (or, many) of God's angels to join his rebellion. Once thrown down *to* earth, these fallen angels' powers were unleashed *upon* the earth.

82   In John 8:44, Jesus does say that Satan "was a murderer from the beginning," but exactly what "the beginning" refers to is not conclusive. Was it the beginning of all Creation (as in John 1:1)? Or, the beginning of humankind? Or, the beginning of Satan's rebellion against God? There are several "the beginning" references in John, and most of them refer to the beginning of Jesus' ministry (6:64, 8:25, 15:27, and 16:4), not the beginning of time/creation. Because Jesus speaks of Satan as being "a murderer," many assume that this refers to Cain's murder of Abel (Gen. 4:1–8), but there is nothing to prove this. It is possible that Satan put into King Herod's heart to murder children in Bethlehem in an attempt to destroy Jesus (Mat. 2:16–18)—the "beginning" of Jesus' earthly life—but there is no way to prove this, either. But the apostle John does later equate a "murderer" with one who hates his "brother" (1 John 3:8, 15). It is possible, then, that Jesus spoke of Satan's *hatred* rather than any literal murderous event. This actually makes more sense, and thus "the beginning" would refer to Satan's fall—whenever it happened—which filled him with hatred for God, His Son, and those made in His image (i.e., all people).

83   Consider, for example, what Paul says in 2 Cor. 6:14–16. Just as this is true for Christians on earth, so it is true for spiritual beings in the spiritual realm. There is "no fellowship" between good and evil or between God and Satan.

84   Oldridge, *The Devil: A Very Short Introduction*, 8.

85   This is what we see in God having raised up Pharaoh in order to serve His purpose (Exod. 7:1–3, Rom. 9:17–18). God did not *force* Pharaoh to be evil, resistant, and unbelieving; Pharaoh did all these things of his own free will. However, God *knew* that Pharaoh would (left to himself) become this kind of person, *and* that Pharaoh would harden his heart against any message from God. Since God needed such a man to carry out His divine will, God provided for him to become the ruler of Egypt. But this is a very different scenario than God *creating* Pharaoh to be evil: this robs Pharaoh of his own free will; it also puts God in the position of ruining people through no fault of their own. This latter scenario violates everything we know about God in Scripture.

86   Some have suggested that the "condemnation" here is what one receives *from* the devil, rather than a sharing in the condemnation *of* the devil. Your Bible translation may offer an alternate reading because of this suggestion. However, Satan already condemns (in his heart) all people, and his condemnation has no effect on our standing with God. Paul is clearly warning candidates for the eldership—the subject under discussion in this passage—not to become *like* Satan, rather than trying to avoid or even be concerned with Satan's disapproval of them.

87   Many cite Isa. 14:12–14 and draw literal conclusions from this passage to depict the fall of Satan. The descriptor, "star of the morning [or, shining one]" is derived from Hebrew, *helel*, which has been translated into Greek as *eosphoros*, and then into Latin (in the Vulgate Bible) as "Lucifer." The context of this passage is a prophecy of God's judgment against the nation of Babylon; "Lucifer" clearly refers to the king of Babylon. But some think that this is a veiled reference to what happened to Satan. In the most general sense, it *is* (because it parallels what else we know about him); in a specific or doctrinal sense, it is *not* (because the basis for this is unprovable or inconclusive). Another possible parallel reference to Satan might be in Ezek. 28:1–19, which is a specific reference to the king of Tyre, and alludes to the fall of Adam (in the Garden of Eden) rather than the fall of Satan. However, it is not hard to see similarities between the three scenarios.

88   Some of the early church "fathers" believed Satan was envious that Man was made in God's image, and thus deceived Man and caused him to sin; thus, Satan fell when he caused Adam to fall—or, Satan's fall was directly attributed to (and the result of) his having deceived Adam and Eve (Kelly, *Satan: A Biography*, 182). There are assumptions with this view, to be sure, but it does represent the traditional belief about Satan's "fall."

89   Someone might respond, "Well, the religious world is overflowing with all these same things"—and, if we are talking only about the "religious world," this is true. But what often poses as "Christianity" today can be a far cry from what the Bible teaches. True Christianity is not based upon human assumptions or opinions; it has no contradictions. Instead, it is based upon heavenly-revealed truth which can be *suppressed* (Rom. 1:18–20) but not *destroyed*. Whatever God's truth has revealed about the spirit realm—including the existence of it—rests upon information and authority that far exceeds any modern narrative, however confident that narrative appears to be.

90   As I understand it, this account (in Rev. 20:1–3) is not the removal of *all* demonic power, but does illustrate the great *limitation* of it. This stands in contrast to the great freedom that Satan had while Jesus and the apostles were active in their ministries, so that *their* power (of God) would be shown as superior to all of *Satan's* power. This explains the great explosion of demonic possession during Jesus' ministry, and why we no longer see this happening today. Some say that Satan *has* been completely subdued, or (according to Preterism) he has already been destroyed, and that all the wickedness in the world is "residual evil" being propagated by evil people. This, of course, undermines all of Jesus', Paul's, Peter's, John's, and James' warnings in the NT to believers about Satan: if he has no power, then who are we *fighting* against (Eph. 6:12)?

91   God not only spoke the world into existence through His omnipotence [lit., all-powerfulness] but He can also completely destroy whatever He has created. In fact, He has promised to destroy the physical creation when the plan of salvation has fully run its course (2 Peter 3:7–10).

92   Thomas Aquinas (14th century theologian), in his *De Malo* ("On Evil"), believed that Satan and his demons could not actually put thoughts into people's minds, nor read thoughts. They can, however, affect people's "spirits and humors [i.e., bodily fluids, which the ancients believed affected one's temperament]" by picking up on people's behavior and preying on their imaginations. This perceptive ability allowed demons to "stimulate their victims to emotions of lust, anger, and so on" (Kelly, *Satan: A Biography*, 301; bracketed words are mine). This point is provided not because I believe it entirely, but to add historical perspective.

93   Among some of the early church "fathers" was a belief that the ransom payment *was* made to Satan. "Around the year AD 180, Irenaeus implied that the ransom was paid to Satan, who had held men and women in bondage since persuading them to disobey God: in effect, Jesus offered Himself to the Devil in return for his human captives. This idea was made explicit by Origen and Gregory of Nyssa in the 3rd century, and was later incorporated into the work of Augustine. The ransom offered to Satan was not honoured [*sic*], however: as Jesus was the Son of God, Satan could not possibly keep Him in his power. Thus, the doctrine led to the conclusion that God had deceived

his divine nature like a hook inside a bait: 'the Devil, like a voracious fish, gobbling up the bait swallowed the hook of the Godhead...and was caught.' Augustine adapted this simile in the early 5th century, when he described the cross as 'the Devil's mousetrap'" (Oldridge, *A Very Short Introduction*, 26). "In this redemption, Christ's Blood was given [to Satan] as a price for us. By accepting it, however, the Devil was not enriched, but bound, so that one might be loosened from his hands" (Augustine, quoted in Kelly, *Satan: A Biography*, 216; bracketed words are mine). All this is nonsense, and (if taken seriously) blasphemous. Neither God nor Christ deceived Satan or anyone else, otherwise they would have had to become *like* Satan to do so. Yet, it is always amazing to what lengths men will go to try to explain something apart from the teachings of Scripture (1 Peter 2:21–22).

94   If you would like to know more about God's divine attributes, I recommend my book, *Seeking the Sacred* (Waynesville, OH: Spiritbuilding Publishers, 2009); go to www.spiritbuilding.com/chad.

95   *Strong's* (electronic), G2666.

96   We cannot peer into this realm on our own, but there have been occasions where God has shown people this realm. For example, Paul was invited to see into the "third heaven"—that is, into God's world—through a vision (2 Cor. 12:1–4). Similarly, John was caught up in the Spirit—again, in a vision—to "see" the spiritual realm in a way that God chose to reveal it to him (Rev. 4:1ff).

97   In Psalm 115:8, the psalmist says, "Those who make them [idols] will become like them, everyone who trusts in them." Similarly, those who give allegiance to Satan become like him, whereas those who give allegiance to Christ become like *Him*. We take on the nature, identity, and disposition of heart of whatever it is that we follow.

98   This quote may come from John Wooden (1910–2010), the Hall of Fame coach for the UCLA basketball team, but I believe it to be much older, possibly from Abraham Lincoln, or Lincoln's era.

99   You should not confuse addictive cravings—which admittedly can be extremely powerful and seemingly irresistible—with the decision to *consent* to those cravings. At some point, every addict says "yes" to what he or his body wants to do. Addiction always begins with and is perpetuated by personal *choices*; it is never a justification for sinful behavior. God gives no such permission in His word. Being addicted to *anything* is like being under a spell: Satan is the spell master, and the darkness is the thing which holds one captivated. Addicts who have the ability to say "no" are not victims, but self-made prisoners.

100   "We tend to see sin as an endless series of individual wrongs by individual people. There's truth in that, of course, but it's not the whole

picture. Biblically, any sin and all sins are linked together and related to the original human rebellion (Genesis 3 – 11) against God that triggered God's loving wrath. In scripture, while individual sins are certainly taken into account, sins are seen as part of a universal network—they are seen as part of a single rebellion by a single human family" (Jim McGuiggan, *The Dragon Slayer: Reflections on the Saving of the World* [McGuiggan Publishing, 2004], 92).

101 Someone might argue here that if Jesus created all things, then He must have created the world of darkness. Such a conclusion contradicts what has been revealed in Scripture. God created the physical world and called it "very good" (Gen. 1:31). But Man's sin corrupted this world and brought all kinds of trouble, corruption, and misery into it. God did not create trouble, corruption, and misery, but these are what exist in the absence of His presence and fellowship. So it is with the world of darkness: it is not part of the "very good" Creation, but it is the result of the intelligent creatures of His creation—namely, angels and human beings—turning away from God and seeking something else. It is like saying of a well-lit room, "The darkness in this room is just waiting to take over as soon as these lights are turned off." The darkness only exists when the lights are turned off, because when "the Light shines in the darkness," the darkness cannot overpower it (John 1:5). Satan did not sin because of something good that Christ had made; he sinned because of something evil apart from Christ, which is the power of sin itself. If there is no law, "there also is no violation" (Rom. 4:15)—i.e., any violation of what Christ did, said, or established is itself an unholy creation not of God, but of those who turn away from Him. Similarly, God did not create divorce, but divorce does exist whenever people abandon the marriage relationship that God did create. In a sense, Satan entered into a room filled with Light, but chose to reject the Light, and immediately "it was night"—just as when Judas chose to leave the Lord during the Last Supper (John 13:30). Satan has been in darkness ever since, and ultimately will be consumed by that darkness when God removes from him every ounce of power, authority, and free will.

102 I am not discounting either church services or the Christian religion here. Rather, I am simply pointing out the fact that Jesus' mission must never be summarized by an appeal to these things. Faithful Christians engage in both of these, but they also realize that Jesus' objective far transcends either one.

103 While it is not my point yet to talk about *how* one is "born again," Paul cites immersion in water (baptism) as the visible demonstration of this great spiritual transformation in Rom. 6:3–7.

104 Paul clarifies that the Father who *gave* His Son "all authority" is Himself exempted (1 Cor. 15:27–28). In other words, the Father did not give *away* all His authority as the Supreme and Sovereign Being, but *delegated* all of His authority to His Son.

105 *The Passion of the Christ*, directed by Mel Gibson, produced by Newmarket Films, 2004. It has grossed over $600 million worldwide; the budget to make the film was $30 million. Gibson's own production company, Icon Productions, had to fund the film's production and marketing (another $15 million) because, as he said, "This is a film about something that nobody wants to touch, shot in two dead languages"—i.e., Latin and Jewish Aramaic (*Wikipedia*, cited Sept. 2, 2021).

106 Interestingly, the role of Satan in Gibson's movie was actually played by a woman, actress Rosalinda Celentano.

107 God requires justice for any animal that takes the life of a man (Gen. 9:5, Exod. 21:28–36). But the serpent's crime was not merely of inflicting physical harm (or even death) upon a human. Its crime was a moral deception—something an ox, for example, is incapable of doing. And, because of the moral nature of the crime, it deserves not only a singular punishment, but a perpetual curse.

108 In *The Passion of the Christ*, at the end of the scene where Satan speaks to Jesus in the Garden, Satan releases from underneath his cloak a serpent, which slithers to Jesus who is lying on the ground. Jesus suddenly stands up, and, while never losing eye contact with Satan, stomps on the head of the serpent—a theatrical nod to Gen. 3:15. This is pure fiction, to be sure, but is also an interesting way to convey what was about to happen.

109 There is an allusion here, too, of the disobedient Israelites who were bitten by the fiery serpents while in the wilderness (Num. 21:6–9). Their wounds *were* fatal, unless they looked upon the bronze serpent which Moses had made and lifted up on a pole. Jesus' superiority over the Israelites is two-fold: first, Satan's "bite" was not a punishment for His sin, since He was sinless; second, He does not derive His life from the Israelites or anything they could do for Him (see John 3:13–15), but by virtue of His divine nature as the Son of God.

110 Yet, even angels of God were not told everything that was going to happen to bring about God's eternal plan of redemption. They themselves "longed to look" into the fulfillment of the prophecies which the Holy Spirit gave to the prophets to speak (1 Peter 1:12). And, it is through Christ's *church* that the revealed word of God has been disclosed to angels, not the other way around (Eph. 3:10). In other words, angels are higher and more powerful than us, but this does not mean they always *know* more than what we know. And, if this is true about God's heavenly angels, then it stands to reason that it is even *more* the case with fallen angels, including Satan himself.

111 Christopher Hitchens, noted atheist, found the idea of Jesus' sacrificial death to be immoral and therefore completely reprehensible. "Ask yourself the question: how moral is the following? I am told of a human sacrifice

that took place two thousand years ago, without my wishing it and in circumstances so ghastly that, had I been present and in possession of any influence, I would have been duty-bound to try and stop it. In consequence of this murder, my own manifold sins are forgiven me, and I may hope to enjoy everlasting life... In order to gain the benefit of this wondrous offer, I have to accept that I am *responsible* for the flogging and mocking and crucifixion, in which I had no say and no part, and agree that every time I decline this responsibility, or that I sin in word or deed, I am intensifying the agony of it" (*God Is Not Great: How Religion Poisons Everything* [New York: Twelve/Hachette Book Group USA, 2007], 209). Hitchens' view both misrepresents the situation and overlooks many critical details. He does not see, for example, the connection *between* his sins and Christ's sacrifice, and thus excuses himself from culpability. He, like Peter (Mat. 16:21–23), condemned the idea of Christ's unjust death, yet he failed to understand the "eternal purpose" that it carried out (Eph. 3:11–12). He, along with many others, was oblivious to the divine love, mercy, and grace that compelled Christ to take upon Himself what we all deserved for our own sins. It is also interesting to me that Hitchens talks about what is "moral" without ever explaining the definition or origin of "morality." Having read numerous books written by atheists, I have found this kind of presumptuous and unqualified reasoning to be typical of them.

112 There *does* exist a scenario in which we may *not* face physical death. If we are "made alive together with Christ" (Eph. 2:5), and Christ returns to receive us to Himself before we die, then we will *never* have to experience physical death (1 Thess. 4:13–18). This is what Jesus meant in John 11:25–26 and what Paul meant in 1 Cor. 15:51–52. But, aside from that unique and extraordinary event, we will all face our mortality at some point in time.

113 McGuiggan, *The Dragon Slayer*, 11.

114 Satan tempted Jesus to turn stones into bread, cast Himself down from the pinnacle of the Jerusalem temple, and to worship him. Jesus, of course, denied all such requests. Yet, during His ministry, Jesus *did* create loaves of bread out of nothing; He *did* prominently make His presence known in the temple; and He *did* worship Someone outside of Himself—not Satan, but God the Father. He did these things not at Satan's bidding, for He would never obey such instruction, but He did so because it was the right thing to do to reveal Himself as the Messiah.

115 The phrase, "[He will] rule all the nations with a rod of iron" (Rev. 12:5), indicates the paradoxical nature of Christ's reign. The word "rule" here in the Greek [*poimaino*] is the same word elsewhere translated as "[to] shepherd" a group of people (as in Acts 20:28, 1 Peter 5:2, and Rev. 7:17). Thus, His "rule" is that of a Shepherd *over* His own people, but the "rod of iron" indicates His ability to destroy the enemies *of* His people (see also Rev. 2:27 and 19:15).

116 At this point, "the woman"—the remnant of Israel, which has been joined by all those who are faithful to God through Christ (i.e., His church)—is providentially cared for by God for the period of time in which she will face a severe persecution by the dragon and his allies (Rev. 12:6).

117 Michael [Hebrew, "(he) who is like God"] has been mentioned in Scripture before: see Dan. 10:13, 21, 12:1, and Jude 1:9. He is described as "one of the chief princes" of heaven (Dan. 10:13), and his position indicates that even among the angels there is a hierarchy of power, position, and authority.

118 A Calvinist will argue differently. Calvinism claims that every person's future destiny has already been decreed by God's sovereign and unchangeable decision. Thus, before you were even born, God decided whether you would be saved or lost, and there is nothing in the world (literally) that you can do to change this. However, this is not an honest representation of Christ's gospel, but a perversion of it. I have described and responded to the Calvinistic doctrine in chapter 17 of my book, *The Saving Grace of God*, and I strongly recommend it; go to www.spiritbuilding.com/chad.

119 I say "outside of God the Father" because it was the Father who *gave* all authority to His Son. Paul explains this in 1 Cor. 15:27-28: in giving all authority to His Son, the Father is excepted from His Son's authority. God did not give *away* all His authority, but He legally *delegated* His authority to His Son.

120 The so-called Doctrine of Original Sin claims that we are all born sinful. More specifically, it claims that we are all born guilty with Adam's guilt—we have inherited a sinful nature (a.k.a. "total hereditary depravity") from Adam, our common ancestor. Simply put: since we are all allegedly born sinful, guilty, and bound for hell, therefore we all need to be "saved" as soon as possible so that we do not die in this condition. This doctrine provides the basis for the baptism of infants and children in several allegedly "Christian" religions, yet it is a false doctrine based upon a false premise. It rests almost entirely upon Rom. 5:12: "Therefore, just as through one man sin entered into the world, and death through sin, and so death spread to all men, because all sinned...." Paul did not say we are all born guilty of Adam's sin; this has been read into the text. He says that Adam introduced sin into the family of man, and that death—both physical and spiritual—will be the consequence of that sin. While physical death is inevitable (since the curse placed upon Adam affects all who are born of him; see Gen. 3:19), spiritual death is contingent upon each person sinning of his own volition. Just a few chapters later (Rom. 7:8-11), Paul says: "But sin, taking opportunity through the commandment, produced in me coveting of every kind; for apart from the Law sin is dead. I was once alive apart from the Law; but when the commandment came, sin became alive and I died; and this commandment, which was to result in life, proved to result in death for me; for sin, taking an opportunity through the commandment, deceived me and through it killed

me." Nowhere in the NT does it say that we are born into sin, born sinful, guilty of Adam's sin, have "total hereditary depravity," or have a sinful nature. It does say that when we sin—a choice we make, not Adam—then we become guilty of violating God's moral law. Recall Rom. 5:12 again: "because *all sinned*" (emphasis added)—Adam's sin opened the door to our own sin, but each one of us walked through it on our own in due time. If we had not yet sinned (the case of an innocent child), we do not yet need saving; once we have sinned, we stand condemned by God and are in need of a Savior. Our only salvation is "in Christ"—NT language for "in a covenant relationship with God through Jesus Christ." Thus: "If Christ is in you, though the body is dead because of sin [because of the curse placed upon Adam—MY WORDS], yet the spirit is alive because of righteousness" (Rom. 8:10).

121 For more detail on the objective nature of sin, I recommend reading "What Sin Is and Is Not" in my book, *The Gospel of Forgiveness* (Waynesville, OH: Spiritbuilding Publishers, 2011); go to www.spiritbuilding.com/chad.

122 I am not saying that the magnitude of punishment *in* our spiritual ruin is equal, but that "death" comes to all who sin. In other words, there may be different levels of punishment in the outer darkness, just as there seems to be different levels of reward in heaven. All this belongs to a different discussion. Suffice it to say for now that regardless of what exactly one suffers *in* his permanent spiritual death, *all* suffer to some degree.

123 The question with which many have wrestled through the ages is: Was Jesus *prevented* from sinning, or did He actually *choose* not to sin when He was tempted? If He was prevented from sinning, then this gives Him (it has been said) an unfair advantage over the rest of us. But if He chose not to sin, then (it is implied) He actually *could* have failed, but simply chose not to. There is no answer to this question that will satisfy everyone. However, I propose: Jesus could *not* have sinned, not because He was an automaton that was programmed only to be righteous. Rather, He could not have sinned because He could not violate His divine nature and still be the Son of God. The same can be said of the Father Himself: He cannot sin, *not* because the opportunity does not exist, but because He will never be unfaithful to who He is—"He cannot deny Himself" (2 Tim. 2:13). I realize that there is a bit of mental wrangling here that makes this difficult to comprehend (for myself as well as anyone else), but there is, as I understand it, no better answer that does not distort Jesus' divine nature.

124 I'm speaking here of those who are old and mature enough to be held accountable to God on their own cognizance, so to speak, not to those who are too young or of insufficient mental capability to be responsible for themselves. Young children, for example, are innocent before God; they do not need "saving" because they have not yet sinned. We are not to "save" those who are not in trouble. But at some point, every person who is of

sound mind, given enough time and opportunity, does commit sin against God. This is the intended meaning of my statements here.

125 I have no intention of denying citations of other people's work; unfortunately, I am unable to locate the author of this extraordinary quote.

126 If you would like to learn much more about the Holy Spirit, I strongly recommend my book, *The Holy Spirit of God: A Biblical Perspective* (Waynesville, OH: Spiritbuilding Publishing, 2010); go to www.spiritbuilding.com/chad.

127 Dan Barker, an atheist, was once a "born again Christian" in a denominational church, but became disillusioned with its fakery, duplicity, and dogma. Thus, he "discarded" his faith in God and claimed that "there is no need for a god." "I did not lose my faith. I gave it up purposely....I lost faith in faith" (*Godless*, 40). This is not true. Barker lost faith in a certain *brand* of "faith," but he still

believes in things that he cannot see, cannot physically verify, and cannot know for certain—including the alleged absence of God's own existence. "Faith is what you need when you don't have certainty" he says later (*ibid.*, 69); even though he cannot know for certain that God does not exist, he claims that His non-existence is "truth" (*ibid.*, 67). Like many atheists, Barker believes that one must give up reason, intelligence, and truth in order to become or remain a Christian. Yet, denying the Creator and putting all of one's faith in the Creation is not a hallmark of wisdom and open-mindedness, but just the opposite (Rom. 1:18–23).

128 To see all these books and workbooks, go to www.spiritbuilding.com/chad.

129 I have written much more about "heaven"—and the difficulty that we have in embracing it—in two of my earlier books: *Seeking the Sacred* (Spiritbuilding Publishers, 2009), 246–266; and *Christian Thinking* (Spiritbuilding Publishers, 2016), 248–251.

130 Hollywood has done its share to reinforce this misguided idea. There are numerous movies about "going to heaven" (*What Things May Come, Five People You Will Meet in Heaven*, etc.) that are all about reuniting with people in this life, including resolving earthly relationship problems or other personal dramas. Conspicuously, these movies barely mention or even refuse to acknowledge being with the Father or His Son.

131 Yet, we have no problem enjoying a delicious meal, even while knowing that many people in the world are starving at that some moment. Imagine if all those starving people were invited to the same meal—"Come, for everything is ready now" (see Luke 14:16–24)—but they refused it? Likewise, God invites all people to accept His offer of salvation, but most refuse it.

132 Geisler, *If God, Why Evil?*, 113.

133 From Hume's *Dialogues Concerning Natural Religion* (1779); quoted in Randy Alcorn's *If God Is Good* [Colorado Springs, CO: Multnomah Books, 2009], 18; bracketed word is mine.

134 Geisler, *If God, Why Evil?*, 10.

135 The problem of evil is called "the rock of atheism" or "atheism's cornerstone" (Alcorn, *If God Is Good*, 11).

136 There is one exception to this: God can cause animals *and* earthquakes (or any natural events) to bring harm upon people, if it serves His purpose. We see this in Scripture numerous times. This does not suddenly attribute decision-making ability to animals or nature, but acknowledges the Creator's ability to override natural instincts and natural laws in order to advance an objective that we may not always fully understand. Being infinitely greater and wiser than what we are capable of, He does not have to explain Himself for these decisions, and it is not our place to condemn Him because we do not understand them.

137 If you are interested in a more in-depth discussion on God's moral law, I recommend further reading in my book, *The Gospel of Saving Grace* (Spiritbuilding Publishers, 2020); go to www.spiritbuilding.com/chad.

138 Alcorn, *If God Is Good*, 112. William Lane Craig, in *Reasonable Faith*, says: "If God does not exist, then life is objectively meaningless; but men cannot live consistently and happily knowing that life is meaningless; so in order to be happy he pretends that life has meaning.... In a universe without God, good and evil do not exist—there is only the bare valueless fact of existence, and there is no one to say that you are right and I am wrong" (quoted in *ibid.*, 114).

139 Geisler, *If God, Why Evil?*, 13.

140 "The Bible talks about the *entry* of evil into the universe, but evil's ultimate *origin* remains a mystery" (Alcorn, *If God Is Good*, 50).

141 Consider Moses' entreaty to Israel, for example, in Deut. 30:15–20: "choose life" means to side with God and join in His fellowship; to choose "death and adversity" means to oppose Him and suffer the consequences. "In a universe where God is Creator and Judge, doing good is always smart while doing evil is always stupid" (Alcorn, *If God Is Good*, 251).

142 If we simply evolved apart from any supernatural intervention, all talk about "free will" becomes entirely subjective, imaginary, and even ridiculous. It would assume, without any basis or explanation, that we developed a *moral decision-making ability* accidentally and for no expressed purpose.

143 Geisler, *If God, Why Evil?*, 15.

144 Charles Spurgeon once said, "He who demands a reason from God is not in a fit state of mind to receive one" (quoted in Alcorn, *If God Is Good*, 344). It is arrogant and presumptuous for inferior beings to question the intents and actions of a supreme Being; one who feels comfortable doing so only magnifies his arrogance and ignorance.

145 Geisler, *If God, Why Evil?*, 30.

146 In a very real sense, God *has* stood trial before us (people) in the case of His Son being arrested, tried, and tortured for His alleged crimes. Yet the facts remain: He was innocent of every charge; He committed no crime; He never lied about anything (1 Peter 2:21–23); and only because of false testimonies of wicked men was He finally executed. Thus, God was found innocent before all men, and the verdict reached in Jesus' trials has been recorded and preserved for all of humankind to read from that point forward.

147 In a postscript, Ford Motor Company—the bus manufacturer—provided a $40 million settlement to families of those who were killed, since the bus's gas tank was decidedly vulnerable.

148 Harold Kushner, writing from a modern Jewish perspective, claims that God is sometimes *limited* and makes *mistakes*, but He is to be loved anyway. "Can you learn to love and forgive Him despite His limitations?" he asks (*When Bad Things Happen to Good People* [New York: Schocken Books, 1989], 148). This is an absurd position. First, how did Kushner determine that God is "limited" and makes "mistakes," except by his own personal standard of measuring God's actions? And, if God needs to be *forgiven*, then this implies that He has *sinned*, and that we are expecting help and salvation from a God who has the same problem that *we* have. Yet, such nonsense answers are sadly very common in discussions about theodicy (i.e., God's justice).

149 James E. Sellers, *When Trouble Comes* (New York: Abingdon Press, 1960), 49.

150 Alcorn, *If God Is Good*, 283.

151 There are a few biblical examples of this. First, the instructions given to Daniel (Dan. 12:4, 8–9); second, Paul's vision of Paradise (2 Cor. 12:1–4); and third, the vision revealed to John (Rev. 10:4). In all these cases, information *was known* (or *knowable*), but it was purposely unrecorded.

152 On "Java Man," see Howard E. Wilson, "The Java Man," *Truth Magazine* (http://truthmagazine.com/archives/volume2/TM002021.htm); on "Piltdown Man," see http://www.history.com/news/piltdown-man-hoax-100-years-ago; on "Peking Man," see Malcom Bowden, "The Lost Peking Man Skeletons" (http://truthmagazine.com/archives/volume2/TM002021.htm); on "Neanderthal Man," see Dave Phillips, "Neanderthals Are Still Human!",

Institute for Creation Research (http://www.icr.org/article/neanderthals-are-still-human/); all cited June, 2017.

153 Boatman, *What the Bible Says*, 293–294.

154 Luke 16:22 is the closest we have to this: "Now the poor man died and was carried away by the angels to Abraham's bosom...."

155 Cited from http://www.icr.org/article/neanderthals-are-still-human/ (June, 2017). The International Association for Near Death Studies (IANDS) says: "Depending on how restrictively the NDE is defined, studies have indicated that between 12% and 40% of people who go through a near-death episode will later say they had an NDE. It is clear that in the United States alone at least several million people have had NDEs" (http://iands.org/ndes/about-ndes.html). Maybe it's just me, but the calculations here are questionable at best.

156 Boatman, *What the Bible Says*, 276.

157 IANDS, http://iands.org/ndes/about-ndes.html.

158 For what it's worth, I provide the following excerpt: "Where either consciousness or loss of consciousness (including death) is involved, we must distinguish between your private experiences and my private experiences. You (privately) can experience my (public) death; we can both (privately) experience someone else's (public) death: but neither of us can experience his own (inexperienceable) [*sic*] death. You can never actually see yourself unconscious, hear yourself snore, or experience your own being dead, for if you were in a position to have these experiences you would not, in fact, be unconscious, asleep or dead. If you can never experience your own death, it follows logically you can never experience your own dying. 'Now wait a minute,' you might say, 'Granted that I cannot experience my being dead but obviously I am still alive while I am dying and, unless I am unconscious, I can experience that.' No, the fact is that you can never be certain you are dying. 'Dying' takes its only legitimate meaning from the fact that it immediately [and necessarily—MY WORDS] precedes death" (Edwin S. Schneidman, "The Enemy," *Psychology Today* [Aug., 1970], 37; quoted in Boatman, *What the Bible Says*, 272–273).

159 Boatman, *What the Bible Says*, 277. Some claim that during His three days in the tomb, Jesus allegedly preached the gospel to disembodied spirits in order to "save" them (!), citing 1 Peter 3:19–20 as proof. There are a number of contextual and theological errors in such a conclusion, but this does not stop people from believing it. Furthermore, I have offered a biblical exposition of 1 Peter 3:19–20 in my published workbook, *1 & 2 Peter Study Workbook* (2020); go to www.spiritbuilding.com/chad.

160 DeSpelder and Strickland, *The Last Dance*, 575.

161 http://leomacdonald.blogspot.com/2006/11/nde-and-void-kevin-williams-research.html; cited Mar. 12, 2015.

162 "Do better" is apparently a very subjective decision—something God would never accept and the Bible never teaches. One's obedient demonstration of his faith in God is always based upon factual and objective information and action (such as, "I'm doing what God has told me in His revealed word to do"), not subjective feelings (such as, "I think I'm a better person than I was before!").

www.ingramcontent.com/pod-product-compliance
Lightning Source LLC
Chambersburg PA
CBHW031948080426
42735CB00007B/310